PRAISE FOR *NEXT G*

"*Next Generation Retail* is a must-read for anyone interested in the massive $25 trillion retail industry. From customer experience to media, payments, loyalty, the impact of Web 3.0 and supply chain among others, Deborah Weinswig and Renee Hartmann take an incisive and comprehensive look at the trends impacting the sector, while providing a prescient view of what we can expect to see in this ever more complex industry. Truly a superb read which I highly recommend."
Philip Guarino, Board Director, Harvard Alumni Entrepreneurs

"The last few years have not only presented challenges to the retail industry but have also uncovered tremendous opportunities that were never before possible. *Next Generation Retail* is the ideal guide for early and professional retailers, navigating the myriad of changes in the retail industry to innovate for the future and grab market share."
Guy Yehiav, President, SmartSense

"This book and its authors will change your business and life."
Kay Unger, Kay Unger Design

"When you're connected to Deborah, you are connected to the retail industry. You are connected to the trends. The insights. The possible futures. The up-and-comers. The disruptors. The data. Deborah sets a high bar in the industry and is passionate about challenging while pressing for progress."
Justin Honaman, Head of Worldwide Retail & Consumer Goods, Amazon

"Deborah is one of retail's most dedicated students, offering unique insights from her many years of industry research."
Brian Cornell, Chairman and Chief Executive Officer, Target

"Among the thousands of colleagues I have worked with throughout my career, Renee Hartmann stands out among the very best. She is smart, insightful, thorough, quick, charismatic, and I have watched people young and old, junior and senior, as well as many CEOs, gravitate to her. *Next Generation Retail* is a treasure trove of insight for anyone wanting to build a retail business while attracting, converting and retaining consumers along the way. This is a must-read for anyone operating, or looking to run, a retail business."

Scott Kronick, Senior Advisor and Former CEO of Ogilvy Public Relations, Asia Pacific

Next Generation Retail

How to use new technology
to innovate for the future

Deborah Weinswig and Renee Hartmann

KoganPage

Publisher's note

Every possible effort has been made to ensure that the information contained in this book is accurate at the time of going to press, and the publishers and authors cannot accept responsibility for any errors or omissions, however caused. No responsibility for loss or damage occasioned to any person acting, or refraining from action, as a result of the material in this publication can be accepted by the editor, the publisher or the author.

First published in Great Britain and the United States in 2023 by Kogan Page Limited

2nd Floor, 45 Gee Street	8 W 38th Street, Suite 902	4737/23 Ansari Road
London	New York, NY 10018	Daryaganj
EC1V 3RS	USA	New Delhi 110002
United Kingdom		India
www.koganpage.com		

Kogan Page books are printed on paper from sustainable forests.

ISBNs

Hardback	978 1 3986 0964 8
Paperback	978 1 3986 0963 1
Ebook	978 1 3986 0962 4

British Library Cataloguing-in-Publication Data

A CIP record for this book is available from the British Library.

Library of Congress Control Number
2022951474

Typeset by Integra Software Services, Pondicherry
Print production managed by Jellyfish
Printed and bound by CPI Group (UK) Ltd, Croydon, CR0 4YY

CONTENTS

LIST OF FIGURES AND TABLES

TABLES

ACKNOWLEDGEMENTS

I would like to dedicate this book to my parents, who always pushed me to ask the question why and to never stop dreaming. In addition, the Coresight Research team and many friends of Coresight who enabled this book to come to fruition. In particular I would like to thank a few individuals for their contributions to Coresight's expertise in the subject matter: Coresight's Head of Global Research, John Mercer, for his steadfast leadership of the Coresight research and the entire Coresight Research team's commitment to thorough and detailed fact finding and analysis. And to Ken Fenyo and the Coresight advisory team for their deep dives into helping retailers make sense of technological change and how to act on these changes.

Deborah

Thank you to my kids Zeb and Noe who are my biggest supporters and my guides to their digital native generation, even though they mock me for my questions. My husband Sage who always believes in me, while quietly correcting my grammar. And to my parents, who gave me a global outlook and taught me the value of hard work. Thank you to the Coresight team for their commitment to the subject of retail innovation and diligent research and insights.

Renee

We also extend a special thanks to the retail experts who were interviewed for this book. Their insights and outlook were invaluable.

Daniela Ciocan, CEO, Access Beauty Insiders and Unfiltered Experience

Scott Eneje, Co-Founder, Yandi Digital Solutions

Ken Fenyo, President, Research and Advisory, Coresight Research

Daniel Goldberg, Chief Data Strategy Officer, Coresight Research

John Harmon, Senior Retail/Technology Analyst, Coresight Research

Terence Ng, Senior Analyst, Coresight Research

Diane Randolph, Board Member, Retired CIO

Zachary Rubin, Founder, Go Arena

Carol Schumacher, strategic advisor adviser for IR and PR to C-suite and Boards

Andrew Smith, Co-Founder, Think Uncommon

Buddy Teaster, CEO, Soles4Souls

Letitia Webster, SVP eCommerce, Omni Channel and Master Data Mgt., Tractor Supply

Sarah Williams, Shoppable Livestream Host and Producer, T3 Brand Educator and Spokesperson

Janie Yu, Partner, LFX Venture Partners

Introduction

We are writing this book during the summer of 2022, deep in the tepid uncertainty of the global Covid-19 pandemic's 'aftertime' long tail. We are still not out of the crisis, but consumers have largely returned to an updated version of normal operations; with the exception of China and a handful of other countries, most nations have relaxed restrictions on businesses and individuals. While things are still not back to 'normal', they are firmly in a new normal zone.

In this book, we have the opportunity to reflect on the changes that have occurred amongst consumers and in retail since the pandemic began, and we have strong indications of where things are headed after these tumultuous few years. As we created this book, we drew on ample research and decades of experience in the retail industry from Deborah's company, Coresight Research, and its extensive data and industry insights and analysis of the retail sector. Where noted, many of the chapters in this book are adapted from Coresight reports, originally published online and used with permission. We also interviewed industry experts across a wide range of fields, including retail executives, technology innovators, industry specialists and creators who are developing the next level of content across livestreaming, non-fungible tokens (NFTs) and social commerce.

We will share the insights we have gleaned with the reader, and will provide data and industry intelligence, as well as advice and practical suggestions for how to bring these best practices into your own organization. We hope that this book will serve as a toolkit for helping professionals in the consumer industry, retailers and brands alike to analyse their own business and find inspiration from each of the segments we discuss.

Chapter 1 covers the changing nature of today's consumer since the Covid-19 pandemic, via our own pandemic experiences, and how these relate to broader consumer mindsets, consumer behaviours and consumer demands.

Chapter 2 addresses the question we are most often asked concerning the future of retail: How should we plan for the Metaverse? The Metaverse is the next new landscape for retail innovation, allowing retailers to completely break free from the physical world and re-imagine their offering to consumers in a purely virtual world. We examine how brands have begun to break into the Metaverse, how this new landscape will evolve in the future and what retailers can do to adopt the Metaverse into their marketing, brand and commerce strategies. Four Coresight reports were the basis for this chapter: *Playbook: Strategies for retailers to monetize the Metaverse* (14 March 2022), *The Metaverse in Retail: Taking brand recognition, engagement and loyalty to a new level* (24 May 2022), *Retail Tech Landscape: The Metaverse* (February 2022) and *Metaverse's Latest: Decentraland's fashion week* (11 April 2022).

Chapter 3 focuses on the rise of livestream shopping. The livestream shopping phenomenon was first to hit in China, where top livestreamers sell billions of dollars' worth of products in seconds. The craze has now gone worldwide, and retailers are choosing from dozens of technology and traffic providers to develop their own livestream shopping to cash in on the trend. Material in this chapter is adapted from the following Coresight reports: *Understanding the Livestreaming Opportunity: Global retail executive survey findings* (17 May 2022), *US Social Commerce Survey 2022: Capitalizing on social media influence in retail* (4 May 2022), *China versus US Livestreaming E-Commerce Adoption* (21 July 2022), *Six Livestreaming Myths Debunked* (16 January 2022) and *US Livestreaming E-Commerce Survey 2022: Demand for entertainment drives viewership* (19 April 2022).

Covid created an entirely new class of retail with the rise of instant or quick-buy commerce, building a more than $20 billion industry in the US alone in one year following the pandemic. **Chapter 4** looks at how this developed, where the market is going in the future and how retailers can access this market for themselves. The following Coresight reports were utilized when writing this chapter: *From Quick Commerce to Instant Needs: Exploring business models in rapid delivery* (5 November 2021), *Quick Commerce in Europe: Expansion meets consolidation in rapid delivery* (23 February 2022), *Instacart's Next Growth Steps: IPO, acquisitions, rapid delivery and more* (17 February 2022), *ShopTalk 2022 Day Two: Strategic growth opportunities for retail – livestreaming, digital tech, the Metaverse* (29 March 2022) and *Market Outlook: UK grocery retailers – pandemic creates opportunities for instant commerce channel* (25 November 2021).

Employees, investors, and consumers expect sustainability to be addressed at the companies for which they work, in which they invest and by the brands from which they buy. In **Chapter 5** we discuss the development of sustainability in retail and present Coresight Research's EnCORE framework, which is designed to help retailers and brands frame their approach to sustainability. We used the following Coresight reports to inform the material in this chapter: *The Time for Sustainability in Retail is Now* (17 September 2020), *Retail Innovators: CPG sustainability innovations* (27 May 2022), *Playbook: Succeeding with alternative models in retail – resale, subscription and rental* (1 June 2022).

Chapter 6 goes into detail on how content and commerce are blending more than ever before. Historically, retailers have not been content creators, but they are being forced to delve into the content creation model to integrate storytelling and entertainment into the purchase cycle. And as consumers spend more and more time online, brands are seeking ways to connect with consumers on the social platforms they spend time on, in a way that is authentic and engaging. This chapter incorporates the following Coresight reports: *US Social Commerce Survey 2022: Capitalizing on social media influence in retail* (4 May 2022), *Retail Tech Landscape: Social commerce* (15 December 2021) and *US Social Commerce Survey 2021: The impacts of social media, influencers and livestreaming on shopping behaviors* (7 October 2021).

Chapter 7 observes how more consumers are seeking convenience online across a range of activities, whether it be buying groceries, reserving services, ordering takeout or for daily shopping necessities for pickup or delivery. These new consumer habits have led to the development of an entirely new revenue stream for retailers – allowing retailers to market products and services to their customers online and monetize these advertising opportunities in new formats. *The Evolution of Retail Media: Five trends to watch* (25 May 2022) and *Digital Retail Media: A new opportunity for US grocery* (10 November 2021) were both used to inform the material in this chapter.

Prior to the pandemic, consumers rarely thought of supply chains at all, but when the shock of the pandemic hit, 'supply chain issues' became a common refrain among retailers, politicians and consumers alike. The pandemic upset supply chains the world over, prompting companies to consider how to protect themselves from external shocks. Although 2020 should have been a wake-up call to revamp supply chain strategies, companies continued to experience increased disruptions. **Chapter 8** details these issues related to supply chains, drawing upon the Coresight reports: *Playbook: Digitization for faster, closer and more sustainable sourcing* (7 July 2022), *Achieving Agility and Resilience in Sourcing: Five strategies for brands and retailers* (10 March 2022) and *AI in Sourcing: The need of the hour* (30 May 2022).

NFTs have not only disrupted the art industry but have also injected energy and buzz into the retail world. But how are brands really benefiting from NFTs? Is it only marketing spin or are they creating real value? In **Chapter 9** we will examine real world use cases and provide tangible ways in which brands and retailers can and should utilize NFTs in their consumer strategy. It draws upon the Coresight report *Buildings Blocks of the Metaverse: NFTs* (21 March 2022).

Chapter 10 discusses the role of blockchain technology in retail. Many retailers have used blockchain technologies in a variety of innovative ways to improve customer satisfaction, authenticity and operational efficiency. Different blockchains released at different points over the last decade offer distinctive features and capabilities. Partnering with blockchains and incorporating their technologies into offerings can be a powerful strategy to improve customer satisfaction. This chapter adapts material from the Coresight report *Building Blocks of the Metaverse: Blockchain* (4 April 2022).

As more and more consumers experiment with new shopping channels and alternative payment methods, retailers need to develop their existing payment infrastructure to deliver a satisfying digital consumer experience. **Chapter 11** examines these, adapting material from the Coresight reports *Building Blocks of the Metaverse: Payments* (4 July 2022) and *Shifting Payment Infrastructure: The path to frictionless checkout and decentralized commerce* (28 June 2002).

Chapter 12 details how retailers are leveraging their customer data in new and innovative ways by serving customized ads to their consumers, delivering unique experiences and fostering customer loyalty. It is based upon material in the Coresight reports *Retail Tech: What do data and AI mean for retail?* (17 March 2021), *Retail Personalization in 2022: Balancing trust, data collection and privacy* (30 March 2022) and *Measuring the Value of Retail Data Sharing and Analytics* (5 August 2020).

The Covid-19 pandemic has impacted consumer behaviour and resulted in significant shifts in the global retail landscape. Although loyalty programmes have long been a key strategy for retailers to drive growth and retain customers, retailers now need to be more dynamic in their approach to such programmes, adapting to suit the needs of customers in the present climate. **Chapter 13** delves in how consumer loyalty can be enhanced, incorporating the Coresight reports *Retail Tech Landscape: Customer loyalty programs* (19 May 2021) and *Loyalty Programs: How can US retailers drive growth and engagement?* (15 April 2021).

E-commerce has evolved into a cornerstone of the global economy, causing particular disruption in the retail sector over the past few years. The space has evolved in various directions, encompassing legacy behemoths such as Amazon to newer entrants such as Etsy, plus legacy brick-and-mortar retailers such as Walmart expanding online and direct-to-consumer brands such as Harry's expanding from online to launch an offline presence. Just as the retailers themselves have adapted to the changing environment and their ever-evolving competitors, so have the infrastructure and tools to support these companies. **Chapter 14** covers these developments, adapting material from the Coresight reports *Headless Commerce Part 1: The evolving state of e-commerce infrastructure* (8 December 2021), *Headless Commerce Part 2: Addressing profitability issues for mid-sized e-commerce players* (2 February 2022), *Headless Commerce Part 3: Optimizing e-commerce infrastructure* (12 April 2022) and *Retail Tech Landscape: Headless commerce* (12 April 2022).

In **Chapter 15** we assess which key technologies and disruptions are here to stay, which will likely turn out to be fads and what future innovations to expect. We also offer our outlook on which components of retail innovation retailers should address, as they look toward the future of retail.

Finally, **Chapter 16** delves into the following questions: Which of these trends are relevant to your business? How will they affect your industry and how do you make the case to your stakeholders to adopt these new innovations for your retail business? We bring it all together to help you create your own roadmap and navigate how you can help your clients, companies or teammates adapt to next generation retail.

01

The changing nature
of today's consumer

The Covid-19 pandemic shock

So many things have changed after the Covid-19 pandemic that it is almost difficult to even distil all these changes at once. As one of the executives we interviewed in this book, Andrew Smith, Co-Founder of Think Uncommon (2022), put it: the pandemic was a change event. Change events can be emotional and traumatic, and most consumers are still processing what these changes mean to them, and to society as a whole.

Regardless of age, geography or preferences, today's consumer has changed dramatically, and retailers are being forced to shift their strategies to adapt to this breakneck speed of change. Covid only accelerated the changes in consumer demands globally, and retailers are being forced to innovate quickly to address these new needs and preferences. This also applies to their employees.

Since the start of the pandemic in 2020 we have been embarking on an unplanned, non-directed global experiment in consumer behaviour. No one ever thought about what would happen if you locked the world up inside their houses and the mere prospect of going out to dinner, buying groceries or going to the mall might sicken or potentially kill them. While at some times extremely dramatic, the ways that consumers changed their behaviour will be long lasting and unexpected. In some cases, the pandemic accelerated trends that were simmering for years but hadn't quite taken off, while some of the changes were completely unexpected.

Consider QR codes. For years, QR codes were ubiquitous in Asia, but brands and consumers in the rest of the world were unwilling to accept them. We tried to convince retailers to adopt QR code for years as they provide a unique and direct way to seamlessly blend the offline and online world. But the retailers always said no – consumers don't use QR codes. But then came the pandemic and almost every restaurant got rid of their menus in an effort to sanitize the dining experience, and consumers were forced to scan a QR code or go hungry at the restaurant. There was a 94 per cent growth rate in QR code interactions from 2018 to 2020 (Blue Bite, 2021) and a projected 22 per cent increase in the use of QR codes from 2020 to 2025 across the globe (Statista, 2021).

Now, brands, retailers, restaurants and everyone else have fully adopted QR codes into their daily consumer experience. And, it's been a positive development for retailers that still hasn't been completely integrated in all ways to fully embrace the online/offline experience that QR codes can deliver. But now that consumers have fully adopted the QR code, retailers can experiment with new possibilities that were not available prior to the pandemic.

As we started envisioning this book, we knew we would start with the consumer, as the consumer is ultimately demanding and driving all the innovations in retail that we discuss in the rest of this book. And as an exercise in distilling all of this change, we each analysed how our families have changed as consumers as a result of the pandemic. We both had very different pandemic experiences – Deborah and her family were in New York for most of the time, while Renee and her family went on the road and travelled around the West of the United States. Our experiences allowed us to gain perspective from both a rural and urban point of view, and from different lifestyle perspectives.

There have always been several frameworks for evaluating consumer behaviour, with elemental theories like Maslow's hierarchy dictating the behaviour of consumer groups according to economic levels of country of residence. However, while certain components of class structure and economic structure did hold somewhat true during the Covid pandemic, these frameworks were largely turned on their heads. Even billionaires were confronted uncomfortably with considerations of basic survival, and just because someone lives in a wealthy country, there were times when even basic goods like food and shelter were considered under threat. And wealth didn't translate into health, either.

For instance, during the Shanghai lockdowns in 2022, some of China's wealthiest consumers were essentially locked in their houses and were sporadically unable to order food or essentials. Even the most powerful and wealthiest consumers had periods of time when they doubted their access to basic food, health care and well-being. During one of these periods of high uncertainty around food delivery, one of my contacts in Shanghai posted on social media that the delivery of food she received made her happier than any luxury bag she had ever purchased. When some of the world's biggest luxury consumers suddenly must worry about basic survival, this will surely have a long-lasting impact on the way in which they make purchase decisions and their consumer desires going forward.

If we really think about it, each one of us has had dramatic shifts in our consumer behaviour because of the pandemic. It's a worthwhile exercise to think about how your own consumer behaviour and those of your family and friends have changed, and we both found it to be somewhat therapeutic as well. It provides a window into how retailers can adapt to this changing consumer behaviour – whether it was caused by the pandemic, or just the changing nature of today's world environment. Changing consumer behaviour is really hard. But adapting to consumer behaviour is easy and can be a lot of fun for retailers.

For years, retailers have discussed omnichannel retail, but up until the pandemic arrived it was a disconnected, fragmented experience, and one that consumers were not always demanding. Online and offline seemed like completely different experiences, and often had different prices. We felt that livestream shopping was a great connector as it took offline into the online world in a three-dimensional way and felt much more similar to being in a real store. Next, the Metaverse has now integrated a virtual world into that of retail with personalized experiences, products and content. Layer on the magic of QR codes and retail has truly become this omnichannel animal we have been hearing about for two decades. And none of this would have happened at all, or at least not as quickly, had it not been for the pandemic and the dramatic changes it forced in consumer behaviour in a very short period of time.

So, we are left to wonder: how will the events of the years post-2020 change consumer preferences? How will we evaluate these new preferences and predict consumer behaviour? Will we be able to rely on the previous frameworks, or will new ones take their place? Are we truly going to face a paradigm shift?

In this chapter we will be discussing how the consumer has changed since the pandemic. We will delve into consumer mindsets, consumer behaviours and consumer demands. The trends in this chapter will lay the groundwork for the rest of the book where we outline specific strategies for retailers to tap into these changing consumer trends and adapt to the new consumer paradigm. The experiences of Deborah and Renee will also illustrate how their families and friends changed and the impact on retail.

Consumer mindsets

Perhaps the most significant shift in consumer behaviour is not the day-to-day actions of consumers, but rather their mindsets. The pandemic has spurred a mental health crisis, which has brought enhanced awareness of consumers' mindsets and created a global environment that is more in tune with consumer mind space. At the same time, the political and global environment has become more and more toxic, exacerbating issues affecting consumer mindset.

All of these changes have led consumers to revaluate their priorities in life, and for many has clarified what is really important to them. We all see this every day among our friends and family, and also reflected in the data of people leaving the job market completely or switching to new jobs, people moving to new cities and countries and the prevalence of remote work even after Covid restrictions have been lifted.

Prioritizing happiness

The pandemic brought immeasurable pain, suffering and loss to so many families around the world. And even to those families that did not suffer catastrophic losses, almost everyone felt some sort of loss from the pandemic – whether it be losing a graduation, missing years of grandchildren's development, being separated from friends and family or not being able to go to school or send your kids to school. As a result, almost every consumer has evaluated what makes them happy, and they are prioritizing choices that maximize their happiness.

For some people this is choosing to stay in a remote work environment that is less time consuming and enables them to spend more time with family, for some this is exiting the workforce or finding new careers and for others it is simply prioritizing how they want to spend their time.

As Deborah reflects on her pandemic experience, she appreciates the flexibility that the pandemic forced onto her business at Coresight, leading her to start new events, initiatives, podcasts, business lines and even a non-profit that allowed her to think differently about how she works and what she does and who she does it with. And as someone who typically lives on a plane, she had the opportunity to appreciate staying home, spending time with her family, reconnecting with friends, working out and learning to cook (finally!). These experiences changed her mindset and her approach to work and life in irreversible ways, even as she takes to the skies again for business travel.

For Renee, the pandemic has brought on a life change as she and her family moved to Lisbon for a fresh adventure in a new country in August 2022. Her family had been wanting to give living in Europe a try and the pandemic gave her the push to re-evaluate what was important in life, the flexibility of remote work to make the move possible and the recognition that life is short so the time to do the things important to you is now.

Retailers should recognize this fundamental shift in consumers' priorities and choices. Consumers are looking for retailers to help them maximize their time devoted to seeking happiness – whether it's skipping the visit to the retail store altogether, making retail a destination that evokes happiness or providing a physical or virtual space to connect with like-minded people and expand their passions. Also, the role of the sales associate is more important than ever as sometimes consumers just want to connect with someone and that interaction and engagement can be just the motivation for them to visit the store instead of shop online.

Concern and alarm

The pandemic certainly raised levels of concern and alarm among consumers, as everyday acts such as shopping, eating and talking suddenly became potentially harmful or even deadly for some people. Added to this layer of concern were additional events such as wildfires across Australia, Europe and the United States, Russia's invasion of Ukraine, rising political tensions within countries and between countries, a rise in authoritarianism globally and inflation and economic concerns.

Given this backdrop of global uncertainty, it is undeniable that the average consumer's level of stress, concern and alarm has risen. There has never been a higher demand for mental health support – whether it be for adults, children or couples, and it has become a pervasive topic on a daily basis at schools, doctors' offices and workplaces around the world.

Renee and her family were lucky enough to be able to work from home, and her kids were in virtual school for a year, so they had no specific reason to go indoors. So from April 2020 until April 2021 (when the vaccine rolled out) they didn't go indoors anywhere except their house or the Airbnb where they were staying. That meant no grocery stores, no going inside to use the bathroom at the gas station, no runs to Target or eating indoors. Although these habits eventually changed, the mindset will continue for some time.

Renee's kids had virtual school for a full year – which was very challenging as they dealt with isolation, hours and hours of online school and just a vacuum of the in-person fun they usually had with their friends. As they have returned to school they are back playing sports, attending Girl Scouts in person, taking art lessons and hanging on the beach with their friends in real life. Even hearing the word 'zoom' in passing makes them shudder and they will not even consider any virtual classes of any flavour, no matter how interesting they sound on paper.

Deborah's son is an elite gymnast and the gym opened back up in July 2020 so she and her son returned to Manhattan, while her husband and daughter stayed in their house and engaged in activities outside with others or enjoyed books and board games inside. The time spent at the gym had a massive positive impact on her son's mental health. He took the subway to get there and back and life felt pretty normal, albeit he often came home to a burnt dinner which he got somewhat used to. Deborah missed going to the gym so she continued running and often started to look for hills in Manhattan to climb. She and her son also found some weights and worked out together at home. When she was at their house, she started swimming again in the ocean and just felt much healthier and happier. Working out was always her adrenaline rush!

Both of Deborah's children also switched schools (one permanently and one for a period of time) as a result of the pandemic. Her son started high school in a very unique in-school setting, but the children stayed in pods and did not engage with other teachers or children. Their teachers zoomed in from other classrooms and the children appeared to stay on top of their schoolwork and learning. He was allowed to socialize with the kids in the pod and it was a nice way to begin a new school with an immediate set of very good friends. Her daughter started off in a rural public school that was pretty much full engagement with the teachers and kids. She loved it and made friends quickly and was even happier when she figured out how to get a custom lunch in a non-custom-lunch environment. When her school opened back up in Manhattan, it was one week in person followed by one week remote and there was Plexiglas in-between the kids during lunch. It was *not* a great experience and she and many of the other girls experienced anxiety, stress and panic attacks. When she graduated from 8th grade (in 2022), it was incredibly real and sad to hear the girls talk about what it was like going to school during the pandemic. A shocking 50 per cent of the class is leaving (including Deborah's daughter) to go to another school for high school (no surprise).

They aren't the only kids that experienced a difficult time during the pandemic. At Renee's son's public middle school in Los Angeles his English teacher had every kid in her class write down anonymously what they were upset about on a piece of paper at the start of the class, crumple it up and throw it to the front of the classroom. Then she would read each of the papers out loud to the class so that everyone in the class could hear that they weren't alone. All of the kids were having challenges with adjusting back to school. Practically every school in every country has had to adjust to these new challenges during this period. Our fear is a mental health epidemic for these children and its lasting impact. The kids have faced long-term isolation, increased stress and lack of access to mental health resources. One of Deborah's friends in the New York tristate area shared recently that the suicide rate in her son's school is the highest it has ever been.

Companies, families and schools are all still dealing with the mental health challenges that arose from the pandemic, and this issue is front of mind for most consumers as well.

Fragmented interests

Consumers are increasingly fragmented in their interests, needs, habits and mentality. Whether this fragmentation is driven by political interests, nationality, age, geography or interests, consumers are not a homogenous group, and retailers are increasingly struggling to thread the needle to appeal to all consumer groups.

During the pandemic the day-to-day impact on consumers' lives has been dramatically influenced by the region in which they live. Renee and Deborah both typically spend a lot of time in Asia, mainly greater China. Countries in the Asia-Pacific region such as Australia, New Zealand, China and Japan cut themselves off from the rest of the world during the pandemic. We are now seeing that the consumer trends in these countries are becoming less and less globally uniform, and more specific to that country or region in particular. The world is becoming less global in many ways, and there has been an impact on retailers who have global footprints.

Even in the United States, where you lived during the pandemic had a major impact on your experience. In Florida it was hard to tell that there even was a pandemic happening, whereas in New York it was impossible to ignore. In fact during the pandemic Deborah found herself reconnecting with old friends from New York who had experienced the 9/11 crisis together. The pandemic was a similar crisis to endure together in New York.

When she went down to Florida for a board meeting in February of 2022, well over 50 per cent of the people she met had moved there from New York during the pandemic.

In today's world, young consumers rarely watch network or cable TV, instead turning online to places like YouTube and TikTok for their entertainment, while older adults align to their favourite streaming channels, news organizations and online publications, further fragmenting interests and diving deeper into their own silo of news, entertainment and cultural touchpoints. Retailers are no longer able to reach a broad spectrum of consumers, and need to adopt a multi-pronged approach to reaching consumers on the platform they use, aligned with talent that appeals to them and their interest group, all while being careful not to offend the other factions. Also, as a result of an increase in the number of news sources, many consumers are finding information that confirms their beliefs, right or wrong. For example, if you want to find evidence that the world is flat, it is pretty easy to become a believer according to a 'news source' somewhere.

Forging connections

As soon as people were not able to connect with others in person, people around the world started finding creative ways to get together and maintain human connections. We are all now way too familiar with Zoom – happy hours, baby showers, funerals, school, meetings, conferences, company bonding experiences, tradeshows, board meetings, doctor's appointments, employee education and virtually anything else we used to do in person has pretty much been done on a Zoom or similar video conference technology at this point. Why did this happen? It's simple – humans need other humans, whether it's for work, school, companionship, support, treatment, shopping or even legal proceedings. We simply are not set up to live alone.

During the pandemic we all experienced this realization and we all took the initiative to find these connections in new ways – whether it be a socially distanced happy hour in a driveaway, a Zoom call with college friends or family games nights.

Deborah forged new connections with liked-minded retail executives to create a non-profit called RetailersUnited, which was originally founded to get personal protective equipment (PPE) into the hands of those who needed it. With her supply chain background, she was able to mobilize PPE and transportation and there were many who supported her. She created solutions for managing the pandemic from a retailer point of view, whether it be procuring PPE for communities in need, addressing supply chain challenges or finding ways for retailers to help their communities. Connecting with other executives during a time of need when everyone was focused on doing good was invigorating during the pandemic and created an almost family-like community that has endured after the crisis. The good of RetailersUnited continues as the organization is working with Parsons and New York Fashion Week to bring over six Ukrainian designers.

Creating community

Consumers are seeking communities. The local community is often being replaced with online communities and special interest groups, linking people with similar interests. Many consumers find community among others who share the same passions, such as you see in the streetwear community or crypto community. Consumers bond over finding and securing hard-to-find limited edition items – whether they are a limited edition hoodies, sneakers or NFTs. Having status has always been important to humans, and with the online and offline worlds merging like never before, consumers are spending at rates higher than expected in retail. As Deborah has always said, nobody is going to be running around the Metaverse naked!

Gaming also often fulfils this need for consumers when they find friends via *Fortnite*, *Roblox*, Twitch or Discord. Renee had several friends whose teens started dating someone they met on Discord during the pandemic. The massive success of *Animal Crossing* during the pandemic and the fact that most gaming consoles were nearly impossible to buy showcased just how important this need for community within the gaming world became at this time.

And in the non-gaming world, groups often formed around specific interests like hiking, running, ceramics, travel, art and music. In extreme situations, we have seen lonely people become radicalized by extreme groups online, mostly because the person was seeking a community.

During the pandemic, Deborah was doing up to three online events per day at times, connecting with the retail community and sharing ideas. She started participating in Clubhouse, where she found that the community really lifted everyone up. However, today she doesn't even have Clubhouse on her phone anymore – showing how communities can thrive when people need them, but can also be short-lived when circumstances change.

The erosion of traditional communities, and increasing fragmentation of consumer mindsets has spurred the demand for new types of communities to arise where consumers find comfort and belonging that fulfils their needs.

Consumer behaviour

Consumer behaviour is changing rapidly and retailers are scrambling to catch up. Some behaviours shifted rapidly out of necessity during the pandemic. These shifts were not temporary, and have led to a major reshuffling of consumer behaviour and trends.

Pursuing passions

Consumers developed new hobbies and passions during the pandemic, and while some were short-lived, many stuck. Whether its gardening, cycling, camping, playing an instrument, cooking or creating, consumers have realized the power of hobbies and passion, and these passions will drive retailers in their niche to satisfy these passions, educate consumers on how to improve and accompany them as they become experts at their passions. A study by Lending Tree found that 6 in 10 Americans took up a new hobby during the pandemic (Schulz, 2021).

During the pandemic Renee took online cooking classes, learned ceramics and doubled down on her passion for travel as she and her family drove all over the West Coast, staying at Airbnbs and camping along the way. Over a six-month period, they stayed at more than 15 Airbnbs, sometimes for a week and sometimes for up to a month. They travelled across a wide range of states and through both urban and rural areas including Utah, Idaho, Wyoming, Montana, Washington State, Oregon and California. And, of course, they bought a lot of gear for these adventures: inflatable kayaks, drones, horseback riding helmets, camping gear and more.

Deborah also took up new hobbies and rekindled old passions. She practiced yoga and went running (reliving her prior track days) and took online courses ranging from curators helping her better understand the works of Cezanne to cryptography and dog grooming (some human grooming too). She enlisted her family (some begrudgingly) in regular family workout sessions and took up cooking – something she has always stayed far away from prior to the pandemic. These habits have stuck and she now regularly works out with her family and cooks much healthier as opposed to grabbing a frozen dinner!

We all took up some passions during the pandemic – some of which will likely stay for a long time, and some of which may go to the wayside, but there has never been a time in the world where so many people developed new hobbies and passions at once, and this will have lasting effects in the retail world. Retailers can tap into these and extend the reach of their platforms.

One of the executives we interview later in the book, Carol Schumacher (2022), gave us the example of US do-it-yourself (DIY) retailers (Home Depot, Lowe's and Tractor Supply). Prior to the pandemic they mostly carried trees and flowers in their outdoor section. Today they have a huge section for people who are growing their own vegetables and fruit. Home gardening has seen a massive boom since the pandemic, and although it will likely not remain at its peak, consumers' behaviour has fundamentally changed in this area. The urban farmer is real and we see many examples (mainly Deborah sees them) of people growing all kinds of vegetables and herbs indoors in Manhattan!

Retailers should examine where they can tap into consumer passions and hobbies and not only sell them things to enable these passions to come to life, but create a community around these groups, offering education, connection and joy. And, if the right kind of community is created, consumers will bring their friends and they will keep returning. We are seeing more and more loyalty programmes come to life as a result of community.

Nesting at home

One of the most fundamental behaviour changes as a direct result of the pandemic is that consumers are spending *much* more time at home. While this was true universally during the height of the pandemic, it has continued after restrictions have been lifted. While some companies have quickly brought employees back to the office, many employees plan to stay at least partially remote indefinitely. And some employees have decided that they will only accept a remote job, with no desire to ever return to the office.

This change has had a massive impact on consumer spending. It drove a huge uptick in the value of homes as people decided to move, either to find a better experience at home, take advantage of being able to work remotely or simply wanted a change of lifestyle. It saw people invest in the comfort of their home – remodelling everything from home offices to outdoor spaces to home expansions. People spent on comforts to make their home enjoyable – outdoor movie areas, comfy couches and bigger and better kitchens. And home decor boomed as the office environment was moved to the home. Some employers even provided allowances to improve home offices. The Twitter account Home Rater ranks people's at-home backgrounds when they are on TV, giving points for colour-organized bookshelves, pristine kitchens and enjoyable art. There were also stories of people having inappropriate items in their backgrounds and people getting called out for iT!

Deborah remembers a call she had during the pandemic with the then CEO of Intel Bob Swan. He talked about how our business relationships were going to be forever changed since we were going to enter the homes of those whom we had only known professionally previously. Deborah can think of many moments where she really learned a lot more about people whom she had worked with for many years. Some would have their kids on their laps during calls, some would yell at their kids, some would be on the other side of a webinar while the doorbell rang over and over and then their wife came in and told them who was at the door, and it was all shared with a large audience. Her favourite was when in the middle of a webinar the door rang and the executive got up and answered the door! Even better, he told the audience about what was being delivered from UPS and the home repair he was embarking on.

During the pandemic, Renee also did a *lot* of online shopping – more than normal. She bought things to make her home more comfortable: bean bag chairs from Wayfair & Lovesac, a rocking chair from Pawleys Island Hammocks and her favourite pandemic purchase: a gas fire pit, without which she is not sure she would have made it through the first few months of the pandemic. She had other pandemic-inspired purchases that were an epic failure as well – the inflatable pool her kids only used once which ended with a dead rat floating in it, the Pogo stick her daughter never used and some impulse purchases of outdoor furniture for a short-lived experimental outdoor space.

Consumers are going to continue to value their home space for some time after the pandemic. Though interest rate hikes will likely dampen the real estate market for a bit, we expect to see consumers continue to find ways to spruce up their existing home for entertainment, work and comfort.

Health and wellness

In general, consumers are more aware of health and wellness than ever before. For many consumers the Covid pandemic brought enhanced aware-ness of eating healthily and boosting immunity, whether via vitamins, supplements, intravenous therapy or other alternative methods. For some consumers fitness became more important than before, with an enhanced desire to be in shape, using wearables for monitoring and purchasing equip-ment to further develop new fitness pursuits. And, for some consumers, health concerns continue to dictate the way in which they conduct their day-to-day life, avoiding crowded places, taking extra precautions and changing their habits. These trends will continue after the pandemic and will influence consumer decisions.

Deborah leaned into health and wellness during the pandemic – she took up running so that she could get out of the house and get some exercise since her gym was closed. In addition, she started to walk the dogs many times a day to the point that they were not even very excited to go out! She was an early buyer of Peloton and really enjoyed the challenges. While she was on the phone with clients, she would ask them for their Peloton username and they would follow each other and ride the same classes together. As someone with celiac disease, she saw huge health benefits from cooking at home and not going out to eat. And when she went to the doctor her numbers were the best they had ever been in her adult life. She felt the best she has in a long time and many of these habits she is trying to continue practicing. While she has returned to the gym, she now often exercises twice a day and the positive impact on reducing stress and improving mental health will have lifelong benefits.

Renee also embraced health and wellness during the pandemic. She hiked, walked and kayaked outdoors, and did the Peloton app on those cold rainy days. She bought both an Apple Watch and an Oura ring to monitor vitals and began paying attention to which foods boosted immunity and made those at home. And she watched her friends do exactly the same types of things in China as they posted home-cooked fresh food, dance videos and running race accomplishments on their WeChat feed.

The health and wellness trend was fairly universal during the pandemic, even if the adoption of the trend was unique to each country or location. Consumers have changed the way they behave to be more conscious of their health and wellness choices – in the food they eat, the activities they do, the products they consume and the technology they utilize.

Digital consumption

It's safe to say that nearly every person's digital consumption increased during the pandemic. Remember those weekly notifications from your phone during the pandemic documenting your screen time? They were laughable at best.

Whether you were young, old, a digital native or a digital newbie, you could not function without digital consumption during the pandemic. It was used for ordering groceries, shopping online, connecting with friends, working, school, streaming entertainment, gaming and just looking things up and following the news. And it was consumed on a variety of devices: computers, smartphones, tablets, TVs, virtual assistants (such as Amazon's Alexa) and even via home systems and appliances.

Renee and her husband stopped policing their kids' screen usage as much as they did prior to the pandemic. And unsurprisingly their usage went way up. During the pandemic the kids were forced to take their social and school interactions online for the most part. But her kids have been back to a mostly full in-person school and schedule for more than a year now.

And here's the interesting wrinkle: they still play with their friends virtually – whether on *Fortnite*, *Roblox*, AmongUs or just calling each other and watching YouTube videos together. Her 11-year-old daughter is just as happy to have a virtual playdate with a friend as a playdate in real life. For one year the kids relied primarily on virtual friendships, and they are just as comfortable in the online world as in the offline world. Even when they are hanging out with their friends in real life and at school, they are all talking about the memes they saw online or laughing at the latest YouTube humour. This was true pre-pandemic, but has intensified.

While Deborah is not much of a consumer of movies or shows, she worked on a project that required her to watch TikTok (her daughter was beyond ecstatic) and she even learned some of the dances (never posted). She also helped a professor at HBS write the TikTok case, which was enlightening. In terms of her kids' digital consumption, she walked into her son's study in late March 2020 to find him playing Xbox. It turned out almost every boy in the class was too! At this point, she and her husband realized that the kids needed to have much greater access to devices to stay in touch with friends. Similar to Renee's family, they stopped monitoring the amount of time they spent on them.

As one of our interviewees in the book, Diane Randolph (2022), put it: 'the pandemic forced people who had only ever interacted in the physical retail channel to the digital channel'. And as another interviewee, Andrew Smith (2022), said 'the pandemic trained people with new skills to interact with technology and retail in new ways'.

This shift in digital habits is a big one for the retail world. It is the underlying reason that much of the technological change and innovation that we discuss in this book is even able to happen. Consumers have to be ready for technology to change, and the pandemic greatly accelerated consumers' willingness to accept digital transformation.

Awareness of sustainability

Sustainability has been a developing and growing topic among retailers in recent years, spurring debate about consumer demand, definitions of sustainability and consumers' willingness to pay more for sustainable products. Consumer mindset on sustainability varies widely according to their geography, income level and age, but one thing is clear – sustainability is here to stay, and consumers, investors and employees will be grappling with how they reward and penalize brands and retailers for their sustainability practices.

Globally, sustainability has become more of a direct issue for consumers which is requiring brands and retailers to quickly adapt to this mindset and put their money where their mouth is to do something to address climate change and environmental issues. For example, on a recent Air France flight, the pilot announced the energy consumption of the flight; Olaplex is seeing an increase in demand in China as they disclose the carbon impact of each items; and the well-known environmental leader among brands, Patagonia, supported non-profits around Europe to combat the damming of rivers throughout Europe.

Deborah sits on the board of a company that had to move from organic cotton to recycled cotton and the company experienced a significant increase in sales as a result of this.

Deborah's family started to compost and also fed any vegetables or fruits to the guinea pigs before they went off. In addition, they were much more mindful of anything they had purchased as they were now living with their things 24/7.

One experiment they tried at the beginning of January 2022 was cancelling their Amazon Prime subscription. They had found 10 pencil sharpeners in their daughter's room because every time she needed one she would casually look around and, upon not finding one after looking for five minutes, she would then 'add to cart'. The impact has been so much greater than they ever would have expected. There are about a fifth of the number of boxes showing up at their house, there is noticeably much less stuff in the apartment and the family is spending much less money on basics

In addition, they also started to sell their previously loved items on Poshmark as most charity stores like Goodwill don't repair merchandise. The kids are thinking about how much they purchase as they now see goods from the beginning to the end of their life and they have a much better understanding of the fact that dropping items at a charity store does not guarantee that anyone will ever benefit from them. In addition, Deborah's grandmother was a professional seamstress in her days and had taught Deborah how to sew. Deborah has threaded a needle and repaired items (mainly hems that were pulled out) when the drycleaners were closed, but she is also thinking dramatically differently about how she takes care of her clothes, how often she washes them, and she is fixing things the minute she sees that they are on the road to disrepair.

Almost every executive we interviewed mentioned sustainability as one of the key consumer changes that they are tracking. When we discussed the subject with the Senior Vice President of E-commerce, Omnichannel, and Master Data Management at Tractor Supply, Letitia Webster, she felt that the most powerful force pushing companies to adopt sustainable practices is demand from the consumer. Despite changes in government regulations and shareholder/employee pressure, she believes that consumers' sustainability habits and the companies that they reward for their initiatives will be the drivers of sustainability for the future.

Consumer needs and demands

As consumers' mindsets and behaviours change, they have new needs, and demands for how retailers should meet them.

Omnichannel

The Covid pandemic rapidly accelerated the adoption of omnichannel retail for all consumer groups of all ages and demographics across the world. Whether it's ordering groceries on Instacart, hailing a ride from Uber, getting drive-up service from Target or purchasing via a livestream from your favourite influencer or retailer, omnichannel retail is no longer a choice, it is a given that young and old consumers alike expect from retailers.

Renee and her family's use and expectations of omnichannel retail changed dramatically during the pandemic. While they were at home in LA where things could be easily delivered, they ordered from restaurants for pick-up or delivery to their house (even buying food supplies from restaurants for a period of time), they ordered food delivery from Whole Foods or Instacart and of course they did a lot of online shopping – from Amazon, Dicks, REI, clothing brands, Etsy and anything else they could think of to keep busy during the initial lockdown.

When Renee and her family were in more rural areas there were less options available for fast online shopping and food delivery. Amazon delivered pretty much everywhere they stayed, but often other delivery options just took too long to get there. In most places they stayed, Instacart and online grocery delivery wasn't available, and there was little to no restaurant delivery. In these areas they relied on curbside pickup heavily – sometimes driving up to an hour to find the nearest Safeway or Target so they could order online and do curbside pickup.

In some smaller towns the local restaurants banded together to take orders for pickup once a week or for special occasions like Christmas or Thanksgiving. They were also able to call local shops to buy something over the phone and have them bring it outside. This came in handy when buying fly fishing gear in Livingston, Montana. Even for retailers with no online presence, pickup was a necessity.

Deborah's family had started to buy goods for the impending pandemic as early as late 2019. She had stockpiled bins of dry food, cleaning supplies, and paper products as well as water and PPE. All of the PPE was donated away, but the family only just finished some of the dry goods in mid-2022. When they left the city, they ordered a weekly delivery of organic vegetables and for quite some time they did not need much else since they had so much food. The family would run to the local drugstore for milk and daily necessities. Once the family depleted much of their supplies, Deborah would drive to Aldi every Friday (the local grocer had a very poorly timed remodel in 2020) where the produce was some of the freshest that she had ever seen and she would pick up milk and other dairy items. The family did scramble to buy bikes for the kids and exercise equipment, but was ultimately able to figure it out with the help of the local Dick's Sporting Goods which had put in place an amazing buy online, pick up in-store (BOPIS) programme and great customer service in general.

Consumers have come to expect and demand omnichannel retail not only from the big box retailer, but from small local shops. You often see consumers shopping in person while looking online for information or coupons or at e-commerce sites for price comparison or product information. Prior to the pandemic omnichannel was a retailer's aspiration, but after the pandemic it is a must-have for the consumer.

Speed

A critical lesson from the pandemic is that consumers expect speed and convenience from all retailers as well as accuracy. Same-day delivery replaced next-day delivery as a consumer expectation, for example, and many consumers are looking for delivery in less than 30 minutes, which is why we have seen the rise of quick commerce. Consumers are no longer willing to wait for things to be delivered, for their questions to be answered or for a lengthy checkout. And if retailers disappoint, they will take to social media to tell everyone.

As Deborah was in New York City during much of the pandemic, she had a myriad of options for quick delivery. She got into the habit of ordering from Gopuff for her groceries and daily necessities. While she made this decision for speed and convenience purposes, she found that she was spending less than she did when she shopped in person. She was only buying what she needed, not the impulse items she saw when she was in the store. What impressed her the most about Gopuff is that she would make recommendations and they would actually carry those exact items. What she found a bit infuriating was using Instacart. Items would be substituted even when she checked the do not substitute box. And, for retailers, she felt that they were giving away the customer experience and their customers similar to what retailers do with Amazon.

Consumers have been increasingly demanding faster speeds from retailers, particularly for delivery, but since the pandemic, their need for speed has become even more pronounced. Retailers need to continually evaluate their speed against competitors and find ways to increase speed and convenience for the consumer.

Inclusivity

Despite political and ideological differences, consumers are seeking inclusivity. This has been partially driven by movements such as Black Lives Matter and the #Me Too movement, but it is also from the need to be seen and served as an individual. These needs span everything from gender to race to size and political affiliations. A 2021 survey by McKinsey found that 45 per cent of consumers believe retailers should actively support Black-owned businesses and brands, and two out of three consumers said that their social values now shape their shopping choices (Brown et al, 2022).

Brands such as Beyond Yoga are offering inclusive sizing and showcasing models across the size spectrum reducing the stigma on 'plus sizing' and providing an inclusive environment for all consumers. Fashionova has a size spectrum so everyone can shop together which really makes the most sense. Similarly, we are seeing cosmetics companies adopt broader skin tone shades, driven by innovators such as Fenty who demonstrated the consumer demand to appeal to a wide spectrum of skin tones and customers. We have seen apparel and footwear brands follow suit by developing a broader range of skin tone colours for underwear, outerwear and a redefinition of the colour 'nude'.

Personalization

Recent years have seen a general shift in power away from retailers toward consumers, propelled by the convenience and power of data-driven e-commerce, as they can compare products and prices with ease online. The advent of smartphones increased this trend, putting massive computing power in the hands of consumers at price points as low as $100. The necessities of the pandemic accelerated this power redistribution even further. Consumers being essentially locked out of physical stores enabled them to discover new online shopping channels, many of which use data to offer higher degrees of personalization, leaving traditional retailers behind. Deborah would argue that there is still much to be done in this arena.

Experiential

After two years when consumers had limited options for offline experiences and replaced this desire by buying things for their home or hobbies, they are now hungry for these experiences. As expected, interest in travel, live performances, parties, dinners, movies and just about every kind of in-real-life (IRL) experience has soared after the pandemic.

As Renee reflects on her pandemic consumption habits, she realizes that her family ended up buying things to try to make up for the fact that they were missing out on their usual experiences like travelling, shows, movies, dinners out, theme parks and everything else they usually spent money on and did for fun. Deborah's family bought a lot of board games and books!

But consumers are also seeking experiences in the retail world. Immersive art experiences have grown in major cities as consumers want to see and live something new and different. They are seeking spaces for these experiences, and want to be surprised and delighted by these immersions.

Renee and her family really enjoyed shopping at small boutiques in Denmark during their first post-Covid trip, revelling in the sense of discovery and delight that is hard to replicate in online shopping. She will cherish the time she spent meeting her sister at a popular outdoor mall in Los

Angeles, at long last, where they could eat outside, she could play with her niece and go shopping all at the same time. She had fun trying on dresses in the boutique in Manhattan Beach nearby where the people who work there really consult with you and give you styling tips. She now has come to appreciate the in-person shopping experiences that are additive to her enjoyment, while skipping the frantic trips to the mall to buy school supplies for the kids or search for a specific piece for a new outfit. She wants to enjoy offline shopping, not just do it to get it over with. If it's a chore, she would rather shop online.

Retailers need to adapt to this need and deliver these surprise and delight experiences in innovative and engaging ways, tailored to each consumer mindset, behaviour and demand.

KEY TAKEAWAYS: TODAY'S CONSUMERS

Since life has somewhat returned to 'normal' and we are carrying on with our usual type of experiences like eating out, going to shows, meeting friends, attending conferences, travelling, having meetings and a myriad of kids activities, our consumer behaviour has not completely returned to pre-pandemic ways.

While everyone had a unique pandemic experience and consumer behaviour was affected in individual ways, we see similarities when we compare with our friends and family. Some bought new houses, remodelled their houses, got into gardening, took up new hobbies, focused on their health and in general started concentrating on the small things in life that can make you happy. Some families had horrible, wrenching experiences that led to dramatic changes in behaviour.

RENEE'S PANDEMIC LEARNINGS

- Experiences can bring more joy than things.
- Online shopping is more convenient than offline shopping, unless you can gain a positive experience from the process of shopping.
- Focus more attention on health and wellness (including mental health).
- Enhance awareness of what makes us happy and what doesn't.
- Life is short, do the thing you want to now.

> DEBORAH'S PANDEMIC LEARNINGS
>
> - Be transparent when facing a crisis.
> - If an employee, colleague or friend isn't supporting you, don't be afraid to have a direct discussion with them.
> - Step out of your comfort zone and try new things.
> - Taking better care of yourself makes you ultimately happier and leaves you with the ability to make better decisions.
> - Spend time with the people you care about and do the things that bring you joy.

Both of us had unique experiences during the pandemic, just like everyone else, but these experiences have shaped a global shift in consumer behaviour that will be long lasting. The last few years has supercharged the pace of change in consumer preferences and habits – regardless of age, race, geography or nationality. Each consumer has changed in different ways, but thematic adjustments have aligned so that we can examine the types of changes in the consumer, which establish the foundation for how retailers need to adapt to these changes in real time, and in ways that their target consumer will accept and embrace.

Addressing changing consumer demand

All of these consumer mindsets, behaviours and demands are coming together at a crucial time for retailers, as they evaluate their growth strategies in challenging global political and economic times.

In order to survive, retailers must look ahead and adopt new strategies and tactics to address these changing consumer demands. In the rest of the book we outline specific ways in which we see retailers adapt to the new consumer paradigm, and we link these business model changes directly to the above consumer behaviour shifts and patterns.

The rapid adoption of the Metaverse, NFTs and blockchain by retailers is directly influenced by consumer distrust in established systems, the need for community and the demand for unique experiences that merge the physical and online world in ways that replicate the joy of online games in the real world.

The rise of instant commerce was turbocharged by concerns for health and wellness and demand for speed and omnichannel solutions to allow consumers to prioritize their time for their passions.

Retailers have responded by using artificial intelligence, mining retail data and delivering sustainable options in order to adapt to the fragmented nature of the consumer mindset, align with core values and principles of the consumer and provide a personalized experience.

We will examine real world examples of how retailers are adopting these strategies, the results they have created thus far and where we see the future of retail innovation. Each of these strategies is pinned to these consumer dynamics and the harsh reality that retailers must innovate to meet today's consumer demands, or suffer the consequences.

References

Blue Bite (2021) The state of QR in 2021. www.bluebite.com/nfc/qr-code-usage-statistics (archived at perma.cc/VCP9-HB3U)

Brown, P, et al (2022) The rise of the inclusive consumer, McKinsey & Company. www.mckinsey.com/industries/retail/our-insights/the-rise-of-the-inclusive-consumer (archived at perma.cc/8XFG-N9QJ)

Randolph, D (2022) Interview with the authors.

Schulz, M (2021) 53% who took on a pandemic hobby went into credit card debt as a result, Lending Tree. www.lendingtree.com/credit-cards/study/quarantine-hobbies-credit-card-debt/ (archived at perma.cc/5RW6-V4Y2)

Schumacher, C. (2022) Interview with the authors, July.

Smith, A. (2022) Interview with the authors, July.

Statista (2021) Market size of QR code transactions in various regions worldwide in 2020 with forecasts from 2021 to 2025, Statista. www.statista.com/statistics/1227799/qr-code-transaction-value-worldwide-by-region/ (archived at perma.cc/P2N5-PF92)

02

Unlocking the Metaverse for retailers

LEARNING OBJECTIVES

This chapter will cover:

- an introduction to the Metaverse
- advertising in the Metaverse, including using augmented and virtual reality
- immersive brand experiences in a virtual environment
- working with virtual idols
- creating brand-led NFTs

An introduction to the Metaverse

First of all – what exactly is the Metaverse? It's a widely used term that can indicate a variety of technological adaptations, but at its most basic level the Metaverse is a computer-generated augmented reality and virtual reality where users can interact with one another in a 3D immersive world. This world allows retailers to realize opportunities in consumer engagement and alternative revenue streams that were previously not possible.

The Metaverse is poised for explosive growth. Coresight Research estimates that the digital innovations market could be worth $100+ billion by 2023, driven by hyper-growth in crypto, the Metaverse, NFTs and other related decentralized finance technologies.

There has been a tremendous amount of hype and speculation about the Metaverse across all industries, including in retail. And many ask whether retailers tapping into the Metaverse is simply a public relations (PR) scheme aimed at generating attention and buzz. And while it is true that most Metaverse initiatives by brands and retailers do receive outsized buzz, this is for a reason, not simply for the sake of gaining eyeballs.

The adoption of the Metaverse is yet another technology that has been accelerated by the pandemic. During more than two years of lockdowns, people became more and more comfortable with virtual interactions. Even older generations have adapted to Zoom meetings, cocktail hours, baby showers, birthday parties, virtual conferences and even funerals. During the very intense lockdowns in Shanghai in 2022 colleagues from an advertising agency arranged virtual gatherings where co-workers interacted in virtual worlds as their avatars in order to alleviate some of the boredom and isolation they felt.

And the true adopters of the Metaverse are the younger generation, who have always been very comfortable in the virtual world. Today's teens are inherent digital natives, with most being able to use an iPad with ease by the age of two. The younger generation also fast-tracked their digital development even more during the pandemic. Most kids, even as young as kindergarteners, had to navigate Zoom school, and with in-person gatherings and activities stalled, kids turned to virtual worlds for their social engagement and entertainment.

Gamers played *Fortnite*, *Roblox*, *Animal Crossing* and other multiplayer games with their friends, immersing themselves in worlds that allowed them to explore, create, battle and strategize. In *Animal Crossing* – one of the most popular games during the pandemic – gamers could create their own virtual worlds, create businesses, buy things, design their outfits and interact with other people in their world. With games like these, players didn't miss hanging out in person or interaction as much as they otherwise would.

After this acceleration, both kids and adults alike are more accustomed to virtual worlds, have seen the benefit of online/offline integration in their lives and have become more open to new experiences and interaction online. And they all have high expectations for performance, design and speed.

While the Metaverse may seem a bit obscure to most adults, these technologies and consumer behaviours are completely native and natural to most pre-teens and young adults today – especially after their shared Covid isolation experience.

How retailers can tap into the Metaverse

So, how can retailers tap into the Metaverse? Who are they targeting with Metaverse activities? How can they bring these to life in a way that integrates their brand personality and business model?

To date, we are seeing four primary ways in which retailers are doing this:

1 They can use augmented and virtual reality technologies to build digital advertising campaigns, which have gained steam in recent years due to their ability to target specific customers. As these technologies improve immersion, and with digital traffic featuring avatars from every corner of the globe, extended reality (XR) advertising is becoming a powerful tool for retailers to reach a larger pool of customers.

2 Brands can look to partner with an integrated platform to provide an immersive user experience, which will be crucial for customers spending hours in a virtual environment. As visuals improve thanks to advancements in immersive technologies, retailers must continue to innovate their spaces to stay ahead of the competition.

3 Using virtual idols and real-world influencers (as digital avatar versions of themselves), which are both growing slices of the overall influencer market, retailers are able to build innovative strategies to control the brand narrative and increase product interaction.

4 Because NFTs are so scarce, retailers and brands can mint and sell exclusive digital artwork, objects and apparel as exclusive, limited-time collections. This provides authentication advantages too, as products are verified by blockchain's immutable record of transactions.

Let's dig into each one of these ideas in more depth, to explore specifically how retailers have tackled each of these ideas to date, and how these areas may continue to innovate in the future.

Advertising in the Metaverse

The easiest and most obvious way for retailers to dip a toe into the Metaverse world is to weave advertising campaigns into popular virtual worlds. Because virtual worlds do not come with any pre-existing land, avatars or environment specifications, retailers have the opportunity to reach more consumers and monetize the space, providing customers with stunning imagery and immersive visuals to reinforce their brand. Many brands have partnered with in-game and XR advertising platforms to introduce virtual billboards and launch commercials in the Metaverse to target specific audiences. Advertisers can also make use of in-game features to advertise events and digital objects. Brands could also curate sponsored content in social communities and strategically place products.

As digital traffic increases and user bases grow, virtual spaces – such as *Decentraland*'s Shopping District or *The Sandbox*'s adiVerse (Adidas) – will become highly coveted for themed advertising. In virtual games based on blockchain, advertisers may purchase land space as NFTs to advertise on, or rent the space from landowners.

Other platforms are partnering with advertising firms to improve gameplay. For example, Subway enlisted marketing agency Cadreon (in Turkey) to partner with digital marketing firm Bidstack, bringing in-game advertisements to *Football Manager*, much like they exist in an actual sports stadium (Bidstack 2020). Bidstack has also partnered with UK-based gaming company Sports Interactive, which developed *Football Manager* (Bidstack 2021b). Coca-Cola, McDonald's and Volkswagen have all engaged in similar strategies, which have improved gameplay realism by 95 per cent and increased intent to purchase by 12 per cent on average according to Bidstack (2021a).

We expect game providers to launch new ways to distribute information to users, such as live news. For example, *Bloktopia* (a blockchain game) will feature a radio with themed stations and curated content. 'Bloktopians' will tune into these stations to receive general and targeted news, presenting an opportunity for brands to advertise their Metaverse events and offerings.

Advertisers can also create curated content that is entertaining and targeted at a particular community. As advertisers will be able to target specific demographics and provide on-theme advertisements with entertaining visuals, customers are much more likely to engage with, and even share, advertisements in the Metaverse. Beer brand Miller Lite debuted a Super Bowl commercial hosted by an avatar spokesperson with stunning simulated outdoor scenery in a N bar (Tepedino, 2022).

Many virtual gaming platforms give developers and creators opportunities to build and play their own games within the environments. Such fully immersive games enable advertisers to seamlessly reach their target demographics with strategically placed products. In this manner, advertisements will be less intrusive and can contribute to improved gameplay. For example, Gatorade bottles were featured in unskippable 'press conferences' in *NBA 2K*. Players can also customize their own Gatorade bottles.

Creating immersive experiences in the Metaverse

As the Metaverse continues to evolve, there will be many different platforms available for retailers to partner with, and possibilities for virtual environments and offerings are essentially endless. It will be important for brands entering the Metaverse to consider joining a platform in which their particular offering will be smooth and seamless, or they risk losing customers to competitors that are continuously innovating.

Brands and retailers that plan to implement in-game commerce should consider selecting platforms that feature instant payments, stunning visuals and immersive experiences, and/or interoperability with other platforms.

Partnering with a platform

The Metaverse has been constantly developing, with brands and retailers employing innovative strategies to build a digital presence. In its infancy, *Decentraland* is one of the oldest Metaverse platforms and is most accessible to users (from desktops). As such, many trends with long-term staying power are being established in this virtual world. The first ever Metaverse-based fashion week took place in *Decentraland* in Spring 2022. It saw immersive experiences, NFT collections, fashion and runway shows, virtual storefronts, panels and discussions, and after-parties, with exclusive NFT collection drops.

Such events in virtual environments enable brands to sell products with minimal setup and overhead costs, and change their offerings, experiences and appearances of storefronts on a day-to-day basis.

Around 95 per cent of game developers plan to construct, or are already constructing, virtual worlds, so opportunities to partner with games will be overwhelming, with each environment offering something unique (Improbable, 2022). However, the cost of each in-world currency will vary significantly. For example, worlds such as *Decentraland* and *The Sandbox* have limited land and token supply, driving scarcity and demand.

There are also opportunities to partner with platforms that create the experience for users either in a number of different virtual worlds or as an independent experience. For example, Obsess is a VR shopping platform that works with retailers and brands to create accurate and realistic virtual versions of real stores to expand customer bases globally; virtual stores with experiences and visuals not possible in the physical world; and Metaverse shopping stores in worlds such as *Fortnite* and *Roblox*, and accessible through Oculus. Clients of Obsess include Coach, General Mills, Nars, Ralph Lauren, Tommy Hilfiger and Universal Music Group.

Many virtual worlds are built on blockchain, but there are also games (such as *Fortnite* and *Roblox*) that are not built on blockchain but have similar systems to support NFTs and in-game transactions (V-Bucks and Robux, respectively). Epic Games, the maker of *Fortnite*, has even partnered with LEGO® to build a dedicated Metaverse for kids. Blockchain payment systems offer instant payments and transactions, security, transparency, authenticity and smart contracts (lines of code written into blockchain that automatically execute contracts when pre-existing conditions are met). Without delays from third parties, virtual economies are free to thrive, unlike in the physical world.

Because Metaverse environments are virtual, there is theoretically no limit to what brands are able to provide for customers. Brands and retailers have the opportunity to create immersive experiences for customers to interact in and learn more about the brand, as well as establish a community for people to spend hours in. Avatars from all parts of the virtual world have access to virtual marketing spectacles – whereas, in the physical world, one would have to travel to Las Vegas or Times Square in New York City, for example, to see amazing displays.

Consumer electronics company Samsung created a virtual experience by purchasing a plot of land in *Decentraland* and opening a virtual store where users can learn about its sustainability practices and donate to plant physical trees, have dance parties with DJs and learn about the latest consumer electronics news. Samsung also hosted 'Galaxy Unpacked 2022' in *Decentraland* to launch the S22 smartphone.

As advances in communications technology, such as 5G, improve the speed and performance of headset technology, brands will be able to create fully immersive, physics-defying environments not possible in the real world that help users to feel as though they are truly living in the virtual world. The longer users spend in the Metaverse, the more opportunity there is for economic activity and interaction with brands.

CHECKLIST

There are a number of virtual worlds that brands can turn to for partnerships, including:

- *Decentraland*: *Decentraland* defines itself as a virtual reality platform powered by the Ethereum blockchain that allows users to create, experience and monetize content and applications.
- *The Sandbox:* Blockchain-based *The Sandbox* is a game and virtual world where you can buy, sell, and trade virtual plots of land. *The Sandbox* is built on the Ethereum blockchain, which acts as its foundation.
- *Fortnite*: A gaming system built by Epic Games that is not built on blockchain, but does have similar systems to support NFTs and in-game transactions through its V-Bucks currency.
- *Roblox*: A gaming platform offering multiple games that is not built on a blockchain, but does have similar systems to support NFTs and in-game transactions via its Robux currency.

Creating virtual idols and partnering with real-world influencers

Brands are beginning to create virtual idols (computer-generated models and avatars) to promote their brands and advertise their products in digital campaigns such as short films, commercials, social media advertisements and short videos on platforms such as Instagram, TikTok and YouTube. These Metahumans don't need to take a break, eat or sleep. Many brands are also partnering with celebrities and real-world influencers by creating digital avatars of them and offering interactive experiences to Metaverse users. Virtual influencers are growing elements of the overall influencer market, and are actually in competition with one another.

Top celebrities on Instagram have the chance to earn staggering figures: on average, Instagram influencers with 1 million followers can expect to make up to $670 per post; users with 100,000 followers can possibly earn $200 per post; and those with 10,000 followers can see $88 per post, according to Search Engine Journal (Walsh, 2021).

Although there are only just over 200 notable virtual idols or 'V-Tubers' in existence, as of February 2022 (Hiort, 2022), that number is growing on a weekly basis and the top idols are set to bring in impressive amounts this year. For example, Lu Do Magalu, a virtual human with over 5.8 million Instagram followers, was created in 2003 by Brazil-based Magazine Luiza, a retailer with many consumer-facing brands. Less popular idols are still set to earn high figures. Idol Imma Gram, who has worked with retailers such as IKEA and ice-cream brand Magnum China, has just over 350,000 Instagram followers. These sources of income would be from more than just social media and Instagram; because these influencers are computer-generated, they can be controlled for specific marketing campaigns with a wider range of use than celebrity sponsors and real-world influencers have.

Brands and retailers operating in China have been employing 'virtual idol' technologies for several years, but they have recently gained more steam due to the improving graphics of augmented and virtual reality. Idols can adjust their personalities, appearance and traits to adapt to changing consumer tastes. In China alone, virtual idols were set to drive $52.6 billion in additional sales by 2023, according to China-based data miner iiMedia Consulting – up from $2.0 billion in 2018 (kyletanchua, 2022).

Rather than partnering with celebrities and social media influencers, brands are able to maintain better control of their brand narrative and adjust idol characteristics to match shifting consumer tastes and company values. Because the virtual human can be controlled, appearance, dialogue, timing of posts and number of posts can all be regulated to whatever the brand or retailer believes is the optimal strategy to engage the most customers – whether that be a short film campaign, social media posts or YouTube content. If brands do not wish to create virtual idols to support their products, they can partner with an immersive-technologies firm to create digital avatars for celebrities to interact with fans in the Metaverse.

However, despite the buzz surrounding virtual idols (in China in particular), real-world Instagram influencers and celebrities are still much more popular.

Haptic technology is making it possible for humans to feel virtual objects within the Metaverse, and full-body suits allow users to control their avatars. Facial tracking in headsets allows fans to have deeper levels of interaction and immersion with the digital avatar of a celebrity, as their avatars are able to mimic facial expressions. Singer Justin Bieber partnered with XR entertainment platform Wave to create and control a digital avatar through a motion-capture suit for a virtual concert, which drew an audience of 10 million listeners, according to MusicTech. Many other musical artists, including John Legend, Travis Scott and The Weeknd have used Wave or other platforms to create digital avatars of themselves and host virtual concerts with immersive visuals.

Releasing products through NFTs

A non-fungible token (NFT) is a non-exchangeable unit of data represented by a mathematical formula known as a cryptographic hash, which is stored on blockchain. Many brands have started to partner with NFT platforms to mint and sell customized collections, raising brand awareness and teaching customers and users about products and the company's history. Apparel retailers are beginning to file trademarks and patents to pair digital objects as NFTs with physical items in the real world, driving exclusivity and scarcity, as well as ensuring authenticity. A variety of different brands and retailers, such as gaming giant Atari, the National Basketball Association, Adidas and digital apparel company RTFKT (acquired by Nike), have already generated millions of dollars through NFT collections.

Businesses wanting to mint NFTs have started to collaborate with NFT marketplaces and existing digital brands to design and distribute virtual goods. Some of the popular marketplaces (and blockchains) to sell NFTs are Axie Marketplace (Ethereum), BloctoBay (Flow), Magic Eden (Solana), NBA TopShot (Flow), OpenSea (Ethereum) and Rarible (Ethereum, Tezos).

Adidas recently collaborated with Bored Ape Yacht Club and PUNKS comic to bring limited-edition digital clothing to the Metaverse, also available in the OpenSea marketplace. Gucci, which recently purchased a plot of land in *The Sandbox*, is having its designers utilize in-game tool VoxEdit to design unique items and mint them as NFTs in *The Sandbox* marketplace, available on OpenSea. Gucci also advertised in *Roblox* with a branded game that was served to almost all users on the platform. Consumer goods corporation Procter & Gamble commissioned artists to create digital artwork toilet paper, then formed a partnership with NFT marketplace Rarible to mint and sell the product. Nike acquired NFT apparel and accessory company RTFKT to pair NFTs with physical goods; RTFKT has NFTs listed on multiple marketplaces.

We will dedicate an entire chapter to NFTs later in the book – this is an exciting element of the Metaverse, and one which lends itself to creativity and innovation.

Monetizing the Metaverse

The Metaverse is still in its infancy, but commercial opportunities are starting to present themselves. As immersive technologies improve, user bases will grow globally and people will be more likely to spend hours of their time in the Metaverse as their digital avatars. The opportunity to reach such a large pool of customers with stunning visual offerings not hindered by the laws of physics is an exciting prospect for brands and retailers.

As one of the biggest retail categories, and one intertwined with impulse purchases and projection of personal identity and image, fashion has one of the strongest potential matches with Metaverse shopping. This type of purchasing can take one of two forms – virtual goods such as clothing for use within the Metaverse, and physical goods, with the Metaverse substituting for e-commerce as a digital purchase channel.

A growing number of brands and retailers are trialling fashion sales in virtual worlds. As mentioned earlier, the first Metaverse-based fashion week took place in *Decentraland*. The event saw immersive experiences, exclusive NFT collection drops, fashion and runway shows, virtual storefronts, panels and discussions and after-parties. Brands and retailers sold not only virtual apparel through NFTs, but also sold physical goods via NFTs tied to physical items on the marketplace or by directing users to their websites.

Rarible, which separately runs an NFT marketplace, purchased plots of land in *Decentraland*, where it hosted a diverse suite of brands, creators and NFT artists in a temporary zone dubbed 'Rarible Fresh Drip Zone' specifically for the Metaverse Fashion Week (MVFW). Notable real-world brands that set up shop were PUMA and Fred Segal, which both opened digital storefronts to sell NFTs. Other real-world brands, such as Perry Ellis and Fresh Couture, opened digital storefronts to gain exposure and showcase collections.

Apparel retailer PUMA teamed up with digital asset marketplace ARTISTANT and Middle Eastern fashion designer Regina Turbina to drop its NFT collection and exhibit it in a virtual store in Rarible's drip zone, part of PUMA's 'She Moves Us' campaign. These NFTs, which included digital sportswear, gear and wedding apparel, will be auctioned separately on ARTISTANT.

Fashion retailing giant Forever 21 is one of the few stores to establish a permanent shop in *Decentraland*. In its storefront, the company presented an exclusive collection of avatar wearables designed for *Decentraland*. Designer Charli Cohen, also owner of NFT company RSTLSS, held a space within *Decentraland* where she sold her NFT avatar wearables, with full pricing information displayed in a user-friendly manner in an immersive setting.

FIGURE 2.1 The Metaverse is a virtual and immersive space where users can interact with one another and computer-generated environments in real time for commerce, entertainment or community

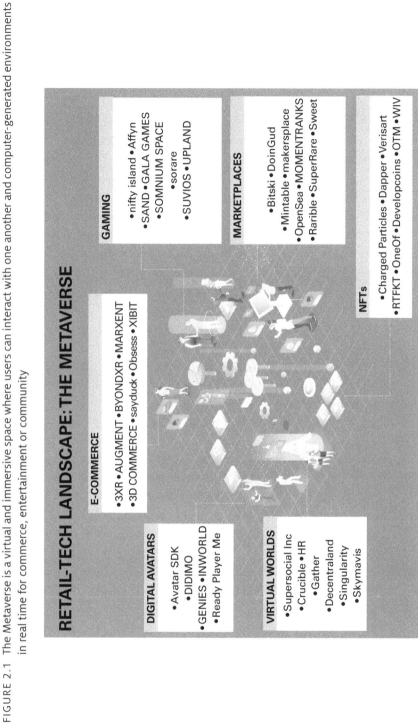

RETAIL-TECH LANDSCAPE: THE METAVERSE

E-COMMERCE
- 3XR • AUGMENT • BYONDXR • MARXENT
- 3D COMMERCE • sayduck • Obsess • XIBIT

GAMING
- nifty island • Affyn
- SAND • GALA GAMES
- SOMNIUM SPACE
- sorare
- SUVIOS • UPLAND

DIGITAL AVATARS
- Avatar SDK
- DIDIMO
- GENIES • INWORLD
- Ready Player Me

VIRTUAL WORLDS
- Supersocial Inc
- Crucible • HR
- Gather
- Decentraland
- Singularity
- Skymavis

MARKETPLACES
- Bitski • DoinGud
- Mintable • makersplace
- OpenSea • MOMENTRANKS
- Rarible • SuperRare • Sweet

NFTs
- Charged Particles • Dapper • Verisart
- RTFKT • OneOf • Developcoins • OTM • WIV

German luxury fashion designer Philipp Plein, Founder of Swiss-based Plein Group, purchased 65 parcels of land in *Decentraland* in mid-February for $1.4 million ($21,540 each on average). During MVFW, Plein debuted 'Plein Plaza', a new permanent attraction in *Decentraland*. In Plein Plaza players can visit a modern museum of NFT artwork and explore NFT collections dropped exclusively for *Decentraland*. During MVFW Plein Group collaborated with 3D artists on virtual catwalks and hosted several parties with Metaverse-native artists.

Estée Lauder was the exclusive beauty brand of MVFW. Also opening a permanent location, the beauty retailer minted a limited quantity of 10,000 NFT wearables inspired by its Advanced Night Repair product. Customers had the chance to 'step inside' the iconic bottle of night repair and receive proof-of-attendance protocol, generating NFTs and digital badges.

Debuting virtual collections and stores were UK-based Selfridges, which provided an immersive journey inspired by its iconic Birmingham store, and Tommy Hilfiger, which partnered with *Decentraland* playground Boson Portal to sell both digital and physical products appearing in its store. Dolce & Gabbana designed an exclusive NFT collection of 20 avatar wearables.

Digital advertising, immersive experiences, virtual idols and NFTs are all examples of unique strategies that brands have employed to establish their virtual presence. The ones that continue to build on these strategies and identify trends with staying power in a timely matter will be able to successfully monetize the Metaverse.

> The Metaverse will be one of the single biggest changes to the retail landscape in the future. It will be a place where consumers can be social and can buy anything they want, anywhere and at anytime.
>
> Terence Ng, Senior Analyst, Coresight Research (2022)

TEN THINGS RETAILERS NEED TO KNOW ABOUT THE METAVERSE

1 The Metaverse is widely accessible to many who use the internet.

2 Gen Z is the first Metaverse-friendly generation.

3 Established Metaverse platforms have a global reach.

4 Demand for virtual land is rising, as land supply in the Metaverse is limited and more brands attract consumers to buy.

5 Brands are creating immersive experiences within 3D games and the Metaverse.

6 NFTs and other digital assets are a new retail revenue stream.

7 Cryptocurrencies enable buying and selling in the Metaverse.

8 Immersive technologies can improve customer experience.

9 The Metaverse can support retailers' sustainability goals.

10 Virtual IP protection will be vital in the Metaverse.

We will deep dive into the key components of the Metaverse throughout the book, but if we leave you with one message, it is that *the time to delve into the Metaverse is now*. Now is the time to experiment, learn and iterate as the Metaverse develops and evolves.

KEY TAKEAWAYS: THE METAVERSE

The Metaverse is still essentially in its infancy and will continue to evolve over time. Given the nascent nature of Web3 and the Metaverse, brands are being afforded a good deal of latitude from consumers as they begin to roll out Metaverse activations. It's a great time to experiment and begin testing and building your brand community. Below are a few ways you can begin to dip your toe into the water:

- Start simple with advertising in a virtual world.
- Create immersive brand experiences in virtual words.
- Partner with a digital platform that attracts your customer base.
- Consider investing in virtual stores or spaces.
- Utilize celebrities and influencers in the Metaverse.
- Create unique NFTs for your brand by partnering or building.
- Monetize the Metaverse by selling digital items or bringing your e-commerce offering to the Metaverse.
- Consider accepting virtual and crypto payments.

References

Bidstack (2020) Case study: Subway. www.bidstack.com/case-studies/subway-x-p161/ (archived at perma.cc/PB37-7JRL)

Bidstack (2021a) *Annual Report & Accounts 2020*. www.bidstack.com/wp-content/uploads/2021/03/Bidstack-Annual-Report-2021.pdf (archived at perma.cc/62NG-YHZL)

Bidstack (2021b) Case study: *Football Manager* 2020. www.bidstack.com/case-studies/football-manager-2020/ (archived at perma.cc/4YS3-3AHC)

Hiort, A (2022) How many virtual influencers are there? Virtual Humans. www.virtualhumans.org/article/how-many-virtual-influencers-are-there (archived at perma.cc/2XKP-YLYZ)

Improbable (2022) New poll by Improbable shows that the Metaverse is perceived as inevitable and the political fight for its future is already on. www.improbable.io/blog/new-poll-by-improbable-shows-that-the-Metaverse-is-perceived-as-inevitable (archived at perma.cc/NH97-9RPP)

kyletanchua (2022) Virtual idols are taking China by storm, tech360. www.tech360.tv/virtual-idols-are-taking-china-by-storm (archived at perma.cc/8U3H-HDCS)

Ng, T (2022) Interview with the authors, July.

Tepedino, C (2022) Miller Lite opens Metaverse bar in *Decentraland*, Rarity Sniper News, February. https://raritysniper.com/news/miller-lite-opens-Metaverse-bar-in-*Decentraland* (archived at perma.cc/U9BA-TA3W)

Walsh, S (2021) 52 Instagram statistics and facts for 2021, Search Engine Journal. www.searchenginejournal.com/instagram-facts/314439 (archived at perma.cc/2BXL-99KT)

03

The rise of livestream shopping

LEARNING OBJECTIVES

This chapter will cover:

- a definition of livestreaming and livestream shopping
- the rise of livestreaming following the pandemic
- the livestreaming ecosystem
- a profile of livestreaming success in China
- an overview of formats of livestreams used by brands and retailers
- debunking six myths about livestreaming
- perspectives and advice from a livestream host

Livestream shopping is already an integral part of e-commerce in China, generating $300 billion in 2021 and accounting for 14.3 per cent of total e-commerce sales, Coresight Research estimates. Coresight expects strong sales through livestreaming e-commerce in 2022, totalling $478 billion and accounting for around 19.5 per cent of e-commerce sales in China (Weinswig, 2021).

Livestream shopping adoption in the US lags behind China. However, the US livestreaming ecosystem is developing quickly. We expect more brands and retailers to use livestreaming as a key promotional or sales channel moving forward, particularly as consumers have increasingly shifted online. Coresight estimates that the US livestreaming e-commerce market will grow from $20 billion in 2022 to $68 billion in 2026 – at which point it will account for over 5 per cent of total e-commerce sales (Weinswig, 2021).

WHAT IS A LIVESTREAM EXACTLY?

Livestreaming is a broad term that covers streaming any live broadcast over the internet in real time, regardless of which platform you are using. When referring to shopping, livestream shopping is when a host presents products during a livestream and viewers can immediately purchase the products easily from the livestream.

The rise of livestreaming post-Covid

The Covid-19 pandemic caused a profound shift to digital services that resulted in significant investments from brands and retailers to remain competitive in the online space. Following the pandemic-led shift to e-commerce and increasing demand for authentic digital engagements from consumers, livestreaming e-commerce (shoppable live video) presents a significant opportunity for brands and retailers to retain consumer engagement online and drive sales through an entertaining and seamless format.

The livestreaming e-commerce landscape has grown increasingly competitive as brands and retailers compete to attract and retain customers by adopting advanced digital tools and creating a streamlined purchasing experience on their owned website or apps. The success of live, interactive sessions depends on community, customer experience and engagement, all of which hinge on a brand's ability to create an effective digital journey for shoppers.

The interactivity of livestreaming enables shoppers to access product information and communicate with the host to receive recommendations and answers to questions, helping brands and retailers to drive customer loyalty and engagement as well as presenting opportunities for them to gather consumer insights and feedback.

The proliferation of livestream shopping events on e-commerce platforms, apps and social media underlines the channel's effectiveness as a customer engagement tool. Brands and retailers are differentiating themselves with adaptive marketing strategies to win in the live-shopping space – with the foundational pillars covering multichannel platforms, frequent schedules, knowledgeable and engaging hosts and creative formats.

Having a regular cadence of livestreaming sessions is a key strategy for brands and retailers to build a base of repeat viewers, fostering new consumer habits. Regular live-shopping schedules enable brands and retailers to become an ongoing part of their customers' lives.

While livestream shopping developed as an alternative revenue stream during the pandemic, some companies are still evaluating various platforms, testing technology infrastructure and refining shopping integration to provide a seamless shopping experience.

As the market grows, new players and formats are emerging online, and brands and retailers are continuing to develop their approaches. In Figure 3.1 we identify three stages in the development of live shopping, from the 'test and learn' approach when shoppable livestreams were first established, to the 'open web' which sees the proliferation of owned video hubs and multi-channel livestreaming. We believe that most brands and retailers are still in stage 1.0 and 2.0, and only a few pioneering companies have entered stage 3.0. As the market becomes more competitive, it is important that brands and retailers develop their livestreaming e-commerce strategies in order to be able to innovate and adapt to consumer preferences and shopping behaviours.

In this chapter we debunk six myths often heard in boardrooms about how to set up livestream events, what consumers value most when it comes to live shopping and the impact on sales of successful digital interaction. By decoding these common myths, we present brands and retailers with critical insights into optimizing their livestream e-commerce strategies to win in the live-shopping space.

FIGURE 3.1 Livestreaming e-commerce development (outside of China)

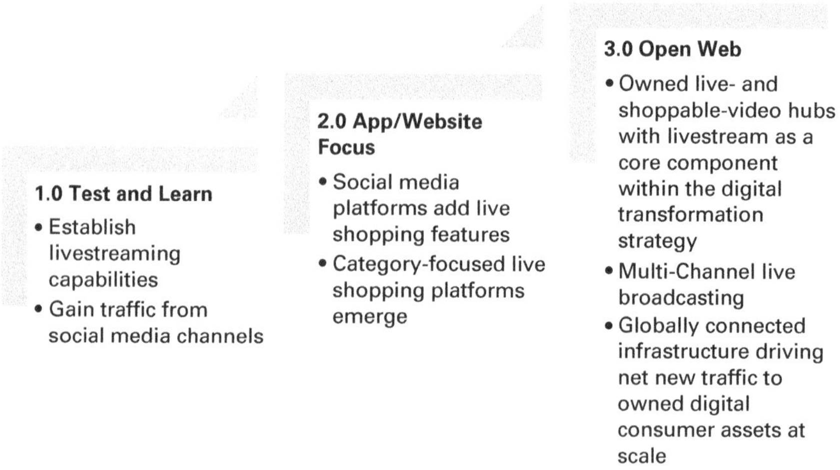

1.0 Test and Learn
- Establish livestreaming capabilities
- Gain traffic from social media channels

2.0 App/Website Focus
- Social media platforms add live shopping features
- Category-focused live shopping platforms emerge

3.0 Open Web
- Owned live- and shoppable-video hubs with livestream as a core component within the digital transformation strategy
- Multi-Channel live broadcasting
- Globally connected infrastructure driving net new traffic to owned digital consumer assets at scale

SOURCE Coresight Research

A profile of livestreaming success: China

With livestreaming already firmly embedded into Chinese consumers' online lives, Coresight conducted a survey of 1,742 consumers in China in Q2 2022 to assess sentiment towards livestreaming in the market. Coresight also conducted a survey of 1,638 US consumers in Q1 2022 asking the same set of questions. By comparing these two surveys we can illustrate how Chinese consumers and US consumers express similarities and differences in the ways that they view the channel. These insights will help us to predict the future adoption of livestreaming globally.

Coresight found that Chinese consumers are very familiar with livestream shopping, with all respondents reporting that they had watched a shoppable livestream (hereafter referred to as 'livestream viewers'). By contrast, less than one-third (32.2 per cent) of US consumers in the Coresight survey reported that they had watched a shoppable livestream (Weinswig, 2022a).

In addition, nearly three-quarters of Chinese respondents reported that they had made a purchase through a shoppable livestream compared to just 15 per cent of US respondents. Among livestream shoppers, there was also a drastic gap in purchasing frequency between China and the US: 52 per cent of Chinese livestream shoppers made purchases at least once a week – 19 per cent higher than the US equivalent subset (Weinswig, 2022a).

Interestingly, Chinese consumers were more focused on the shopping element of livestreaming than US consumers, who predominantly valued the experiences that the channel provided. The Coresight US livestreaming survey found that more than 4 in 10 livestream viewers watched shoppable videos for the entertainment value, and more than 3 in 10 did so to experience a new way of shopping. The proportions of US consumers citing these reasons are 19 per cent and 5 per cent higher, respectively, than in the China survey (Weinswig, 2022a).

While the nature of livestreaming outside of China is more entertainment-based for now, we expect the channel to evolve as brands and retailers focus on differentiating themselves and driving conversion by improving personalization, value and convenience in the livestream shopping journey. To meet demand for convenience in the shopping journey, brands and retailers should look to improve their livestream commerce capabilities, whether on their owned sites or by launching content on third-party platforms. Companies seeking to capitalize on livestreaming should use data and analytics to refine their marketing campaigns and improve their sales performance.

The livestreaming ecosystem

The livestreaming e-commerce ecosystem has evolved since the start of the pandemic, and now includes livestreaming platforms, infrastructure and integration technology.

- *Livestreaming platforms:* Leading social media platforms are enhancing livestreaming commerce functionality with new and improved sales enablement tools to allow in-video purchases, for example. In addition to livestreaming platforms, marketplaces and self-owned websites, as well as dedicated livestreaming sites such as Talkshoplive, provide opportunities for content creators to host and promote live video content.

- *Livestreaming infrastructure:* Brands and retailers can work with technology providers to enter the livestreaming space and enhance their presence. Livestreaming solution providers such as Bambuser, Firework and LiSa offer live-video shopping hardware and software. Other innovators, such as VISX by Omnyway, connect the live shopping experience with a brand's physical store. Buywith can help brands share screens during livestream sessions, so that influencers can jointly host events. And we are seeing the advent of livestreaming shopping festivals by Coresight with its 1010 livestreaming festival, as well as livestreaming platform Verb creating their own festivals.

- *Livestreaming integration:* E-commerce solution providers enable the customization of shoppable videos to target consumers. Brands can leverage influencer networks to extend the reach and engagement potential of their livestream content. Payment providers enable content creators to offer purchase functionality through live video, supporting a seamless shopping journey.

Livestreaming consumer preferences

The 25–34 age group is fuelling growth of the livestreaming channel. The Coresight 2022 Q1 survey suggests that, as these consumers grow more familiar with livestreaming, e-commerce, entertaining and educational content – as well as special deals – will attract them most (Weinswig, 2022d).

Entertainment has become the most popular reason for consumers to watch livestreams, cited by 40.7 per cent of livestream viewers, ahead of

FIGURE 3.2 The livestreaming ecosystem

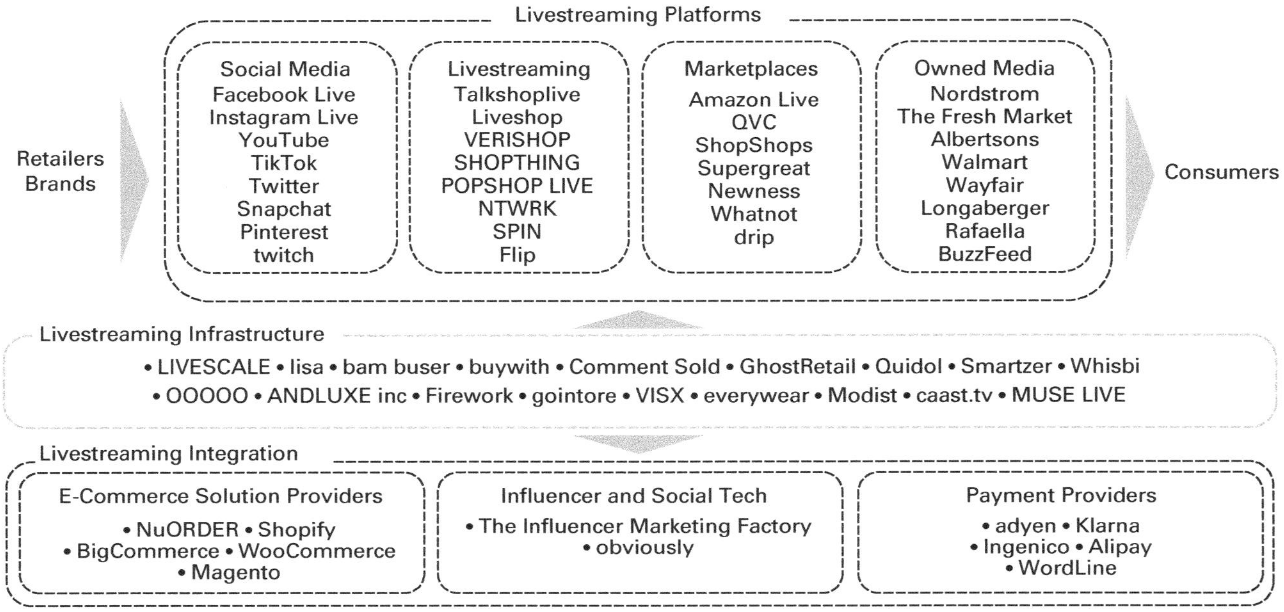

Retailers
Brands

--------- Livestreaming Platforms ---------

Social Media
Facebook Live
Instagram Live
YouTube
TikTok
Twitter
Snapchat
Pinterest
twitch

Livestreaming
Talkshoplive
Liveshop
VERISHOP
SHOPTHING
POPSHOP LIVE
NTWRK
SPIN
Flip

Marketplaces
Amazon Live
QVC
ShopShops
Supergreat
Newness
Whatnot
drip

Owned Media
Nordstrom
The Fresh Market
Albertsons
Walmart
Wayfair
Longaberger
Rafaella
BuzzFeed

Consumers

Livestreaming Infrastructure

• LIVESCALE • lisa • bam buser • buywith • Comment Sold • GhostRetail • Quidol • Smartzer • Whisbi
• OOOOO • ANDLUXE inc • Firework • gointore • VISX • everywear • Modist • caast.tv • MUSE LIVE

Livestreaming Integration

E-Commerce Solution Providers
• NuORDER • Shopify
• BigCommerce • WooCommerce
• Magento

Influencer and Social Tech
• The Influencer Marketing Factory
• obviously

Payment Providers
• adyen • Klarna
• Ingenico • Alipay
• WordLine

SOURCE Coresight Research

both discounts and educational content. This implies opportunities to deepen engagement with consumers with livestreaming, rather than pursue a price-driven, transactional relationship (Weinswig, 2022d).

In addition to low prices and promotions, consumers expect to learn about products and see them in a real-life setting. Marketers should lean into educational content to connect with livestreaming viewers and gain new customers.

Livestreaming platforms

Brands and retailers are increasingly seeking to differentiate their live shopping offerings by livestreaming through their own e-commerce websites rather than livestreaming platforms.

Brands should prioritize a seamless in-video product browsing and checkout process, as the Coresight Q1 2022 survey found that 60.4 per cent of respondents who have watched shoppable livestreams abandoned a purchase due to functionality issues – such as being redirected to another website to complete the purchase (Weinswig, 2022d).

Although social media and video-sharing platforms such as Facebook Live, YouTube Live and Instagram Live dominate the market, brands' and retailers' proprietary websites are gaining recognition. Since 2021, Amazon Live has seen the highest year-over-year growth in recorded user numbers, of 10.8 per cent, while YouTube, 2021's most popular platform, has seen a year-over-year decline. Brands' and retailers' proprietary websites have seen strong growth since the pandemic.

TikTok is aiming to establish an equitable and profitable revenue-share system for retail merchants on its platform. It has added revenue-generating features for its creators in the UK, the US and Canada, and has integrated live shopping features – including in-platform purchase capabilities – in partnership with Shopify. Shopify merchants with a TikTok for Business account can add a Shopping tab to their TikTok profiles and sync their product catalogues to the app to create mini storefronts.

We are seeing a slate of brands and retailers using TikTok to compete in the shoppable-video space. New livestream shopping marketplaces including Spin Live, Popshop Live and Talkshoplive are also emerging to capitalize on the popularity of video content.

Retail companies are devoting a significant budget to livestream shopping. Coresight conducted a survey of 220 companies that are using livestreaming as a sales channel to better understand the retailer's perspective on livestreaming. Half of those surveyed reported that they were spending 10–50 per cent of their total annual marketing budget on livestreaming in 2022, and 28 per cent were spending over 50 per cent on the channel (Weinswig, 2022c). We expect this investment by retailers and brands to continue to accelerate in the near future as technology continues to rapidly evolve and consumers become more accustomed to the livestreaming shopping experience.

Types of livestream formats

There are a number of livestream technology providers that enable consumers to purchase products directly from social feeds, via apps/websites or on dedicated platforms. The format of livestream shopping can vary widely and brands and retailers are increasingly experimenting with the right format to engage their target consumers.

Popular livestream shopping formats created by brands and retailers include:

- *Celebrity/influencer-led livestreams:* Brands and retailers often engage celebrity livestreamers or influencers to host the livestream on the influencer's own channels. These livestreamers have built up a reputation and following on their own channels which provides a huge captive audience for the brands. Livestreamers often create a following for a specific vertical or style, and their followers have a high level of trust in these livestreamers, which leads to a higher intent to purchase.

- *Brand-led livestreams:* Brands and retailers are increasingly hosting their own livestreams which run on their own e-commerce and social channels (rather than on the influencer's channels). This allows the brand to have full production control, full brand control and allows the brand to build up its own audience for livestreaming that they can tap into for future livestreams, rather than relying on an influencer's traffic. This shifts the burden of driving traffic to the brand, but it does allow the brand to create repeat customers and build an engaged fanbase that it can tap into for future events. Examples of brand-led livestreams run the gamut, but some good ones include a founder discussing their inspiration for a product, a showcase of the creation of a product from the factory or workshop where it is made, product designers discussing the craftsmanship of the product or product testers demonstrating how a product is tested.

- *Brand sales person-led livestreams:* Brands are often finding out that while influencers do typically have a large audience base, they are not always the best salespeople for a livestream. Shoppable livestreams often sell the most when the hosts are trained in sales techniques, and they provide clear calls to action and sales prompts. Most consumers have probably watched a QVC show or an infomercial, which are more similar to a livestream than an Instagram story. As a result, brands are tapping into their own sales staff to run livestreams. Their salespeople are already trained in the brand and products, and understand the consumer mindset. Salespeople often have customer lists they can market to, and they can also tap into the brand's audience for a livestream on the following pages.

- *Expert host-led livestreams:* Consumers oftentimes trust an independent expert more than they do a brand spokesperson. For products where third-party endorsers are valuable, such as medical experts (dermatologists, doctors, cardiologists), style setters, technical reviewers or others, having a third-party expert can make a huge difference in the engagement and sales of a livestream.

Debunking myths about livestream shopping

When speaking with executives in the retail industry we often hear questions related to livestreaming, and sometimes the prevailing knowledge of the sector includes myths that are widely believed, but not always true. We debunk six of these prevailing myths about livestreaming on the following pages.

SIX MYTHS ABOUT LIVESTREAMING

Myth 1: Live-shopping marketplaces dominate the livestreaming e-commerce space

Myth 2: Producing live video takes the same effort as TV commercials

Myth 3: Broadcasting on social media will drive sales conversion

Myth 4: Livestreaming is primarily a tool to promote deals

Myth 5: Investing in celebrities translates to sales

Myth 6: Sales conversion is the only metric that matters

Myth 1: Live-shopping marketplaces dominate the livestreaming e-commerce space

Brands and retailers often consider live-shopping marketplaces, independent business-to-consumer (B2C) website/apps, as a live-shopping campaign destination. However, such marketplaces are not the most popular live-shopping destinations among US consumers, according to Coresight Research survey data (Weinswig, 2022d). Brands and retailers should incorporate owned websites into their livestream strategies as the core ecosystem, with social media platforms driving audiences into their website, to gain maximum benefit.

For example, Amazon Live, the live-shopping channel of e-commerce giant Amazon, is one of the most recognizable live-commerce platforms in the US. Amazon has over 300 million active users globally, presenting huge potential for livestream sales among its existing customer base. But Amazon is faced with challenges in driving traffic into livestreams, resulting in lower engagement than social media channels. According to a Coresight Research survey of US consumers (and additional estimates), Amazon falls behind major social media platforms YouTube, Facebook and Instagram in terms of popularity, and ties with TikTok (Weinswig, 2022d). Twenty-eight per cent of US livestream viewers in the Coresight survey reported that they had watched a shoppable livestream on Amazon Live, compared to 45 per cent for YouTube (Weinswig, 2022d).

New live-shopping marketplaces are also emerging to capitalize on the popularity of shoppable-video content, but they have yet to sustain high traction, according to tracking data from digital intelligence provider Similarweb.

Although social media currently represents a key livestreaming destination, this channel might not necessarily steer high performance for marketers (see Myth 3).

Hosting livestreams from a brand or retailers' owned websites represents a strong opportunity for conversion and growth in the live-shopping space as adoption of this selling format increases. Brands and retailers should incorporate owned websites into their livestream strategies as the core ecosystem, with social media platforms driving audiences to their website, to gain maximum benefit.

Myth 2: Producing live video takes the same effort as TV commercials

Companies commonly believe that the video quality of livestream content should be on a par with television commercials and so livestreaming requires million-dollar investments in building studios with professional audio-visual installations. However, this is not the case. Viewers prioritize content, and look to livestreaming to connect with influencers and brands, often deprioritizing production value. For example, when a host talks about a product they truly value or have real experience using, viewers can gain insight into the product as if they are getting recommendation from a trusted friend, boosting authenticity and establishing a stronger emotional connection between the host, the brand and the viewers.

The technical requirements for livestreaming are therefore highly accessible, as only a smartphone, good lighting and user-friendly software are needed to get started, not a professional studio and video team. Selecting a full-suite provider with programming, curation and creator access drives ease of implementation.

Myth 3: Broadcasting on social media will drive sales conversion

Social media may be used as part of an omnichannel strategy to boost brand awareness, but livestream viewership, engagement and conversion have been historically low. Although social media platforms are useful in attracting a broad range of viewers, we see three key challenges with using this channel to drive sales:

1 *Social media lacks seamless purchase functionality, leading to low add-to-cart rates.* While social media platforms are popular among livestream viewers, traffic from these channels does not always translate into sales – particularly if the purchasing process is not seamless, coupled with privacy and security concerns for buying directly on social media. Coresight Research's social commerce survey found that nearly 9 in 10 respondents who use social media for product research or discovery give up on making a purchase at least sometimes due to a platform's lack of in-built checkout functionality (Weinswig, 2022d). For livestreaming specifically, streamlined in-video purchasing functionality is key to driving ultimate conversion.

2 *Social media offers limited data tracking.* Hosts do not have direct access to viewer/conversion data when livestreaming through social media. Owned websites, in contrast, give brands and retailers access to and control of first-party data in real time, to better understand and analyse their customers and improve future livestream sessions.

3 *Displayed ads and influencers offer typically lower return on investment than targeted ads.* Viewers of livestreams on social media are not necessarily engaged shoppers that would make purchases; they often simply watch content for entertainment and remain predominantly engaged to interact with friends instead of brands. Furthermore, they may not be the relevant target consumer of the brand or retailer and so would be unlikely to buy through the livestream. Additionally, social platforms inherently seek to drive any conversion to sale. When their 'intent crawlers' identify a buying signal driven through an algorithm or as a result of brands running a livestream, competitive ads will often be served within a few seconds and in close proximity to the paid livestream content. This is not ideal for driving brand differentiation or if the desired outcome is creating a unique dialogue with audiences.

Social media platforms are actively improving their functionality to address the above limitations and increasingly tap into the rise of livestreaming. However, an end-to-end platform originating from the retailer or brand's website, where intent to buy is highest, is proving to drive far higher conversion.

Myth 4: Livestreaming is primarily a tool to promote deals

Consumers that have watched shoppable livestreams recognize multiple benefits of the channel, one of which is indeed looking for a good deal. However, discovering new products, learning more about products, excitement and convenience were also all cited by more than 30 per cent of livestream viewers in the Coresight survey, demonstrating the varied value that the channel provides to shoppers (Weinswig, 2022d).

Brands and retailers should diversify their livestreaming strategies to focus beyond price and connect with engaged consumers – driving repeat visits via 'shoppertainment' and providing access to shopper data. Executed on a brand or retailer's website, the blend of shoppable short-video and livestream entertainment with streamlined purchase capacity is effective in driving digital consumer engagement and conversion.

Among the earliest adopters of this strategy are department stores and CPG (consumer packaged goods) brands such as Kraft. Kraft Heinz, one of the largest CPG brand owners in the US, began hosting livestream shopping sessions on its own website in November 2021. The brand connected with parents and their children with a seasonal Heinz Halloween exclusive pop-up experience in partnership with Firework. The live campaign was amplified across social channels, as well as the Firework Publisher network.

According to data provided by Firework, Kraft Heinz was able to drive over 675,000 views over the first seven days, exceeding the company's expectations for 25,000 total videos by 27 times, while producing 18 times better engagement than Kraft Heinz's three times expectations (total of 17 million impressions across all platforms) (Weinswig, 2022b).

Myth 5: Investing in celebrities translates to sales

Working with celebrities or influencers to host livestream sessions can boost sales for brands and retailers. However, it is not as simple as that. Brands and retailers must look to engage with influencers that bring an appropriate fanbase; as we mentioned earlier in relation to social media, many celebrities' followers may simply watch livestreams for the entertainment, rather than be engaged shoppers.

Celebrity livestream endorsement is also developing a perception of anti-authenticity within younger skewing demographics; product experts, employees and passionate fans are preferred as primary livestream hosts and participants.

In order to ensure that celebrities' followers lead to high sell-through livestreaming, brands and retailers must look to create an authentic connection with consumers and build trust in their brand and products. This can be accomplished by communicating with the digital consumer audience within a brand or retailer's website.

The livestreaming ecosystem in China provides a model for working with influencers, with top livestreaming hosts Viya and Austin Li having built success by gaining audience trust: shoppers believe that these influencers are working on their behalf to find the best products and deals. Store employees can also make valuable hosts, as they can help online shoppers find products, explain options and features and order out-of-stock items. Shoppers view virtual video assistance – particularly in fashion and large-format stores – as enhancing the shopping experience, underlining the need for retailers to find and train motivated, well-prepared and well-equipped employees.

AT&T provides a live-video service on its website for inquiries and placing shopping orders. Users can receive recommendations on a new phone or advice and expertise on choosing a phone plan for their family. The expert can demonstrate product features and offer the best deal for switching from another cellphone provider (Weinswig, 2022b).

Myth 6: Sales conversion is the only metric that matters

Although a high sales volume is every seller's ultimate goal, livestreaming provides opportunities for brands and retailers to learn about their customers and improve their offerings, through live viewer feedback.

Brands should implement data-tracking capabilities to gain deep and accurate insights into consumers and acquire more leads from livestreaming channels: tailored promotions can drive both revenue and profitability. For example, merchants on Chinese livestreaming e-commerce platform Taobao Live have been leveraging real-time data monitoring to reward live audiences with instant deals when their interaction reaches a certain level, such as free delivery when viewers respond to a quiz. By recommending items to the customer with a suitable promotional cadence, brands' livestreaming will meet predefined promotional goals.

INTERVIEW
Sarah Williams, Shoppable Livestream Host and Producer, T3 Brand Educator and Spokesperson (2022)

One of the key questions we get from brands and retailers as it relates to livestreaming is, 'Who should host my livestream?' Many brands instinctively turn to influencers to host their livestreams, since this is the type of talent that they are most comfortable with and know best. While influencers undoubtedly have their own community and following, which is great for driving traffic to livestreams, most influencers are not direct sellers of products like a salesperson. The second source of hosts most brands turn to are salespeople who work for the brand or retailer already. While these hosts lack the online community of an influencer, they are typically very knowledgeable about the brand, have strong direct sales experience and they know how to ask for the sale and close deals.

As livestreaming becomes more widespread, a new type of host is emerging – one who blends the appeal of an influencer with the selling prowess of a brand salesperson. Think QVC spokesperson for a younger audience with higher consumer engagement and interaction.

Sarah Williams is one of these emerging talents who has excelled in livestream hosting and producing. Sarah originally moved to LA to become an actress – she had always loved comedy and performing. Sarah is a natural in front of crowds, and quickly found a niche hosting events in Hollywood – ranging from red carpet interviews to long-form interview content. While hosting these events, Sarah became extremely adept at making the audience feel comfortable and creating the environment for a relaxed, fun and engaging interview.

During the pandemic, these offline events stopped happening, and Sarah began experimenting with virtual sales events online selling premium hair products. She noticed that initially many brands and retailers used influencers or celebrity talent to host shoppable livestreams. However, these events tended to not be product-focused enough, and the celebrity hosts weren't able to answer product questions in a live setting. Given Sarah's offline event hosting background, she began to try the format out as a host and producer herself and was able to create highly engaging and educational content.

Sarah first started livestreaming on the Amazon platform and she experimented with various formats and approaches. She has adapted her approach along the way, and she hosted more than 100 livestream events in one year alone.

We talked to Sarah about what she has learned from this process, and what types of advice she would give to brands and retailers seeking to dip their toe into the livestreaming space.

While many people may associate livestream shopping with an older customer, similar to the more traditional QVC customer, Sarah told us that a number of livestream shoppers are young. Younger consumers are so comfortable digitally, and especially with the video format after hours spent on YouTube, TikTok and other video platforms, that the livestream shopping format is a natural extension for them. Livestream shopping allows the consumer to have the convenience of shopping from home, with the interactive experience of shopping in-store.

When targeting livestreams to a younger audience, Sarah tells us that the tone should be very different. One app that has succeeded in reaching Gen Z consumers is Supergreat. The key to their success has been in establishing a strong community and has been able to blend the already popular format of podcast style content with livestream shopping to create more of a conversational approach that is more interactive, and less of the host talking 'at' the audience.

When asked what format Sarah recommended for brands to use in their livestreaming activations, Sarah did not choose one specific approach, but rather recommended some tactics to keep in mind when each brand is deciding the right fit for their own customer and brand identity. If the brand chooses to use a celebrity or influencer for their livestream to gain credibility and eyeballs, she recommends adding a co-host to the livestream to pair popularity with deep product knowledge and selling skills. Influencers and celebrities often seek to keep their content as authentic and non-commercial as possible so that their consumers trust their opinions – this is often the opposite tactic of a direct sales approach.

Sarah sees the future of livestreaming developing in a few different ways:

- Brands will adopt livestreaming on their own site – both in one-to-one and one-to-many formats.

- Brands will accelerate the adoption of using one-to-one selling tactics online, allowing their salespeople to interact with customers virtually in a consultative selling experience.

- New apps will arise where consumers will engage in livestreaming via a virtual mall or marketplace, allowing consumers to access multiple livestreams in one place (similar to Alibaba's Tmall in China).

When planning your livestream, Sarah recommends that each livestream be centred around four key pillars:

- sales

- brand and product education

- community building

- authenticity

And it's important that brands and retailers remember that livestreams are 'live'. Much like the TV show *Saturday Night Live*, anything can happen at any time. Even the best-laid plans can change once you go live, so it's important for the hosts to have these pillars to come back to when things change during the livestream.

Sarah reminds brands and retailers that this is the Wild West in terms of livestream development, which makes it the perfect time to test and learn what will work for your brand and community.

TEN THINGS RETAILERS NEED TO KNOW ABOUT LIVESTREAMING

1 Livestreaming has shown the highest level of commercial success in China, with other markets growing rapidly, but still a small percentage of the size of China's livestreaming market.

2 Retailers should create a regular cadence of livestreaming in order to create success – it's not a one-time event, it needs to be sustained over time.

3 While consumers in China watch livestreams primarily for shopping purposes, consumers outside of China primarily watch livestreaming for entertainment.

4 Retailers are hosting livestreams on their own platforms (website, social) as well as on partner and social media sites.

5 Livestreaming does not need to be highly produced, and can be done with just a smart phone, high-quality lighting and user-friendly software.

6 Livestreaming on a retailer-owned platform allows for maximum control and targeting, along with rich data.

7 Retailers should test multiple livestreaming hosts to assess which type resonates with their consumer base.

8 Livestream hosts should not only be celebrities and influencers, retailers and brands should look to their own sales staff, founders and third-party experts to enhance brand knowledge and credibility.

9 Brands should create a clear messaging strategy prior to each livestream to ensure the livestream stays on message and produces the intended results.

10 Now is the time to experiment with livestreaming!

KEY TAKEAWAYS: LIVESTREAMING

Livestreaming has emerged as a targeted way to blend entertainment, shopping and experience for consumers in a virtual environment. While many retailers look to the platform for quick sales success, it is advisable that retailers utilize the platform for more than just sales, and seek to optimize their livestreams for consumer engagement, education and as a way to gain customer insights. By taking a broad approach, retailers will be able to test and learn as they launch a series of livestreams, and can learn and iterate along the way.

Below are key takeaways to keep in mind when developing your own livestreaming strategy:

- Set broad metrics for success including sales, engagement and customer insights.
- Evaluate your technology platform and partner for integration, ease of purchase and data/insights provided.
- Ensure you are reaching the right kind of customer who is not only interested in your brand, but has a propensity to purchase on livestreams.
- If you partner with influencers or experts, make sure they are knowledgeable about your product and brand.
- Ensure you are attracting traffic to your livestream, consumers can only participate and buy if they attend!
- Experiment with different livestream formats, engagement tactics, hosts and locations and assess what works and doesn't work along the way.
- Stay up to date on the latest trends and case studies across comparable brands – the industry is evolving quickly.

References

Weinswig, D (2021) 2022 China e-commerce trends: Opportunities under pressure, Coresight Research. https://coresight.com/research/2022-china-e-commerce-trends-opportunities-under-pressure/ (archived at perma.cc/38UT-XWE8)

Weinswig, D (2022a) China vs. US–livestreaming e-commerce adoption, Coresight Research. https://coresight.com/research/china-vs-us-livestreaming-e-commerce-adoption-infographic/ (archived at perma.cc/8DM6-P2V4)

Weinswig, D (2022b) Six livestreaming myths debunked: How to optimize US livestreaming e-commerce strategies, Coresight Research. https://coresight.com/research/six-livestreaming-myths-debunked-how-to-optimize-us-livestreaming-e-commerce-strategies/ (archived at perma.cc/6AGG-JDTD)

Weinswig, D (2022c) Understanding the livestreaming opportunity: Global retail executive survey findings, Coresight Research. https://coresight.com/research/understanding-the-livestreaming-opportunity-global-retail-executive-survey-findings/ (archived at perma.cc/H2UY-Q7QY)

Weinswig, D (2022d) US social commerce survey 2022: Capitalizing on social media influence in retail, Coresight Research. https://coresight.com/research/us-social-commerce-survey-2022-capitalizing-on-social-media-influence-in-retail/ (archived at perma.cc/RK8G-YMZ7)

Williams, S (2022) Interview with the authors, July.

04

Quick commerce

LEARNING OBJECTIVES

This chapter will cover:

- a definition of instant or quick commerce
- an analysis of delivery platform versus vertically integrated instant commerce players
- key instant commerce players
- Instacart case study
- UK Grocers case study
- sustainability and instant commerce
- the future outlook for instant commerce

WHAT IS INSTANT OR QUICK COMMERCE?

Instant or quick commerce refers to e-commerce transactions that are delivered or are ready in a very short period of time – anywhere from five minutes to less than 24 hours. In particular we have seen a huge increase in this activity in the food and grocery markets with the advent of grocery, drugstore or restaurant pickup, grocery and restaurant delivery and purchase online and pick-up via dedicated apps.

Online grocery shopping surge underpins quick commerce demand

Consumers have retained shopping behaviours learned during 2020 – most notably, elevated levels of online shopping. The online grocery boom in 2020 supported the emergence of a micro-industry of instant-need players, competing with more established operators that typically offer longer delivery windows for a share of the expanding grocery delivery market.

The pandemic acted as a significant catalyst in accelerating online grocery adoption, driving fundamental, lasting changes in consumer behaviour. According to data from Coresight Research, around one-quarter of consumers made grocery and CPG (consumer packaged goods) purchases online throughout 2021 – even when consumer avoidance of public spaces hit its trough (Weinswig, 2021a). Coresight Research's US consumer survey in October 2021 found that almost half (48.8 per cent) of respondents had bought groceries online in the past 12 months (Weinswig, 2021a). We expect the online channel to see permanent gains as consumers retain their online shopping behaviours post-pandemic.

Coresight Research estimates that retail sales (predominantly grocery/ essentials) by major players in the overall quick commerce market will total $20–25 billion in the US in 2021. This equates to a 10–13 per cent share of Coresight's estimate for US online CPG sales, which we expect to total around $191 billion in 2021 (Weinswig, 2021a).

This is supported by retailers investing in omnichannel shopping experiences for their customers. Physical retail spaces are being repurposed as micro-fulfilment centres to adapt to shifting consumer shopping behaviour. This is evident in the persistent usage of the buy online, pick up in-store (BOPIS) and curbside-pickup services offered by retailers such as Target and Walmart. Investors are betting big on instant needs, with a host of companies securing significant seed or sequential financing rounds since the beginning of 2021.

Convenience is now more of a retail concept than a retail channel. No longer does a consumer need to walk or drive to their local convenience store to grab last-minute essentials; instead, convenience store selections (and more) come to them via quick-commerce operators. Not only has the quick-commerce sector expanded in terms of geographic coverage and product offerings, but the number of players has boomed. The explosion in industry participants is heavily concentrated on the vertically integrated segment, where players promise deliveries from their own fulfilment centres to urban consumers in as little as 10–15 minutes.

There are significant differences between quick-commerce players – in scale, business model and delivery offering – and with these distinctions come differing advantages and economies.

Instant commerce business models

The quick-commerce landscape includes longstanding same-day delivery platforms that deliver orders from local, third-party retailers, including DoorDash, Shipt, Instacart and Uber Eats (which acquired Postmates for $2.65 billion in November 2020). These companies deliver products (largely grocery items) from third-party retail stores. In some cases, these delivery firms pick the orders while in others they only fulfil delivery. The promise has traditionally been for 'same-day' delivery, although options now range from 30 minutes to several hours.

The instant commerce delivery platform business model

Under the delivery platform model, product inventory is owned by third-party retailers and the delivery operators aggregate these third-party merchants on digital platforms.

ADVANTAGES

- Delivery platforms operate an asset-light model, which does not require fulfilment centres to be deployed or supplier relationships to be established before entering a new city.
- These platforms will usually offer more choice than vertically integrated players, although the overall offer will be driven by the operating hours and the selection of the third-party retailers' stores.

CHALLENGES

- The store-pick model employed by delivery operators is more susceptible to out-of-stocks as the platforms do not have full, real-time visibility into the retailer's in-store inventory.
- Delivery platforms surrender pricing power to third-party merchants (retailers) and some retailers raise prices on delivery apps to help offset the merchant fees that they pay to the delivery firm. Some municipalities cap merchant fees, which can push up consumer fees.

- A reliance on per-transaction fees suggests a relatively straight line for costs as sales grow, meaning delivery platforms have a lesser degree of operational leverage than the dark store model.

Instant-needs players generate their contribution margin largely through the difference between product costs and product sales. For delivery platforms, variable consumer fees are the principal driver of contribution margin. As they operate an asset-light model, they carry lower inventory risks and can scale faster. The substantial order volumes and pace of growth in the sector confirm that consumer demand for immediate fulfilment is there.

DoorDash has adopted a hybrid approach with third-party delivery capabilities (Marketplace and Drive) as well as operating a vertically integrated model through its DashMart dark stores. Each of its 25 DashMart locations carries around 2,000 stock-keeping units (SKUs) and provides both delivery and pickup options.

Among the delivery platforms, Uber's 'Delivery' segment Uber Eats remains loss-making, with an adjusted earnings before interest, taxes, depreciation and amortization (EBITDA) margin (as a percentage of gross bookings, which is akin to gross merchandise volume) of 1.6 per cent in the first quarter of 2021 and 1.2 per cent in the second quarter. Uber's Delivery gross bookings increased by 85 per cent year over year to $12.9 billion in the second quarter; this is worldwide and largely restaurant bookings – on an earnings call, management commented that 'grocery and new verticals' (which includes convenience and alcohol) accounted for about 5–6 per cent of total gross bookings (Weinswig, 2022a).

At DoorDash, adjusted EBITDA as a percentage of gross order volume stood at 0.4 per cent in the first quarter of 2021 and 1.1 per cent in the second quarter. DoorDash reported $10.5 billion in gross order volume in the second quarter, up 70 per cent year over year, largely comprised of restaurant orders. Management stated that 'non-restaurant orders now are totalling over 7 per cent of our total orders' in the first quarter (latest indication). On a statutory basis, DoorDash's EBIT margin was (9.2) per cent in the first quarter of 2021 and (8.0) per cent in the second quarter (Weinswig, 2022a).

The instant commerce vertically integrated business model

With the acceleration of consumer demand for quick commerce solutions, we have seen a number of vertically integrated players join the sector. These operators build their own first-party micro-fulfilment centres (MFCs), akin to dark stores, and engage employees to pick orders as well as couriers to deliver them. Vertically integrated instant commerce companies pick from a range of essential items in their own dark stores and courier them to shoppers, typically within 10–30 minutes. Vertical integration is key to rapid delivery: instant-needs operators procure their own inventory and build out their own MFCs for picking orders.

ADVANTAGES OF VERTICAL INTEGRATION

- Vertically integrated MFCs are optimized for speedy picking and are strategically located as close to customers as possible, enabling instant-needs operators to promise such short delivery times.

- By owning inventory, vertically integrated players also have greater visibility on product quality, inventory supply and pricing.

- Instant-needs companies typically carry a fast-rotating assortment of 1,000–2,000 goods (although Gopuff offers up to 4,000) that are localized to the neighbourhoods they serve. For example, Buyk takes a 'hyperlocal' approach to assortment to ensure that its MFCs stock meets the specific needs and desires of shoppers in each particular area it serves.

- Some operators are planning to flex their SKU range. Instant-needs company 1520, which typically carries 1,500 items, said that it is planning to achieve 3,000 SKUs in the near future, targeting a wider range of consumer needs.

CHALLENGES OF VERTICAL INTEGRATION

- Instant-needs e-commerce depends on a degree of population density (and more so when the delivery time is as little as 15 minutes) and as more players enter the market, the risk of increasing rental costs for MFCs in urban locations could drive upfront investment.

- Setting up MFCs and procuring inventory requires capital investment before entering a new city or market.

- The underlying model of investing in (dark) stores and relying on operational leverage to drive margins has some similarities to traditional brick-and-mortar retail, and comes with similar weaknesses (and strengths), such as volume sensitivity.

In the instant commerce sector, vertical integration enables:

- *Speed*: Delivery in 30 minutes or less due to faster picking and reduced transit time.
- *Availability*: A real-time view of inventory.
- *Pricing*: Balancing competitiveness and margins.
- *Assortment*: Localizing assortments and expanding beyond convenience-store essentials.

We see the impact extending beyond a shift of market share: widespread consumer use of quick commerce could ultimately result in a partial disaggregation of grocery baskets and other shopping trips.

We have seen a boom in funding in the vertically integrated instant-needs segment, which we calculate totals $5.9 billion to date (Weinswig, 2022a). Gopuff has captured over half of that: its valuation jumped to $15 billion after a July 2021 $1 billion fundraiser (Weinswig, 2022a). In the vertically integrated instant-needs segment, Gopuff is the largest and most established player. New entrants focused on shorter delivery times include Fridge No More, Gorillas, JOKR and 1520.

All of the vertically integrated instant-needs players discussed are privately owned. Nazim Salur, CEO and Founder of Getir (not yet in the US market), told *The New York Times* that a neighbourhood can be profitable after a year or two (Nelson, 2011). Similarly, Gopuff management has stated it has achieved profitability in every market that it has operated in for more than 18 months (Weinswig, 2021a). Furthermore, German online grocery and restaurant delivery company Delivery Hero has disclosed a profit contribution of €1.30 ($1.50) per order in its DMart dark-store business (Weinswig, 2021a).

Instant commerce economics: Scale

Scale is a key component of profitability for vertically integrated instant-needs players. Since they are vertically integrated, instant-needs operators can secure more advantageous prices from suppliers as they scale. And, as in regular retail, greater volumes equate to a leveraging of fixed operating costs, driving margins.

Like conventional retailers, instant-needs players generate their contribution margin largely through the difference between product costs and product sales. This is a key distinction from delivery platform models, where variable consumer fees are the principal driver of contribution margin, topped up by fees charged to merchants.

Delivery platforms do not need to build out physical infrastructure or inventories. As a result, these businesses are able to scale relatively quickly. From July 2020 to July 2021, Instacart increased its delivery reach from 30,000 stores to nearly 55,000 stores in North America and is available to over 85 per cent of US households.

To increase network density, delivery platforms are adding new retail partners outside the core grocery business. Instacart has added apparel (H&M), beauty (Sephora), general merchandise (Big Lots) and prescription delivery (Costco) to its portfolio. In addition, Shipt has also expanded beyond grocery to include apparel delivery from Target stores. For traditional grocery players that had outsourced delivery and pickup, diversification will be essential in bringing more last-mile operations in-house. Globally, the online grocery market tends to see retailers take more control of last-mile logistics (such as truck fleets) than in non-food retail.

For all models, greater scale opens more opportunities for secondary revenue streams, notably retail media or in-app advertising. The shift of grocery sales online is driving advertising to where shoppers are – on retailers' websites and apps. Kroger and Walmart are among the established grocery retailers pursuing opportunities in retail media. In May 2020, Instacart launched a new self-serve advertising programme that CPG brands can use to promote their products on its website and app. Furthermore, Gopuff launched its Gopuff Ad Solutions business in June 2021.

At the Groceryshop 2021 conference, Yakir Gola, Co-Founder and Co-CEO of Gopuff, pointed to the company's opportunities in retail media, stating that as an instant-needs platform, it can influence the customer's decision at the moment of consumption (Weinswig, 2021a). DoorDash launched a new advertising offering in October 2021.

Key instant commerce players

In 2011 and 2012, respectively, Postmates (now Uber Eats) and Instacart established the quick-commerce, or hyperlocal, delivery model. Their model is built on working with third-party retailers (or restaurants) for the product itself. These quick-commerce firms are fulfilment intermediaries, traditionally promising 'same-day' delivery, although the lower ranges of this (offered at a premium) have been pushed down to 30–45 minutes. Postmates collects orders from restaurants and retailers and brings them to the customer while Instacart picks and delivers from partner stores on behalf of the customer.

TABLE 4.1 Quick commerce in retail

Key metrics	Vertically integrated instant needs	Delivery platforms – grocery	Delivery platforms – meals	Traditional e-commerce
Business model	Vertically integrated	Marketplace for local grocery stores	Marketplace for local restaurants	Vertically integrated and marketplaces
Product focus	Essentials	Groceries, some non-food retailers	Restaurant meals	Groceries and non-food
SKUs	1,500–5,000	25,000+	N/A	100,000+
Delivery speed	10–30 minutes	Same day (from ~35 minutes to several hours)	30–60 minutes	1–2 days
Curation	High	Low	Low	Low
Localization	Highly localized to individual neighbourhoods	Localized to city	Localized to city	Not localized
Warehousing	MFCs	N/A	N/A	Regional or local fulfilment centres
Delivery methods	Individual and pooled deliveries	Individual and pooled deliveries	Individual and pooled deliveries	Pooled deliveries
Delivery model	Contractors or W2 employees	Contractors	Contractors	Employees/ third-party logistics
Technology implementation	Merchandising, warehousing, logistics	Logistics	Logistics	Merchandising, warehousing, logistics
Market players	Buyk, DoorDash DashMart, Fridge No More, Gopuff, Gorillas, JOKR, 1520	DoorDash, Instacart, Shipt, Uber Eats (incl. Postmates)	DoorDash, Uber Eats	Amazon, many others

SOURCE   Company reports and Coresight Research

Established in 2013, Gopuff took quick commerce and turned it into instant needs, carving out the abovementioned vertically integrated segment, offering delivery in an average of 30 minutes. Following its move into third-party grocery in 2018, DoorDash entered the vertically integrated instant-needs space in August 2020. It has established its own DashMart convenience stores offering delivery of essentials in 30 minutes or less.

More recently, 15-minute commerce operators have intensified instant needs in terms of speed promises. Operators such as Fridge No More, JOKR and 1520 have entered the market, borrowing the vertically integrated model to promise delivery in as little as 10–15 minutes.

Table 4.1 compares vertically integrated firms with delivery platforms. We have added in a comparison with meal delivery platforms and the traditional e-commerce model, too.

Following the influx of new entrants, the instant-needs space is looking unsustainably over-supplied and profit-challenged. Consolidation, with some nascent players falling out of the market, looks inevitable given the glut of businesses competing on such similar selling points and often on the same turf. This will likely be compounded by longer-standing players (from both the first-party and third-party sides) continuing to expand aggressively.

It is challenging to discern a medium-term path to profit for small operators promising ultra-fast deliveries and no fees. Coresight survey data suggests that consumers are currently willing to trade off some delivery speed for low or no fees and competitive product prices. Longer term, reduced competition in a more concentrated market – and one with a greater proportion of consumers accustomed to quick commerce – suggests that there will be greater opportunities for firms to pass reasonable costs on to customers. However, emerging players in a capital-intensive sector will need to have the financial support to survive such a consolidation.

CASE STUDY
Instacart

Instacart is perhaps one of the best-known instant-commerce companies. It received a huge boost in usage from the Covid pandemic. Instacart allows consumers to purchase from (mostly) grocery stores by using the gig economy to have shoppers shop on behalf of the consumer and then deliver to their house. Instacart's app allows shoppers to communicate with consumers and enables the consumers to approve substitutions or provide input to the shopping process.

In addition to its core offering of grocery shopping on demand, Instacart has broadened its offerings beyond just delivery, recently announcing 'The Instacart Platform' suite of enterprise tools, which provides e-commerce, fulfilment, in-store functions, advertising and insights to other retailers. The offering is particularly appealing to small grocers, which cannot afford to make the technology investment to go online. Instacart is betting that the trend for instant-commerce in the grocery sector will continue to expand. Instacart's CEO Fidji Simo expects online grocery penetration to approach the 30 per cent figure of other retail segments (Weinswig, 2022b).

Instacart's competition has increased due to investment from Amazon, Walmart and instant-needs retailers, which target a younger demographic. On its new platform, Instacart can manage advertising on other grocers' websites, and Fidji Simo highlighted the potential of retail media, commenting that the ultimate grocery business model could evolve to one in which retailers run their online grocery businesses at breakeven and earn a profit on their advertising (Weinswig, 2022b).

CASE STUDY
UK grocers: A new wave of ultra-fast delivery

Prior to the pandemic, online grocery was mostly fulfilled and delivered by established supermarkets (with items picked from stores and then delivered via vans to consumers) or by online-only players. Since the onset of the pandemic, UK restaurant delivery aggregators such as Deliveroo and Uber Eats have capitalized on more people ordering groceries online and have partnered with various supermarkets to deliver products for more or less immediate delivery.

The onset of the pandemic brought aggressive expansion of a new breed of delivery startups – primarily in London – with the promise of grocery delivery within 10–15 minutes via bike or moped. Key players to have launched London operations following the pandemic in 2020 include:

- Dija – November 2020 (acquired by Gopuff in August 2021)
- Getir – January 202 (Getir announced that it had agreed to acquire Weezy)
- Gorillas – March 2021
- Jiffy – April 2021
- Weezy – July 2020
- Zapp – January 2021

These players built their own, hyperlocal, delivery-only fulfilment centres (also known as dark stores) and cut out the retailers for sourcing products. Moreover, they deliver through fully employed riders in contrast to the gig model employed by other on-demand delivery operators.

The operators vary slightly when it comes to charging customers a delivery fee. Gorillas charges Londoners £1.80 ($2.46) to deliver its products with no minimum order value. In contrast, Getir does not charge a delivery fee, but has a minimum order value of £10 ($13.7).

Ultra-fast delivery players typically carry a product assortment of about 1,000–2,000 goods, which is much smaller than the range of 15,000–20,000 found in grocery stores. The hyperlocal nature of their business model enables them to pick and reach customers quickly, in many cases being quicker than the shopper going to store themselves.

The rapid delivery operators have plans to launch operations beyond London. In addition to six warehouses in the capital city, Weezy plans to open more across the UK. Dija plans to expand its service beyond London by acquiring Cambridge-based delivery startup Genie. Moreover, Jiffy plans to open over 20 warehouses across the UK. After its London launch in March 2021, Getir intends to expand its operations in Birmingham and Manchester (Weinswig, 2021b).

Nearly all of these superfast grocery delivery platforms have raised significant seed or sequential financing rounds. For example, Getir's valuation jumped from $850 million to $7.5 billion following three funding rounds between January and June 2021. Similarly, Gorillas achieved unicorn status in March 2021 with a $290 million Series B funding (Weinswig, 2021b).

According to financial data provider Pitchbook, on-demand grocery operators have attracted more than $14 billion in investments since the start of the pandemic and over $8 billion from January to April 2021, surpassing 2020 levels (Weinswig, 2021b).

As the instant delivery via dark store model is still emerging, the companies operating in this space are still loss-making, which can be attributed to the high level of discounts to attract customers, as well as investments in real estate, marketing and technology. However, early signs are encouraging. As part of its acquisition of UK-based instant delivery startup Fancy in May 2021, Gopuff highlighted it has achieved profitability in cities where it has been operating for more than 18 months (Weinswig, 2021b).

Additionally, looking to rapid commerce operators in other markets, Berlin-based prepared food/grocery retail delivery operator Delivery Hero disclosed a profit contribution of €1.30 ($1.50) per order in its DMart dark store business (Weinswig, 2021b).

We believe that basket sizes and order frequency will rise if consumers come to trust in instant commerce services and products, eventually improving their unit economics. However, operators may face difficulty in increasing delivery fees once a regular order habit among consumers has been created, especially given the competitive environment. Additionally, on-demand delivery works best in areas with high population density and as more platforms enter the market, the risk of increasing rental prices for dark stores could increase upfront investment.

The chance UK grocers had during the pandemic to reset their relationship with UK consumers should not be underestimated. The industry has served consumers well when they needed it and there will likely be a lasting benefit to this, both at an industry level and at company level, despite a return to on-premise consumption.

Implications for retailers and instant commerce players

We expect that the instant-commerce trend will continue past the pandemic as consumers become accustomized to the players, convenience and time-savings they experienced during the pandemic. As retailers consider how to adapt to this new environment, we have identified several watchouts for retailers and instant commerce players:

- Retaining the loyalty of shoppers who switched to them at the start of the pandemic should be the priority for traditional retailers. Revamping loyalty programmes, boosting healthy product assortments and making stores easier to navigate is vital for retailers.

- With the influx of funds into the ultrafast delivery space, the market has reached the point of saturation, with many startups operating with the same underlying technology and broadly offering the same products. As the sector matures, we anticipate some consolidation in the near term, as evidenced by Gopuff acquiring small UK grocery delivery operator Fancy and Dija and Getir announcing its acquisition of Weezy.

- Discounters have got back on their feet after a tough 2020. However, grocery e-commerce has traditionally been an Achilles heel for discounters as costs associated with picking, packing and delivering orders sit uneasily with their no-frills model. Amid the pandemic-induced online demand spike, grocery discounters should look toward a more aggressive omnichannel approach to stay competitive, including acquiring a delivery startup or tech startup to overhaul their entire online operations.

- Amid the rise in online shopping, grocery retailers are focusing on artificial intelligence, highly personalized engagement and innovative technologies to grow stronger and more resilient in the face of change. Technology vendors must capitalize on the environment and pitch the importance of their solutions for grocery retailers' pain points.

The substantial order volumes and pace of growth in the sector confirm that consumer demand for rapid fulfilment is there. Given their different business models, delivery platforms and instant-needs players will have different impacts – the former relies on partnering with legacy retailers while the latter competes with those retailers for share. The competitive pressures are already prompting major chains to embark on ventures into immediate fulfilment.

However, we see the impact extending beyond a shift of market share: widespread consumer use of quick commerce could ultimately result in a partial disaggregation of grocery baskets and other shopping missions – pulling purchases out of larger, more regular shopping trips and into standalone, 'as-needs' purchases. This would echo multi-year trends that we have seen in other markets, including in Europe in recent years, where expansion of convenience formats propelled a partial fragmentation of the traditional weekly shop into multiple, smaller grocery trips. This could be replicated in the US – the distinction now is that this would be driven by a new retail model rather than a rival retail channel.

Looking forward, we believe online grocery has a bright future, driven by pandemic-induced stickiness, the addition of new capacity and market expansion through the instant commerce sub-channel. As such, retailers have a unique opportunity to capitalize on shifting trends and the still-evolving e-commerce experience. They will have to balance participation with the underlying economics to ensure that higher participation does not negatively impact their businesses. Additionally, the struggle with online among discount retailers means it could become an important competitive weapon in traditional retailers' arsenal.

INTERVIEW

Carol Schumacher, strategic advisor for investor relations and public relations to C-suites and boards (2022)

Carol has spent the majority of her career in the retail sector. She served as Walmart's Global Investor Relations Officer for 11 years, and also held senior leadership positions with The Home Depot.

When asked about what the future of retail will hold, she believes that sustainability will increasingly be one of the core values for the future – not just because of companies feeling like they need to report on sustainability, but because consumers are demanding greater change.

By looking into efficiencies within the retail store and e-commerce landscape there are opportunities to make incremental sustainability gains that many retailers are currently overlooking. Looking at changes that have affected both operations and customers in a variety of ways, she cited the prevalence of self-checkout, especially at Walmart stores. When this technology first launched, consumers were wary of it and often relied on employee associates to help them through the checkout. But today most customers can check out by themselves and frequently also scan items as they shop due to its convenience and speed.

Walmart also continues to see growing acceptance of pickup in store or home delivery among customers. This creates efficiencies in shopping as one worker typically shops for multiple orders at once, not only cutting down on time from consumers, but also adding less redundancy in the workers' jobs, as many move from behind the checkout counter to shopping in store for customers.

And as retailers optimize delivery from the store, they can find ways to make the process more sustainable, such as driving hybrid or electric cars, planning efficient driving routes to use less gas or the use of delivery drones or other methods to increase efficiencies when compared to consumers driving themselves to and from the store.

Retailers see several advantages from sustainability initiatives and can achieve multiple goals; they can become more sustainable without necessarily adding costs to the retailer or raising prices for the consumer. Retailers will continue to look for ways to incentivize their customers to choose delivery and options that increase efficiency and deliver sustainability benefits.

For example, there is a Kroger in Dallas that is experimenting with a virtual food court called Kitchen United Mix where you can mix and match your orders from different food vendors, and Kroger will package it up for you, and you can pick up your order or have delivered in one bag.

Carol sees technology as a game changer in making these efficiencies even more possible, as they allow for cost reduction, improved employee satisfaction, enhanced consumer experiences and more sustainable outcomes. And as technology accelerates there will be even more opportunities for these changes to occur, whether they be in seamless checkout via RFID, NFT-enabled barcodes or advances in robotic technology.

Carol has the following advice to retailers as they seek to enhance the customer experience, increase efficiency and find sustainable outcomes:

- Enhance creativity in how you message the use of new technology.

- Pay attention to the experiential factor for your consumers – and how you communicate with them. Do more than send emails and post on social media.

- There have been many advances in supply chain, but also significant disruptions, during the past two to three years. Leverage your supply chain even more. Look for and analyse how you can increase efficiency and sustainability within your supply chain to drive ongoing sustainability benefits.

TEN THINGS RETAILERS NEED TO KNOW ABOUT QUICK COMMERCE

1 The quick commerce market exploded following the pandemic.

2 Speed is the key reason that consumers are choosing quick commerce.

3 There are two primary business models for quick commerce: a pure delivery model and a vertically integrated model.

4 The quick commerce industry has seen tremendous investment in the sector since the pandemic.

5 As the market matures, consolidation is occurring within the industry.

6 Quick commerce can enhance a company's sustainability efforts.

7 Retailers are experimenting with ways that quick commerce can enhance the purchase experience.

8 Quick commerce can augment supply chain efficiencies, as well as improve employee workflow.

9 Technological improvements have allowed for rapid improvements in the quick commerce sector.

10 Consumer demands for quick commerce have continued past the peak of the pandemic and we expect consumers to continue to utilize quick commerce in the future well past the pandemic.

KEY TAKEAWAYS: QUICK COMMERCE

Consumer behaviour has been irreversibly shifted as a result of the pandemic and consumers have become accustomed to new ways of shopping that provide near instant delivery. Instant commerce is not right for every business, but in some industries it has completely changed the ways in which they operate. As you evaluate how quick commerce can change your business, keep the following takeaways in mind:

- Consumers have shifted their delivery expectations to a much shorter time frame across industries from restaurants and groceries to drugstores and hypermarts.
- There are a number of different business models for quick commerce players – ranging from full vertical integration to partial to delivery platform.
- Understand who are the quick commerce players in your sector and geographies and look for ways to partner with them.
- Evaluate how quick commerce can increase efficiencies in your business – starting from the consumer and encompassing your workers, supply chain and processes and procedures.
- Look for opportunities to increase your sustainability measures via quick commerce.

References

Nelson, E (2011) Groceries in 10 minutes: Delivery start-ups crowd city streets across globe, *The New York Times*, 27 July. www.nytimes.com/2021/07/27/business/groceries-in-10-minutes-delivery-start-ups-crowd-city-streets-across-globe.html (archived at perma.cc/VSZ4-DL6D)

Schumacher, C (2022) Interview with the authors, July.

Weinswig, D (2021a) From quick commerce to instant needs: Exploring business models in rapid delivery, Coresight Research. https://coresight.com/research/from-quick-commerce-to-instant-needs-exploring-business-models-in-rapid-delivery/ (archived at perma.cc/P8BH-EYSJ)

Weinswig, D (2021b) Market outlook: UK grocery retailers – pandemic creates opportunities for instant commerce channel, Coresight Research. https://coresight.com/research/market-outlook-uk-grocery-retailers-pandemic-creates-opportunities-for-instant-commerce-channel/ (archived at perma.cc/R7WA-9KWM)

Weinswig, D (2022a) Quick commerce in Europe: Expansion meets consolidation in rapid delivery, Coresight Research. https://coresight.com/research/quick-commerce-in-europe-expansion-meets-consolidation-in-rapid-delivery/ (archived at perma.cc/2C7B-LUXL)

Weinswig, D (2022b) Shoptalk 2022 day two: Strategic growth opportunities for retail – livestreaming, digital tech, the Metaverse and more, Coresight Research. https://coresight.com/research/shoptalk-2022-day-two-strategic-growth-opportunities-for-retail-livestreaming-digital-tech-the-Metaverse-and-more/ (archived at perma.cc/V73A-D3MB)

05

Advancing sustainability

LEARNING OBJECTIVES

This chapter includes insights and discussion around the following five components of the Coresight EnCORE framework:

- environmental engagement, including selected environmental regulations and standards
- circular models, with examples of recycling and resale programmes from Eileen Fisher, Uniqlo, VF Corporation and more
- optimized operations, covering sustainability in resource consumption as outlined by the United Nations (UN)'s Sustainable Development Goals, including water, energy and fuel
- responsible supply chains, with a focus on environmental impact
- excellence in reporting and communicating to build consumer trust and loyalty and become a champion of sustainability in retail

We also discuss the state of the resale market and highlight examples of innovative startups driving advancements in the sustainability industry.

The time for sustainability in retail is now

Interest in sustainability did not go away with the arrival of Covid-19; it was just momentarily superseded by concerns of health, employment, household finance and access to essentials. Consumers' values and priorities have shifted: with less need for new fashion, some consumers have increased their focus on brand values that resonate with them personally, from inclusivity to manufacturing origin. This shift has resulted in heightened consumer awareness of sustainability; Coresight Research's survey of US consumers in August 2021 found that for 29 per cent of respondents, sustainability was more of a factor when shopping because of the crisis (Weinswig, 2020b).

Investor interest is growing as well. Investment management firm BlackRock noted that as investors sought to rebalance their portfolios during coronavirus-led market turmoil, they increasingly preferred sustainable funds over more traditional ones (Weinswig, 2020a). In the first quarter of 2020, global, sustainable, open-ended funds (mutual funds and exchange-traded funds) brought in $40.5 billion in new assets, a 41 per cent increase year over year. US sustainable funds attracted a record $7.3 billion for the quarter (Weinswig, 2020a).

For businesses, the pandemic has revealed the fragility of global supply chains and disparate workforces. The business community is looking to achieve environmentally sustainable practices that do not add cost but instead provide cost savings. The good news is that many sustainable business practices are profitable in the intermediate to long term, although they involve some upfront cost and require the learning of new processes and ways of doing business.

Employees, investors and consumers expect sustainability to be addressed at the companies for which they work, in which they invest and by the brands from which they buy. Consumers expect it – and demand it – and use social media to out companies that are remiss. According to the Boston Consulting Group, 75 per cent of consumers believe sustainability is 'very important', with more than a third willing to walk away from their preferred brand due to lack of sustainability initiatives (Weinswig, 2020a).

SO, WHAT IS SUSTAINABILITY?

Sustainability means different things to different people. Its original meaning was simply that a process could be repeated over and over without ever running out of raw materials – i.e. the practice could be sustained indefinitely. The UN's World Commission on Environment and Development is perhaps the most-quoted on the definition of sustainable development as 'development that meets the needs of the present without compromising the ability of future generations to meet their own needs' (Weinswig, 2020a). This definition originated in 1987 with the *Brundtland Report*, which introduced sustainable development and how it could be achieved.

In recent years, sustainability has come to mean much more, and the term now tends to include areas such as environmental practices, social responsibility and even corporate governance.

According to the US Environmental Protection Agency (EPA):

Sustainability is based on a simple principle: Everything that we need for our survival and well-being depends, either directly or indirectly, on our natural environment. To pursue sustainability is to create and maintain the conditions under which humans and nature can exist in productive harmony to support present and future generations.

(Weinswig, 2020a)

Navigating sustainability for retail

Navigating the sheer volume of issues that fall under the umbrella of sustainability is daunting. In this chapter we simplify this for retail by narrowing the scope of sustainability to an environmental focus.

Supply chains are often the low-hanging fruit when it comes to delivering greater efficiency and driving sustainable practices: it is all about reducing waste, but greater efficiency and lower resource consumption can also mean lower costs. A long-term strategy with sustainability built in can deliver on the triple bottom line: people, profits and the planet – the three Ps. In fact, corporations that plan with climate change in mind secure an 18 per cent higher return on investment than companies that do not do so, according to Challenge.org (Weinswig, 2020a).

The three Ps result in a fourth P – progress. Retailers are in a unique position to drive change, given the large number of vendors with which they work: retail has a unique ability to influence sustainability practices across a large number of industry players.

EnCORE framework for environmental sustainability in retail

Coresight Research has developed the EnCORE framework to help retailers and brands frame their approach to sustainability. The framework comprises

FIGURE 5.1 Major milestones in the evolution of sustainability

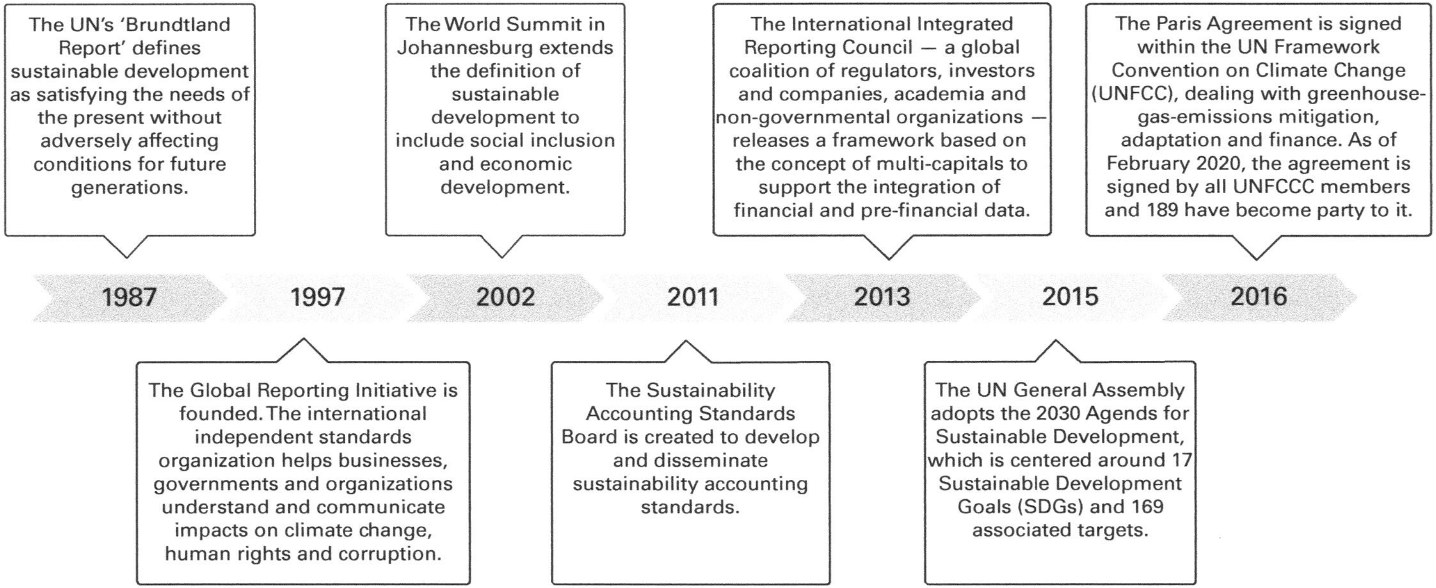

1987
The UN's 'Brundtland Report' defines sustainable development as satisfying the needs of the present without adversely affecting conditions for future generations.

1997
The Global Reporting Initiative is founded. The international independent standards organization helps businesses, governments and organizations understand and communicate impacts on climate change, human rights and corruption.

2002
The World Summit in Johannesburg extends the definition of sustainable development to include social inclusion and economic development.

2011
The Sustainability Accounting Standards Board is created to develop and disseminate sustainability accounting standards.

2013
The International Integrated Reporting Council — a global coalition of regulators, investors and companies, academia and non-governmental organizations — releases a framework based on the concept of multi-capitals to support the integration of financial and pre-financial data.

2015
The UN General Assembly adopts the 2030 Agends for Sustainable Development, which is centered around 17 Sustainable Development Goals (SDGs) and 169 associated targets.

2016
The Paris Agreement is signed within the UN Framework Convention on Climate Change (UNFCCC), dealing with greenhouse-gas-emissions mitigation, adaptation and finance. As of February 2020, the agreement is signed by all UNFCCC members and 189 have become party to it.

SOURCE Coresight Research

five components (see Figure 5.2), providing a model through which retailers can begin to internalize a sustainability strategy (Weinswig, 2020a).

In the following sections, we outline the five components of EnCORE, discuss how companies can make progress in each of them and provide examples of companies that are taking the lead.

En: Environmental engagement

Environmental engagement is the starting point to developing a sustainability strategy, and it begins with awareness of how your industry impacts the environment.

The key component of environmental awareness is understanding – of one's own operations and supply chain (both internal and external processes), plus peer practices and incremental industry shifts. Businesses should seek

FIGURE 5.2 The EnCORE framework

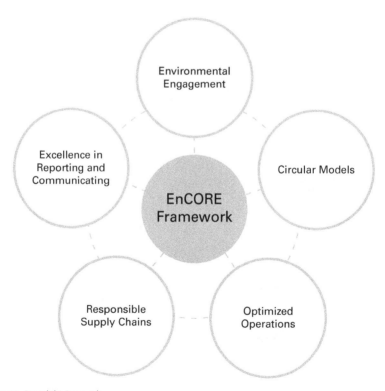

SOURCE Coresight Research

the opinions of all stakeholders, including employees and investors, and seek to understand consumer demands and preferences on sustainability.

There are four ways in which retailers and brands can take advantage of external sources to bring knowledge, awareness and experience into their organizations:

- Lean on external research and draw on third-party information to deepen understanding of industry priorities and to build awareness of consumer demands. From a strategic perspective, external research informs and validates business decisions, improving the ability to gain competitive advantage.

- Engage advisory groups or specialist consultants to assist with a company review – providing input, conducting analysis and identifying risks and opportunities as well as offering assistance in developing sustainability objectives and creating an action plan. Look at sustainability strategies across other industries for inspiration.

- Work with environmentally focused non-governmental organizations for examples of how to operate using fewer resources.

- Join with retail peers to determine sustainability best practices and leaders. Review corporate environmental and sustainability reports of best-in-class corporate citizens. Stay informed on new processes, technology, innovation and solutions.

Once retailers understand the issues, they should be bold. Companies should develop a plan around the sustainability issues where they can have an immediate and direct impact, while establishing a longer-term sustainability strategy and vision comprising specific sustainability goals. Retailers should look to collaborate across their business ecosystem and work with vendors, service providers and other retailers to improve the environment. By increasing the number of companies addressing environmental sustainability in business operations, costs should decline and profits improve.

C: Circular models

Retailers and brands can adopt circular models to minimize the environmental impact of their products and maximize the recirculation of materials back into use.

As opposed to a linear business model, in which inputs come in one end and products out the other, circular models emphasize the optimization of resources and the elimination of single-use products – so many materials re-enter at the start of the cycle. The key to building circular models is to design waste out of processes across the supply chain and choose materials that can be used in closed loops – i.e. materials are brought back into the production process, and resources are continually repurposed in a recycle and re-use loop.

Retailers striving towards zero waste should measure consumption, waste and recycling rates to find opportunities for improvement, and often, the end of a product's life is a good place to start. Product quality and durability are requisite for a successful circular business model, and warranties and repair services are a means of extending a product's life. For example, VF Corporation offers warranties and repairs through its Eagle Creek, Eastpak and The North Face brands, while Clothes the Loop is active at approximately 150 The North Face stores worldwide for shoppers to extend the life of clothing from any brand in any condition.

Rental and resale services tap into consumers' growing demand for sustainable business models, complemented by the growth in the sharing-economy mindset (exhibited by the success of Airbnb and Uber Technologies). Retailers are increasingly adding resale services to their offerings to capitalize on this trend – driving store traffic, attracting new consumers and promoting a circular economy at the same time.

Sustainable end-of-life processes include recommerce, recycling, upcycling and recovery programmes that reuse or repurpose products, often deconstructed and incorporated back into the production cycle. The apparel market provides numerous examples of such programmes:

- Patagonia's recycle, repurpose and repair programmes.

- Trove, Recurate and ReUpp work with retailers to recover their brands.

- Everlane's reuse of materials to create sustainable cashmere and denim.

- Clothing brand Eileen Fisher was an early advocate of sustainability. It champions the notion of 'buy less, make less' as a sustainable solution and moved the apparel industry from a 'take–make–waste' model toward a circular one. The Eileen Fisher brand launched its take-back programme, Eileen Fisher Renew, in 2009 – through which it resells used Eileen Fisher items. The programme has taken back approximately 1.4 million units; this represents less than 2 per cent of the total number of units produced since the company's 1984 founding, suggesting significant opportunity. According to the brand's founder, Eileen Fisher, it 'employs about 30 people in Renew [as of April 2020]… and it is a profitable piece of the business'. Additionally, Fisher believes that take-back initiatives present a 'huge opportunity for a lot of companies' (Weinswig, 2020a).

- Re-imagining, re-inventing and disrupting existing business models for more sustainable solutions is fundamental at VF Corporation and its brand portfolio. In addition to piloting rental and recommerce (The North Face Renewed), a focus on sustainable design led to the 2019 launch of Future-light at The North Face, the brand's most efficacious technical product line as well as its most sustainable material (or the product with the smallest footprint). The North Face worked with like-minded suppliers and vendors in the development of Futurelight, which is constructed with 90 per cent recycled materials. Furthermore, VF Corporation has trained 36 per cent of its European design team in circular design principles. By beginning with circularity at a product's inception, VF Corporation can extend the useful life of materials, which is key to reducing the company's total environmental footprint (Weinswig, 2020a).

Technology has delivered some solutions in the form of digitally native rental and resale services that have grown rapidly, enabling consumers to monetize clothing, accessories, jewellery, home goods and art that they no longer want – and which otherwise may end up in the landfill.

Meanwhile, taboos against second-hand goods have also dissipated, benefiting online startups such as ThredUP and The RealReal, in addition to thrift stores and consignment services. This has also spawned many new rental programmes. Although rental services involve additional shipping and product dry cleaning, it is still a greener option than fast fashion, which results in overproduction that has detrimental effects on the environment.

Consumer acceptance of second-hand goods is gaining momentum in other sectors, too:

- Outdoor retailer Recreational Equipment Inc (REI) sells used sleeping bags, tents, apparel, portable showers, bags, ski poles, snowboards and other gear and recently expanded its rental programme to 75 per cent of its brick-and-mortar stores.

- At VF Corporation's Kipling, a rental model is in pilot as the company targets large-scale commercialization of brand-led recommerce and rental circular business models.

- US furniture and home décor retailer West Elm partnered with Rent the Runway to offer modern décor under the Rent the Runway concept, enabling short-term home décor rental with the option to buy later. Products include hand-selected bundles of pillows, throws, shams and quilts.

Charitable donations and give-back programmes are another form of recycling that offers retailers the opportunity to build stronger ties with the community while also tackling a problem, and retailers can secure tax breaks as well:

- Uniqlo's recycling programme distributes wearable items to refugees and disaster victims, while unwearable clothing is made into paper products and plastic fuel pellets.
- VF Corporation's Timberland and its non-profit partner, Circularity, provide footwear for people in need in the US. In the UK, Timberland partners with TRIAD, a network of more than 1,500 charity clothing banks and charity shops.
- Zara provides used clothing to non-profit projects.

Sustainable options exist for excess inventory too. Rather than sending overages to the landfill, retailers should consider price markdowns, which would lower the impact on the retailer's bottom line. Another option is selling to an off-price retailer such as Burlington, Marshalls or TJ Maxx, or to online discounters such as bluefly.com and overstock.com. These value retailers have seen increasing traffic in recent years as consumers seek out national brands at value prices while engaging in a treasure-hunt shopping experience. Ideally though, retailers and brands should better align supply and demand to reduce overages.

O: Optimized operations

Supply chain aside, there are many opportunities for retailers to optimize operations using a more resource-efficient infrastructure and decarbonization technologies. Greater efficiency throughout the entire lifecycle cuts resource use and reduces a retailer's environmental impact.

The 2030 Agenda for Sustainable Development was adopted by all UN Member States in 2015. It is described by the UN as a 'blueprint to achieve a better and more sustainable future for all' and is centred around 17 Sustainable Development Goals (Figure 5.3). Retailers can use the SDGs as a baseline to assess their sustainability profile and build a more sustainable business model.

A number of the Sustainable Development Goals (SDGs) explicitly deal with the environment; we discuss these in more detail on pages 88–90.

FIGURE 5.3 The United Nations' 17 Sustainable Development Goals of the 2030 Agenda for Sustainable Development

1 NO POVERTY	**2** ZERO HUNGER	**3** GOOD HEALTH AND WELL BEING	**4** QUALITY EDUCATION	**5** GENDER EQUALITY	**6** CLEAN WATER AND SANITATION
7 AFFORDABLE AND CLEAN ENERGY	**8** DECENT WORK AND ECONOMIC GROWTH	**9** INDUSTRY, INNOVATION AND INFRASTRUCTURE	**10** REDUCED INEQUALITIES	**11** SUSTAINABLE CITIES AND COMMUNITIES	**12** RESPONSIBLE CONSUMPTION AND PRODUCTION
13 CLIMATE ACTION	**14** LIFE BELOW WATER	**15** LIFE ON LAND	**16** PEACE, JUSTICE AND STRONG INSTITUTIONS	**17** PARTNERSHIPS FOR THE GOALS	SUSTAINABLE DEVELOPMENT **GOALS**

SOURCE Adapted from the UN

WATER

The 'clean water and sanitation' goal (SDG #6) seeks to address the world's dwindling drinking water supplies, which have been affected by increasing drought and desertification. Installing meters and tracking water usage throughout operations and the supply chain can help identify where the greatest opportunities are to cut water use. Low-flow technology, for example, can save water with minimal impact on the user experience. Water-efficiency treatment systems that return water for reuse after purification also reduces water usage – in addition to cutting costs.

ENERGY

Demand for cheap energy and an economy reliant on fossil fuels has led to climate change, which the UN addresses under 'affordable and clean energy' (SDG #7). Investing in solar, wind and thermal power can help companies reduce their carbon emissions.

Technology can provide the means to reduce energy and material consumption. Examples include power capacitors, high-efficiency laundry machines, smart refrigerators and kitchen appliances, and power strips.

Lighting is an important element in physical retail, creating an ambiance that impacts the shopping experience and thus sales. However, lighting accounts for 35 per cent of energy use in the US. The US Department of Energy estimates that energy-efficient light bulbs could save $120 billion in annual energy costs (Weinswig, 2020a). LED lights use only 12 watts for the same amount of light as a 60-watt incandescent bulb – and last 21 times longer. LED lights are more expensive up front, but they are cheaper in the long run thanks to the lower energy use.

Numerous retailers, such as IKEA, Sephora (owned by LVMH) and Walmart, have installed LED lighting, invested in solar energy and committed to timelines to achieve climate positivity. Furthermore, in addition to implementing longer-lasting LED lights, retailers including Dollar Tree and Kohl's have implemented smart lighting systems to lower intensity during peak hours of the day, when natural lighting is greater. In 2019 alone, Kohl's achieved energy savings of 31 million kilowatt-hours through its smart lighting system, equating to approximately $4 million in cost savings (Weinswig, 2020a).

Lighting is not the only way to reduce operational costs of brick-and-mortar stores; heating and ventilation systems account for high energy usage too. Dollar Tree has introduced the use of a direct outdoor air system, which can reduce system operating costs by 50 per cent compared to variable air volume systems.

Efficient lighting and other means of energy reduction are examples of how retailers can cut costs through sustainable infrastructure – smart buildings that reduce resource consumption. For example, insulation in roofs, walls and floors keep stores cool in the summer and warm in the winter, thereby cutting energy costs as well as carbon emissions.

Tapestry (parent company to Coach, Kate Spade and Stuart Weitzman) is optimizing its operations in alignment with SDG #7 to reduce its carbon footprint. The company is measuring its impact via Scope 1 (direct) and Scope 2 (indirect) carbon dioxide equivalent (CO_2e) greenhouse gas emissions – targeting a 20 per cent reduction by 2025. The company achieved an overall 0.4 per cent reduction in CO_2 emissions across all stores from 2018 to 2019, as retrofitting stores with LED lights offset the impact of its 240,000-square-foot increase in total store space. Tapestry's distribution centres reduced emissions by 2.2 per cent in 2019 as well (Weinswig, 2020a).

FUEL

'Responsible consumption and production' (SDG #12) looks for firms to cut waste throughout the product lifecycle, from design to production to distribution, while delivering the same functional value (for example, a video conference may deliver the same outcome as air travel). In considering a product's end-of-life at its conception, designs can be created with recirculation in mind, while looking for opportunities to minimize resource consumption.

Electric and hybrid vehicles offer greater fuel efficiency and can significantly reduce greenhouse gas emissions (depending on how local electricity is generated, from coal or renewable sources). These vehicles are evolving rapidly, and retailers are shifting away from gas- and diesel-powered transportation. At the end of 2018, there were over 1 million electric vehicles on US roads, and the Edison Electric Institute projects that this number will reach 18.7 million in 2030 (Weinswig, 2020a). France and the UK have a 2040 deadline for automakers to end sales of new gas-powered vehicles, and China, Germany and India may follow suit.

NFI, a third-party supply chain solutions provider, is an early adopter of sustainable supply chain business practices. The company has implemented a variety of clean technologies and equipment to reduce its carbon footprint in North America and drive its own and its customers' sustainable supply chain initiatives. NFI has been recognized by the EPA as a SmartWay Partner and a SmartWay High Performer, reflecting its green trucking initiatives. The company is currently partnering with electric vehicle manufacturers to test these vehicles in Southern California, deploying battery-electric trucks between the Port of Los Angeles and local distribution centres. The cost of maintaining and running these trucks is cheaper than the diesel alternative, but the upfront capital investment is higher (though decreasing with scale). For now, subsidies in California aid the investment, and NFI intends to split the cost savings with its clients.

One-day deliveries are more environmentally damaging than deliveries with longer timelines due to added trips, so many retailers offer the option of more environmentally friendly deliveries that are later or consolidated.

Amazon has pledged to make half its deliveries net carbon neutral by 2030 and 100 per cent by 2040, which will include the use of drones. American entrepreneur Jeff Bezos also committed $10 billion to his initiative, the Bezos Earth Fund, to fund non-governmental organizations and scientists working to address climate change.

The transportation sector can play a significant role in reducing carbon emissions, from using fuel-efficient aircraft to truck routing and capacity optimization. Retailers can look to work with third-party logistics providers that optimize transportation with multi-modal delivery and load capacity considerations. Smart technology can plan vehicle routes, share vehicle information with road networks and optimize inventory to minimize waste.

Some retail companies have made transitioning away from fossil fuels a top priority, as the price per barrel of oil often ranges widely. Target predicts that such a move will save the company $200–300 million by 2040 (Weinswig, 2020a).

R: Responsible supply chains

A responsible supply chain is a key part of any retailer's sustainability strategy. This value chain has perhaps the most environmental impact and so offers opportunities to find less-resource-intensive processes, more responsible sourcing, enhanced raw-material traceability and greater overall transparency for the consumer.

MATERIALS
The retailer should incorporate non-polluting chemicals and eco-friendly raw materials from product design throughout the value chain – all the way to delivery of the product to the customer.

To achieve this, retailers could consider using compostable, biodegradable or recycled materials. Compostable material disintegrates through microbial activity or with decomposition treatment such as ultraviolet light, heat or oxygen, without emitting toxins. Biodegradable material naturally disintegrates without any soil toxicity. Eco-friendly materials, such as viscose, decompose with no environmental impact – something that cannot be said about polyester, plastic or nylon.

Partnerships can advance supply chain sustainability. Stella McCartney, a frontrunner in sustainability and ethical sourcing, has partnered with Italian label Candiani to create 100 per cent biodegradable denim products made from biodegradable ingredients and plants. In addition, the denim also uses less water and energy during production.

Patagonia and REI, both founding members of the Sustainable Apparel Coalition (in a 2009 partnership with Walmart) maintain that partnering with other brands and suppliers is the best way to drive improvement in a shared supply chain.

The Patagonia Supply Chain Environmental Responsibility Programme aims to measure and reduce the environmental impacts of manufacturing its products and materials at supplier facilities worldwide. Utilizing industry-recognized tools and certification programmes such as the Higg Index (developed by the Sustainable Apparel Coalition) and the 'bluesign system', Patagonia's programme recognizes environmentally responsible partners in the supply chain, approves and manages new and active suppliers and eliminates suppliers that do not meet its minimum requirements.

REI is a founding member of the Outdoor Industry Association Sustainability Working Group, an industry forum of 300+ outdoor brands, suppliers, manufacturers and other stakeholders. This group recently launched Climate Action Corps, which is supporting brands in measuring, reporting and collaboratively reducing greenhouse gas emissions.

Blockchain technology makes it easier to trace materials and products to deliver greater transparency. By eliminating the need for a payment intermediary/agent, blockchain facilitates faster transactions by allowing peer-to-peer cross-border transfers with digital currency. Retailers can leverage blockchain technology to better track and trace in the supply chain, as well as to enhance inventory management capabilities by creating a link to an item's digital identity: each time physical custody changes, blockchain records it.

SUPPLIERS

In mapping a supply chain, sustainable sourcing also means integrating suppliers that similarly address environmental performance factors. Suppliers down to the lowest component level should be encouraged to adopt the same sustainability strategy.

PULL SUPPLY CHAIN STRATEGY

Brands and retailers can migrate to a pull supply chain, in which customer demand drives manufacturing. A typical push supply chain is driven by long-term, although often faulty, projections based on inadequate data. A pull supply chain is leaner, minimizes waste and emphasizes the *consumption* of goods rather than the *making* of goods. For demand to prompt a manufacturing process to start, an integrated supply chain spanning all required production inputs is necessary. Real-time information-sharing abilities for multiple stakeholders, beginning with customer purchase across production, operations, supply chain and logistics, can reduce waste, manufacturing overages and inventory liquidations, better match supply and demand and improve full-price selling.

PACKAGING

Packaging needs a sustainability overhaul as well. Sustainable packaging not only reduces the use of single-use plastic, but also reduces the amount of waste going into landfills. Recycled paper or cardboard, plant-based or non-GMO (genetically modified organism) compostable packaging, and renewable packaging made from cork or wood pulp are all more sustainable solutions, from a waste point of view.

Cosmetics retailer Lush uses biodegradable cork container pots which are antibacterial, fire-retardant and water-resistant, and production is sustainable. The company plants trees to later harvest bark for the pots, stripping the bark in a rotating system that does not harm the trees. The cork grows back in nine years for re-harvesting.

In another example of advancing sustainability in packaging, Tapestry is aiming to use 75 per cent recycled content in its packaging across all three of its brands by 2025 (Weinswig, 2020a).

E: Excellence in reporting and communicating

Consumers are demanding more transparency across the supply chain than ever before. Companies that provide this build consumer trust and loyalty. Increasingly, retailers and brands that share greater granularity across business processes are communicating and taking responsibility for their choices, demonstrating a willingness to be held accountable for their actions.

Communicating corporate commitment to sustainability and transparency includes audits, stakeholder engagement and being a role model in the industry – a champion of sustainable business practices with a focus on people and the planet.

A sustainability audit evaluates a company's operations and practices against established standards. Developing a sustainability initiative means examining existing policies, setting benchmarks and establishing performance metrics. Companies can bring in expert consultants to assist with specific initiatives, assessing the value chain for compliance and developing short- or long-term projects. Sustainability audit checklists can address a variety of issues, including governance, workforce treatment, community engagement and environmental impact (such as waste reduction, water and energy conservation, and evaluation of production and supply chain processes).

The most common supply chain certifications are International Organization for Standardization (ISO) 9001 and ISO 14001. Companies for which sustainability is integral to their business strategy look for suppliers that are ISO-compliant. ISO 9001, Quality Management, establishes policies and procedures for planning and executing in the core business area; ISO 14001, Environmental Management, specifies requirements for managing environmental responsibility and provides a framework. Together, these standards address business issues and connect consumer demands on product transparency to the end result.

Retailers can demonstrate accountability and a commitment to sustainability through regular communication with stakeholders – customers, shareholders, staff and the community – to provide updates on the status of initiatives and audit results. This contributes to stakeholder trust in the brand, confidence and engagement.

A good communications programme can also enhance consumer education and empowerment, enabling shoppers to make better-informed choices. The same holds true for staff. To achieve sustainability goals, companies need engaged employees.

With enhanced traceability, retailers can track where materials are grown and even follow them through production. Retailers that share this kind of information with consumers can build trust, as consumers feel they are making better-informed sustainability choices.

Investor communications can also be a key competitive differentiator. Ensuring the investment community is current on corporate progress toward sustainability goals can better position a company. Factors to consider include metrics on waste reduction, carbon emissions, supplier sustainability audits, yearly comparisons of fuel consumption, electricity consumption, waste disposal, water consumption and environmental incidents (spills, discharges). The list is long, but investors want this information to understand risk and enhance investment returns.

Finally, companies should communicate by being an advocate of good corporate citizenship with a sustainable business model. They should look to engage business partners and advocate industry-wide goals of transparency in reporting. Retailers can help other companies to activate EnCORE by becoming an example for the industry and a champion of sustainable goals and programmes, including by providing transparency and excellence in reporting.

For example, Unilever CEO Paul Polman announced to shareholders at the beginning of his 10-year tenure that the company would adopt a long-term business model that would contribute to society and the environment. He even advised shareholders to put their money elsewhere if they did not agree. The result was the Unilever Sustainable Living Plan, created in 2010, which decoupled the company's growth from its environmental footprint. Today, Unilever is on track to meet most of its commitments, including reducing its environmental impact by half, improving health and well-being for 1 billion people, and enhancing the livelihood for millions of its employees, suppliers and retailers.

In Unilever's most recent performance summary through 2019, the company reported that it had reduced CO_2 emissions at its factories by 65 per cent in 2019 versus 2009 – thus achieving its goal of a 50 per cent reduction by 2020. The company also achieved a 96 per cent reduction in total waste sent for disposal in the same time period, despite significantly higher volumes. Furthermore, Unilever's 'Sustainable Living Brands', or those which it says have an environmental or social purpose – Dove, Lipton, Hellmann's and Vaseline – have outperformed average growth at Unilever, at a rate of 69 per cent faster than the rest of the business in 2018 (Weinswig, 2020a).

EnCORE is designed to be a repeating cycle, whereby the final component of one company's EnCORE cycle – excellence in reporting and communication – can spark the first stage of another company's cycle – environmental engagement. The framework can therefore trigger gains that extend beyond any one company adopting its approach.

Actions for retailers to take

- *Get educated*: Understand one's own operations and supply chain and its impact on the environment. Discover peer standards and industry shifts. Know the relevant SDGs, legislation, regulations and information sources.

- *Benchmark your enterprise*: Find relevant peers, exchange learnings and goals. Determine best practices and copy. Sustainable goals should not be competitive but collaborative. Appropriate benchmarks include the UN's SDGs and the Sustainability Accounting Standards Board for Food Retailers and Distributors or Multiline and Specialty Retailers and Distributors.

- *Build a plan*: Conduct a sustainability assessment and internal review, identify priorities, risks and opportunities. Establish sustainability goals that include reductions in greenhouse gas emissions and use of natural resources, as well the implementation of more efficient transportation and better use of water and energy – plus involvement in the community.

- *Be bold*: Develop a sustainability plan that designates responsible departments, allocates funding, establishes a timeline, sets short- and long-term milestones, implements policies and measures success. Do not forget to engage with stakeholders and communicate the plan, evaluating progress and reporting results as you go.

- *Lower costs*: Reduce water usage, reduce energy use and cut waste. Long-term investments should include renewable energy technology and electric vehicles.

- *Track metrics*: Use audit tools such as software and checklists to measure results against goals, schedule regular audit team inspections and supplier audits.

- *Timeline*: Assessment should take four to six months and developing a sustainability plan can take six to nine months. Technology investments and installation will take three to nine months. Publish annual progress reports that cover actions taken, results and next steps.

- *Revisit your plan and iterate*. Sustainability is a journey. Achieve goals and make new ones. Be realistic and stretch by setting applicable and challenging targets.

- *Engage employees* and make it fun.

- *People, profits and the planet* = progress.

The fashion resale market

Supported by the shift from fragmented store-based distribution to online platforms, resale is set to continue gaining share of total fashion sales. Resale constitutes buying and selling previously owned goods, which may be new, but are more often gently used.

The US fashion resale market has evolved from a single-billion-dollar market in 2008 to a $22.3 billion market in 2021. We expect the market to reach $25.9 billion and $29.7 billion in 2022 and 2023, equating to 16 per cent and 15 per cent growth, respectively (Weinswig, 2022b).

The majority of brands and retailers are still experimenting with the resale model to see its impact on company's overall profit margin, operational costs and customer loyalty. Macy's management told Forbes that when it worked with ThredUP in 2019 to convert a 500-square-foot shop in one of its stores into a resale shop that the shop has had no discernable impact on Macy's backstage discount sales in that location. Rather, the shops were attracting new customers, especially younger consumers. Macy's is currently extending its pilot to more stores, which may indicate that the resale model is benefiting Macy's business. However, we expect the impact of resale business on profit margin is still minimal.

We believe that those that bring the resale business in-house (such as Nike) will likely achieve better profit margins than brands and retailers that work with third-party marketplaces because of lower operational costs and more branding effect.

Challenges for the fashion resale market

We expect the US fashion resale market to grow with a compound annual growth rate (CAGR) of 16.9 per cent from 2018 to 2023 (Weinswig, 2022b). The market is growing fast, though there are a few challenges that may negatively impact the top-line performances of resale companies: 1) insufficient inventory (products, including insufficient styles and sizes) that lead to customer disappointment, 2) ineffective marketing, and 3) difficulties in retaining customers (how to convert browsers into shoppers and how to gain repeated shoppers). From the cost perspectives, challenges lie in the long horizon of investment in operations, technologies and marketing. But companies such as ThredUP and The RealReal remain confident about the returns of these investments and profitability on a longer term.

Opportunities for the fashion resale market

We expect to see more corporate shake-ups and consolidations coming down the pipeline, which may give rise to stronger conglomerates that include the resale business. The increased consumer interest in the resale market, along with retailers' visions to expand business reach and operational efficiency, will prompt many retailers/companies in the resale space to re-evaluate their capabilities and overall portfolio in the long term, which will lead to consolidations, reconstructions, mergers and acquisitions, and therefore more sales and sooner profitability.

For small brands that have strong brand positioning and stable sales growth, such as BaubleBar (a luxury jewellery and accessory brand), working with third-party resale platforms may be a good starting point to uncover new revenue streams. But for small brands that do not have strong differentiators/luxury positioning, sustaining an e-commerce model could be better than trying something new (the resale model).

> The resale market will grow exponentially versus the traditional retail market in the future. How fast it grows will depend on supply chain, technology, but mainly the C-suite. I expect that resale growth could be 2–3x that of traditional retail.
>
> Buddy Teaster, CEO, Soles4Souls (2022)

CASE STUDIES
Sustainability disruptors

Driven by high consumer demand for environmentally friendly products, sustainability has become an integral part of CPG brands' product design, causing increased innovation across various CPG categories. Currently, startups are driving this innovation with their competitive new products. These innovators make for an insightful look into how to drive sustainability standards forward and meet consumer demand for reduced environmental impact in the retail industry.

We expect more creative, sustainable products to emerge and both new CPG startups and established brands to incorporate eco-friendly goals into their businesses.

by Humankind

by Humankind is a personal care CPG business that produces plastic-free products, including deodorant, shampoo and mouthwash. The company challenges other brands in its category with its high sustainability and wellness standards.

by Humankind aims to reduce packaging consumption for personal care products with its monthly, subscription-based refill model. After a customer purchases a reusable, refillable container, by Humankind supplies them with regular product refills. By doing so, the company states it eliminates single-use plastic by 90 per cent compared to other companies (Weinswig, 2022a).

by Humankind also takes pride in its 'high-performance' products, including its deodorant, which kills odour-causing bacteria 40 per cent faster than other leading natural deodorants, according to the company (Weinswig, 2022a).

Competitive advantage: Sustainability, the direct-to-customer model and natural ingredients

In a world where sustainability is increasingly important to consumers, by Humankind continues to find ways to cut down on waste and environmentally harmful practices. As well as reducing plastic use with its refill model, the company uses biodegradable, bamboo-fibre-based materials for shipping packaging. Through a partnership with Pachama, a forest project developer, by Humankind has also been carbon neutral since 2019, offsetting all production and shipping emissions by replenishing forests.

The direct-to-customer (DTC) refill subscription model also helps maintain consumer loyalty, as customers need to initially invest in the company's refillable containers, creating a sunk cost. However, consumers' investments are rewarded not only with more sustainable personal care products, but also with packaging and design that ensures the products arrive quickly and have a long shelf life. For instance, by Humankind's shampoo and mouthwash refills are dehydrated and concentrated, making them easy to ship and ensuring they last longer than most of their liquid-format competitors.

In addition to its sustainability efforts, by Humankind uses natural ingredients while ensuring compliance with scientifically proven personal care standards. This provides a competitive advantage as many natural personal care brands compromise on industry standards in order to focus on the provenance of their ingredients or the format of their product. For example, by Humankind's toothpaste tablets contain fluoride, an FDA-approved ingredient deemed essential for preventing tooth decay and cavities but is rarely included in competitors' toothpaste tablets.

Calyxia

Calyxia is a microcapsule and biodegradable plastics company that partners with homecare and sustainable agriculture brands. Its non-toxic, biodegradable EnviroCaps have no microplastics (a fragment of plastic less than 5 mm in length) in them. While the product is primarily used by scented laundry detergent manufacturers, it has potential application in many other industries as well.

How has Calyxia disrupted the market?

In 2018, Calyxia's EnviroCaps became the world's first non-toxic and readily biodegradable fragrance microcapsule designed for use by laundry care product manufacturers. EnviroCaps provide long-lasting fragrance performance in laundry care and replace current microplastic-based fragrance microcapsules, according to the company.

Competitive advantage: Sustainability and technological edge over competitors

There are an estimated 24 trillion pieces of microplastics in the ocean, according to a 2021 study from Kyushu University (Weinswig, 2022a), while land-based microplastics deteriorate soil quality, leading to decreased crop yields, according to the UN Environment Programme. As a result, many consumers and producers view reducing microplastic use as a sustainability priority. In addition to their lack of microplastics, Calyxia's biodegradable EnviroCaps go through a more environmentally friendly production process, saving energy and water compared to the manufacturing of other microcapsules.

EnviroCaps are highly versatile and have the potential to be incorporated into a variety of household cleaning products and industries, including agriculture, electronics, automotive and transportation. The company can control the microcapsules' size and porosity, allowing for a timed release (via chemical triggering) of the ingredients within and prolonging the product's in-use lifespan by more than 10 times. EnviroCaps' ability to extend the lifespan and biodegradability of plastic materials has also led the startup to begin work on an extensive portfolio of products, including coatings, composites, foams and 'crop protection', according to its official website.

Med-X

Med-X is a chemical and pharmaceutical company developing innovative, all-natural pest control solutions with its Nature-Cide brand. Not only is Nature-Cide 100 per cent non-toxic and environmentally safe, but it also outperforms top pest control products, according to the Florida Mosquito Association.

How has Med-X disrupted the market?

Med-X's patented Nature-Cide all-natural pest control uses a blend of environmentally friendly essential oils that outperforms top pest control products without the risk of poisonous exposure.

A third-party study, published in the Florida Mosquito Association's official journal, proved the effectiveness of Nature-Cide. The study named the product the top-performing mosquito insecticide, bettering both the study's top green competitor, Essentria IC3, as well as the three best-selling synthetic pyrethroid mosquito insecticides. These achievements could disrupt the pest control market, as mosquito control is a top global health priority – 17 per cent of all infectious diseases are vector-borne, meaning they are carried by organisms that can transmit them to humans, according to *Scientific American* (Weinswig, 2022a).

Competitive advantage: Safe and effective formula

According to the New York State Department of Health, a toxic substance is 'a substance that can be poisonous or cause health effects', and products that many consumers use daily, including pesticides, can 'also be toxic'. As such, many see traditional, chemical-intensive pesticides as a potential health risk. However, Nature-Cide's pesticide uses 100 per cent non-toxic, natural and environmentally safe ingredients in its formula, such as clove and cottonseed oil, giving it a significant advantage over traditional pesticides.

Nature-Cide is also registered with EPA offices in the 39 states that require it, lending it a legitimacy that non-registered brands cannot match.

MyForest Foods

MyForest Foods, formerly known as Atlast Foods, is a food brand creating plant-based meat substitutes. It stands out in the vegan meat market due to its mycelium-based technology that can replicate whole-cut animal meats, while most other plant-based meats only mimic the minced texture of ground meat. Its first signature product is MyBacon, a plant-based bacon substitute.

How has MyForest Foods disrupted the market?

Mycelium – the vegetative root structure of mushrooms – features long branching fibres, allowing it to replicate traditional meat cuts in both texture and flavour. Combined with fats, flavourings and other ingredients, MyForest Foods' MyBacon replicates the taste and texture of real bacon, providing an opportunity for disruption in the plant-based meat market. In the future, the company plans to disrupt the steak market using the Beefsteak Polypore mushroom.

While MyForest Foods has limited distribution currently, it plans to expand its production capacity soon via a partnership with Ecovative – a mycelium technology company – to supply the CPG, foodservice and grocery industries with plant-based meats.

Competitive advantages: Scalable, environmentally friendly and healthy

Mycelium has a rapid growth rate – producing enough to create a 100-foot-by-10-foot sheet in 10 days – and its texture can be altered through the tuning of porosity, texture, strength, resilience and fibre orientation. Growing and processing mycelium for MyBacon takes only 13 days, a substantial advantage compared to the months or years it can take for farmers to raise animals for slaughter. Furthermore, the entire process produces far less greenhouse gas emissions than traditional meat processing.

MyForest Food's mycelium ingredient is rich in fibre, vitamins, protein, amino acids and minerals, according to the company. In contrast, bacon is notorious for its high-fat and low nutrition content. The nutritional advantages of MyBacon and its similarity to real bacon make it a potentially worthwhile addition to the wellness consumer's diet.

waterdrop

Austria-based drink startup waterdrop has created the 'world's first microdrink', a dissolvable cube made from compressed vitamins and natural fruit juices after sugar and water components have been removed. The company's products are made from real fruit and plant extracts sourced directly from farmers around the globe, and are free from artificial flavours, sugar, gluten and lactose. The microdrinks come in 10 different flavours – each containing different vitamins and minerals – with each flavour pack containing 12 dissolvable cubes.

How has waterdrop disrupted the market?

The company claims that its microdrink design eliminates 98 per cent of unnecessary packaging and CO_2 emissions compared to the manufacturing process used in traditional drinks. As a result, in 2021, waterdrop became the fastest-growing CPG brand in Europe – having surpassed $100 million in sales within five years of its 2017 launch date – according to a company press release (Weinswig, 2022a). It began selling in the US the same year.

Competitive advantages: Sustainability, emerging tech use and DTC model

Waterdrop not only provides a sustainable alternative to other beverages due to its minimal packaging, but the company has also become plastic-positive through its five-year partnership with Plastic Bank, which removes one plastic bottle from the environment for every microdrink pack sold. Since the start of the partnership, the CPG brand has helped eliminate over 30 million plastic bottles from landfills. The company also sells steel, glass and bamboo water bottles – as well as other reusable beverage accessories – which account for 20 per cent of its revenue and help reduce plastic bottle use. Furthermore, microdrinks' smaller volume-per-drink ratio makes them easier to transport, cutting supply chain and fuel costs.

On the technology front, waterdrop recently debuted the LUCY 'smart cap' for its reusable bottles, which filters water through a UV-C system, destroying up to 100 per cent of potential germs, according to the company. The cap also flashes at regular intervals, reminding users to drink water, and is linked to a mobile app to track water consumption.

The small size of waterdrop's microdrink packages makes them ideal for DTC subscriptions, boosting consumer loyalty and helping the company avoid competition on crowded retail store shelves.

Summary

Driven by high consumer demand for environmentally friendly products, sustainability has become an integral part of CPG brands' product design, causing increased innovation across various CPG categories. Currently, startups are driving this innovation with their competitive new products. In 2022 and beyond, we expect more creative, sustainable products to emerge and both new CPG startups and established brands to incorporate eco-friendly goals into their businesses.

INTERVIEW
Andrew Smith, Co-Founder Think UnCommon (2022)

Andrew has focused his career primarily on designing processes and change. In the past several years, Andrew has concentrated on sustainability and how processes and change can impact a business' sustainability efforts with companies he founded, Sproutly and Think UnCommon. He also spent 11 years at Telstra where he headed customer experience, retail operations and retail innovation.

Andrew has come to think of the pandemic as a change event, and that we are all now living in a post-change-event time. He sees the pandemic as an event that changed the way people behave, and trained people with new skills to interact with technology and retail in new ways.

Change events by their nature are very emotional – and Andrew thinks that most people have still not fully healed psychologically from the change event of the Covid pandemic.

In the US in particular, this trauma was turned into an argument, whereas in other countries it was a trauma that the country faced largely together. Change events are traumatic and tend to make people pull into their core values more. As a result, we are seeing people come out of the pandemic with slightly different values and needs. Consumers are wanting to see changes in the ways that brands treat the environment, their employees and their customers.

But Andrew cautions that noise does not necessarily equate to action. Humans are not good at changing their behaviour – how many times have people made resolutions to drink less wine and go to the gym more, only to see those resolutions break quickly? Sustainable actions by consumers suffer from some of the same challenges of drinking less wine and going to the gym more often – 85 per cent of consumers rate sustainability as important and 56 per cent of consumers say that they will change companies based on sustainability performance, but we see a much smaller proportion of those consumers making actual consumption changes based on a company's sustainability efforts.

Andrew caveats that self-motivated change takes time, but it will happen. Right now, the biggest gap between consumer ideals of sustainability and consumer action in sustainability is that consumers do not believe that sustainability should cost more. However, in reality, creating sustainable products often (but not always!) does cost more than making non-sustainable products.

There are three ways to bridge this gap:

1 It could become cheaper to be sustainable, via technology, innovation or advances in materials or supply chain processes.

2 Consumers could become more willing to pay a premium for sustainable products.

3 Companies will have to accept the higher costs of sustainability and not pass these on to the consumer.

Andrew believes that the most likely scenario going forward is likely a mix of all three factors, especially in the short term. Andrew believes that as the market for sustainable products grows, competition will naturally enter the market and push prices down, just like it does for all markets. He also believes that the younger generation has less of a stigma against second-hand products, which helps to push the entire industry towards more sustainable practices.

When asked for his advice to retailers as they enhance their sustainability efforts, Andrew offered the following pieces of advice:

• Businesses need to stop thinking of sustainability as a lofty long-term goal. Often it is very difficult to turn 2050 goals into immediate action – sustainability needs to be a short- and long-term goal to be successful.

- Sustainability needs to be weaved into the fabric of the company; it cannot be just one person's job. Often Andrew sees companies declare a lofty long-term goal, appoint a Sustainability Officer, and then move on with business as normal. At Ikea the Chief Sustainability Officer is the CEO. Sustainability is not an initiative; it is a change in the way your business operates. It starts with changing processes and procedures and regular measurements.

- Don't be afraid to market your progress to consumers. Andrew sees some companies like Best Buy who have made impressive progress in achieving their sustainability goals but do not always market these to consumers, while other companies have accomplished far less and are actively marketing their achievements to consumers.

TEN THINGS RETAILERS NEED TO KNOW ABOUT SUSTAINABILITY

1 A company's sustainability practices have an impact not just on its consumers, but also on its employees, the industry and all other companies in its supply chain.

2 Retailers should join industry associations and other methods to band together with like-minded companies to pursue sustainability initiatives.

3 As consumers become more accustomed to buying second-hand products, retailers should look to the resale market for revenue growth and sustainability improvements.

4 Many retailers are using creative solutions to reduce energy consumption in their supply chain and operations such as lights in the retail store, fuel usage for delivery and material consumption.

5 Sustainable packaging is typically an area for low-hanging fruit in sustainability initiatives, and one that is highly visible to the consumer.

6 Investors are becoming increasingly attuned to company's sustainability efforts, and ESG has become a key area for companies to enhance transparency and reporting.

7 Retailers should look to startups in their industry for inspiration on sustainability initiatives – this is often where innovation is driven.

8 Sustainability initiatives need to be driven by top leadership, and should be the responsibility of the entire organization – not just the sustainability department.

9 Advancements in blockchain can have an impact on a company's sustainability efforts, especially within the supply chain.

10 Technology improvements are leading the way to lower-cost sustainability initiatives.

KEY TAKEAWAYS: SUSTAINABILITY

- As with many aspects of retail, the Covid pandemic dramatically affected sustainability throughout the world, adding even more impetus to business leaders to improve their efforts in sustainability. And although consumers' actions have not fully caught up with their intentions, the future projection is clear: consumers (and some governments) are demanding more from brands, and businesses need to quickly adapt and step up to the challenge.

- Coresight has developed its EnCORE framework to help companies adapt their businesses to be more sustainable, consisting of:

  o environmental engagement

  o circular models

  o optimized operations

  o responsible supply chains

  o excellence in reporting and communicating.

- As in most industries, startups are at the forefront of innovation. Businesses should seek to engage with innovators in sustainability to share knowledge and partner.

- To make real progress in changing an organization, sustainability efforts need to be weaved into the fabric of the company, starting at the top, and should not just be one person's or department's job.

References

Smith, A. (2022) Interview with the authors, July.

Teaster, B. (2022) Interview with the authors, July.

Weinswig, D (2020a) The time for sustainability in retail is now, Coresight Research. https://coresight.com/research/the-time-for-sustainability-in-retail-is-now/ (archived at perma.cc/8LAP-ZBRQ)

Weinswig, D (2020b) US survey update: How Covid-19 has impacted consumers' attitudes toward sustainability (full report), Coresight Research. https://coresight.com/research/us-survey-update-how-covid-19-has-impacted-consumers-attitudes-toward-sustainability-full-report/ (archived at perma.cc/G843-X5MM)

Weinswig, D (2022a) Retail innovators: CPG sustainability innovations, Coresight Research. https://coresight.com/research/retail-innovators-cpg-sustainability-innovations/ (archived at perma.cc/4KKV-GF67)

Weinswig, D (2022b) US fashion resale market: A $26 billion retail opportunity, Coresight Research. https://coresight.com/research/us-fashion-resale-market-a-26-billion-retail-opportunity/ (archived at perma.cc/5698-8ZA7)

06

Driving social commerce through compelling content

WHAT IS SOCIAL COMMERCE?

Social commerce refers to brands and retailers leveraging the power of social media to market and sell their products and services online – which has become ever more important following the pandemic-led acceleration in e-commerce. Social media has evolved from a channel that simply connects people to a destination for shopping. Coresight Research's annual survey on social commerce, conducted in March 2022, revealed that 9 in 10 US consumers use social media and 65 per cent use social media as part of the shopping process (discovering, researching and browsing products, or making purchases). Furthermore, 55 per cent of all respondents reported that they make purchases through social media (Weinswig, 2022).

LEARNING OBJECTIVES

In this chapter you will learn how brands and retailers are using social commerce to close the loop between content and commerce, including:

- an overview of social commerce
- trends driving social commerce adoption
- monetization tools for creators
- social media platform shopping events
- tech companies launching new shoppable platforms
- the convergence of gaming and shopping
- a deep dive into the technology companies shaping social commerce development

Brands and retailers are increasingly looking to integrate more shoppable features into their social media channels to offer a frictionless shopping experience to consumers, who enjoy the convenience of completing transactions through a single platform. A Coresight consumer survey found that 60 per cent of respondents who use social media for product discovery/ research will 'sometimes/occasionally' abandon a purchase due to a platform's lack of built-in functionality (Weinswig, 2022). It is therefore crucial for brands and retailers to offer an end-to-end discovery-to-purchase solution to remove friction in the shopping journey and drive conversion.

Social commerce trends in retail

Storytelling enables brands to facilitate strong communities, based on genuine common interests. This connection between fandom and retail adds another layer to the dimension of storytelling – especially as brands and retailers look to forge a path into the virtual-first shift driven by Web 3.0. We see three key trends driving the adoption of social commerce:

Monetization tools are fuelling a surge in creators

Marketers are increasingly investing in creators with smaller and highly engaged followings; the marketing allocation has shifted toward niche communities. Video and social platforms like YouTube and TikTok have introduced creator funds, and now are introducing new monetization features for creators. Livestreaming creators can make money through a diverse and rapidly growing portfolio of options – from receiving ad revenue and tips, to creating sponsored and premium content and selling merchandise, channel memberships and subscriptions.

In December 2021 TikTok introduced a set of new features for its creators to generate revenue from their content. While the short-form video platform already supported virtual gifts during livestreams, its new Tips and Video Gifts features allow creators to accept payments and gifts when they are not livestreaming. These functions rolled out along within the 'Creator Next' programme, which brings together all TikTok's creator monetization tools. The move came about as the race to capture creator talent is heating up across the livestreaming landscape. Leading social platforms Facebook, Instagram, Pinterest, Snap and YouTube are all offering funds to attract and retain creators.

Meta also rolled out a suite of new features in December 2021 to allow creators to interact with live audiences and monetize their content. The company is trialling a new mechanism whereby users can buy 'Stars' to tip creators during livestreams using Facebook Pay. Additional creator tools include the capacity to share external website links, support for more co-hosts and a professional mode profile for creators to better engage with their followers. The platform has also launched its 'Stars Fest' programme, highlighting a range of creator livestream events throughout the month.

Social media giants' livestreaming events are attracting brands and shoppers alike

Brands and retailers have flocked to a series of new live shopping marathons on social media platforms like TikTok and Instagram to bolster their young audience. Companies partnered with influencers to improve retention and streamline the sales process, while viewers were able to instantly purchase the products they discover without leaving the platform.

On 8–9 December 2021 TikTok UK held a two-day livestream shopping event called 'On Trend', which featured in-platform purchase capabilities for viewers. This built-in live shopping feature was developed in collaboration with Shopify and also enabled merchants to use TikTok for marketing campaigns developed directly from the Shopify dashboard. The sessions were hosted by a variety of celebrities and influencers with participating brands and retailers including Charlotte Tilbury, JD Sports, Lookfantastic and L'Oréal Paris.

Instagram ran a series of live shopping events during the holiday season in 2021 called 'Holiday Pop-Up Shop LIVE' on its app featuring creators and personalities like Nia Sioux and Lisa Rinna. Product categories included beauty, fashion and lifestyle. Viewers were able to click on the host page's profile to access the shop tab and browse all products for sale.

Tech companies' partnerships are reshaping the competitive landscape

As livestream shopping becomes more widespread, e-commerce platforms and livestreaming tech providers have joined forces to expand live shopping capabilities, provide seamless commerce tools and monetize creators' content. New shoppable ad videos, automated inventory solutions and in-video purchase are innovations they have brought into the space.

French live video shopping provider Caast.TV announced a partnership with a French cloud-based e-commerce software company Mirakl in December 2021 to enable merchants to embed seamless livestreaming e-commerce content on their websites. The partnership has enabled the retail giant Carrefour to accelerate its live commerce strategy, with its website now seeing 18 million unique visitors per month. The new live commerce solution has also been employed by leading retailers in France including Boulanger, Cultura, Fnac Darty and Kiabi, with automated inventory syndicating and customized videos integrated into each relevant product page.

Chinese short-video platform Kuaishou announced a strategic partnership with China's largest on-demand food delivery firm, Meituan, to facilitate its expansion into local lifestyle services. Meituan established a mini programme on Kuaishou to allow its users to navigate products, services and coupons provided by Meituan merchants. The partnership was also seen as a response to the central government's push for interoperability among tech companies, and comes after a difficult year in China's internet industry. ByteDance's Douyin has been rapidly developing services that include, for example, food recommendations by internet celebrities through a group-buying link on the video page or in the comments section, a service very similar to that offered by Meituan's Dazhong Dianping.

Gaming and virtual worlds are the new content battleground

Microsoft's announcement that it will acquire Activision Blizzard in a transaction valued at $68.7 billion will take the software giant to third place (by revenue) in the global $175 billion digital gaming market – behind only Tencent and Sony (Redmond, 2022). Activision Blizzard is the home of franchises such as *Call of Duty*, *Candy Crush*, *Diablo*, *Overwatch* and *Warcraft*. The company also has a presence in e-sports through e-sports organization Major League Gaming.

The huge acquisition price underscores the importance of gaming, a market projected to grow at a 9 per cent CAGR between 2021 and 2026, taking it to $240 billion worldwide (Weinswig, 2021). On 10 January 2022, the maker of game *Grand Theft Auto*, Take-Two, announced its acquisition of rival Zynga (developer of *FarmVille*), valuing it at $12.7 billion – with the purchase price representing a 64 per cent premium on Zynga's 7 January closing price (Business Wire, 2022).

On the Activision Blizzard deal, Phil Spencer, CEO of Microsoft Gaming, said, 'Together, we will build a future where people can play the games they want, virtually anywhere they want' (Redmond, 2022). That comment hints that Microsoft is seeking to become the 'Netflix of gaming', although others (not least Netflix itself) are competing in this space, too. In September 2021, Netflix said that it was 'in the early stages of creating a great gaming experience' with the acquisition of Night School Studio (Verdu, 2021). For Microsoft, the purchase comes on top of previous major acquisitions in gaming – including *Minecraft*-maker Mojang for $2.5 billion in 2014 (Stuart and Hern, 2014) and ZeniMax for $7.5 billion in 2020 (Redmond, 2020).

We do not expect Apple to stand still, either. Already, about 70 per cent of all App Store revenue comes from gaming apps, according to 2021 court documents cited by Peterson (2021). However, those are revenues not from owned properties, but from third parties. Microsoft's purchase is likely to prompt greater consideration of proprietary gaming interests at Apple, in turn fuelled by acquisition(s) of gaming giants.

The emergence of the Metaverse, and the potential for convergence with gaming, only add further reasons to own the most compelling digital platforms. Gamers are already in versions of the Metaverse – virtual worlds where consumers can travel and buy power-ups, apparel and other virtual goods with media such as NFTs and payment via cryptocurrencies. While it is still in its early stages, and widespread adoption is far from certain, the development of the Metaverse appears to be the next step in the technology progression of the internet. Should adoption of virtual worlds break out from the gaming sphere, brands and retailers will need to stand ready. Companies should take stock of the digital content they already possess with the goal of repurposing it in the Metaverse. Retailers should also monitor the evolution of the Metaverse and consider using it for virtual gatherings and creating virtual places (such as stores) for consumers to visit.

The social commerce ecosystem

With the rapid rise in social selling, we have seen a number of new entrants to the space driving innovation across multiple areas of the social commerce landscape. We have identified 42 selected startups globally, whose technology solutions support brands and retailers in operating social commerce models, across the following categories:

- social networking platforms
- reselling
- group buying
- video commerce and livestreaming
- social payments integration

We profile each of these below to provide an overview of the technology ecosystem that has emerged to support social selling. The rapid emergence and funding of the number of startups in this sector only further illustrates how dynamic and fast growing this sector has become.

Social networking platforms

Social media, networking and e-commerce companies are increasingly offering social commerce features for product discovery and purchase. Below is a sampling of new companies providing social commerce innovation around the globe, ranging from marketplaces to communities to video shopping.

- Beidian is a Chinese social e-commerce platform that lets users buy and sell products across categories such as clothing, home, food, beauty, and mother and baby products. According to the company, anyone can open a shop on Beidian. The platform connects sellers directly with product suppliers and helps them with their marketing and distribution efforts.

- Funded in November 2018, Chingari is a short-video entertainment platform that also enables users to share videos on third-party social platforms. In February 2021 Chingari launched a social commerce feature in its app. Every video on the Chingari app is analysed frame by frame using computer vision and algorithms to detect objects in the video, which are then matched with a live shopping catalogue. This feature makes live videos shoppable in real time and generates revenue for content creators.

- MX Taka Tak is a community-based video platform that offers fun and entertaining videos on food, sports, gaming and DIY content that can be shared on social media. In March 2021 MX Taka Tak launched My Home, a platform that helps content creators drive growth through social media sharing.

FIGURE 6.1 The social commerce ecosystem

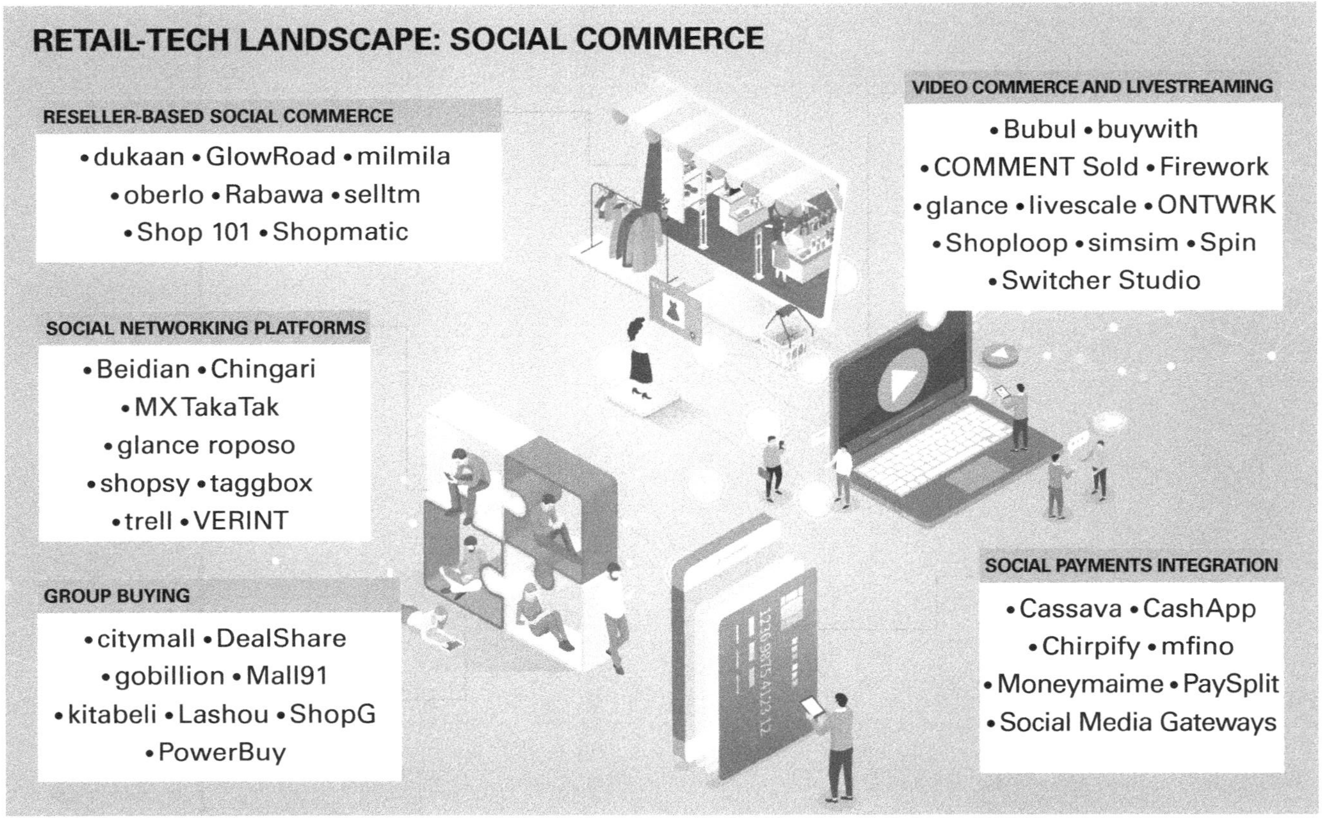

RETAIL-TECH LANDSCAPE: SOCIAL COMMERCE

VIDEO COMMERCE AND LIVESTREAMING
- Bubul • buywith
- COMMENT Sold • Firework
- glance • livescale • ONTVRK
- Shoploop • simsim • Spin
- Switcher Studio

RESELLER-BASED SOCIAL COMMERCE
- dukaan • GlowRoad • milmila
- oberlo • Rabawa • selltm
- Shop 101 • Shopmatic

SOCIAL NETWORKING PLATFORMS
- Beidian • Chingari
- MXTakaTak
- glance roposo
- shopsy • taggbox
- trell • VERINT

GROUP BUYING
- citymall • DealShare
- gobillion • Mall91
- kitabeli • Lashou • ShopG
- PowerBuy

SOCIAL PAYMENTS INTEGRATION
- Cassava • CashApp
- Chirpify • mfino
- Moneymaime • PaySplit
- Social Media Gateways

SOURCE Adapted from the UN

- Roposo is an India-based creator-driven entertainment platform. Creators can share posts related to lifestyle, fashion, food and travel through home-made videos and photos. In October 2021 Roposo launched a live commerce feature that enables users to buy curated products from content creators.

- Walmart-owned Flipkart's social commerce app Shopsy enables consumers on social media to start an online business without any investment. Users can create an account and share product catalogues across the fashion, beauty, mobile, electronics and home categories to their local network of customers through social media channels such as WhatsApp. Shopsy users can also make purchases on behalf of their customers and earn commission, thus connecting e-commerce sellers and consumers through resellers.

- Taggbox Commerce facilitates the collection of social media content such as brand posts, influencer posts or user-generated content from various popular platforms. It then makes this content shoppable, enabling brands to enrich their on-site experience, maximize conversion, and drive revenue and growth.

- Founded in 2016, Trell is an Indian lifestyle, community-based social platform through which consumers can discover lifestyle-related content through blogs and videos. The Trell app, available in eight Indian languages, enables users to share new ideas, experiences and product recommendations across lifestyle categories such as fashion, beauty, personal care, food, travel and gadgets. In October 2020 Trell launched a social commerce feature in its app, allowing users to purchase lifestyle products featured in influencers' videos.

- Verint Community is an online social collaboration platform that uses online communities as forums for driving social commerce and delivering social customer service. Verint Community provides an enterprise social platform with a set of social applications and a social service application programme interface to connect to popular consumer social networks. It helps organizations interact through social channels with their customers and employees, supporting better business decision-making

Reseller-based social commerce

Companies that are helping retailers to sell their products to consumers through resellers, leveraging social media channels, are beginning to shift the dynamics within the social selling space. These new companies are enabling social media influencers to seamlessly create their own shopping experiences, allowing them to establish their own businesses and income streams with low upfront investment. By opening up the ability for social media influencers to sell products, these companies are helping to close the loop between content and commerce.

- Dukaan is a DIY platform that enables merchants, retailers and individuals to set up their online stores using smartphones and start selling through social media platforms Instagram and WhatsApp. It was founded in May 2020. Dukaan also has a reselling platform called Dukaan Plus, through which resellers and social media influencers promote products. Dukaan Plus manages payment and shipping. It features more than 400,000 products across 40 different categories.

- GlowRoad is an India-based social reselling platform that enables millions of individuals, including homemakers and graduate students, to start their own business and earn money. It supports users by giving them access to a virtual shop and millions of products from trusted suppliers, and takes care of payment and shipping facilities. According to the platform's website in December 2021, it has more than 6 million sellers and 18 million buyers and has a presence in over 2,000 Indian cities.

- Founded in 2017 in Bangalore, India, Milmila is a social reselling app that enables individuals to start their own business with zero investment. The platform offers products at wholesale prices across categories such as lifestyle, electronics, home and living, enabling individuals to choose products, add their margins and share products through social media channels. Upon conversion, individuals can earn through profit margins.

- Oberlo is a marketplace that enables entrepreneurs to search and find products to sell online. The platform helps merchants source products online from suppliers, import product listings to their e-commerce store, edit the product listings, add margin and sell to customers through the supplier, which ships orders to them directly.

- Founded in 2020 and headquartered in Nigeria, Rabawa is a social and video commerce platform that connects resellers and aspiring entrepreneurs to manufacturers and wholesalers, enabling them to start their business without any investment. Rabawa provides access to products across 100+ categories such as clothing, jewellery, beauty and accessories, and leverages social media to curate, promote and sell products to end users. The platform also enables reselling through social channels such as Facebook, Instagram, Twitter and WhatsApp.

- Selltm is a social commerce and reselling app that helps individuals sell and distribute products on social networking platforms through resellers and earn through commission. Featured categories include clothing, foot-wear, mobiles, home décor and electronics. The company was acquired by Indian e-commerce giant Snapdeal in 2019.

- Founded in 2015, Shop101 is an online social reselling app that empowers students, homemakers and working professionals to earn from home. The platform sources products from small businesses and retailers across 30+ categories and lists them on its app at competitive prices, according to the company. Resellers can choose from these products, add their margin and share links through social media. When a customer places an order, resellers earn through margins while payment and delivery is taken care of by Shop101. The platform had over 10,000 suppliers and 10 million resellers as of November 2021.

- Founded in Singapore in 2014, Shopmatic is a technology company that provides e-commerce solutions to individuals and small businesses through four channels: chat, social, webstore and marketplaces. Shopmatic enables users to leverage social media channels such as Facebook, Instagram and WhatsApp to share product-checkout links with their contacts for placing orders. It then handles payment and delivery, along with managing the selling channels and technology.

Group buying

Group buying is when companies use social media channels to help consumers avail discounts through buying as a group and deal sharing. In some markets like China group buying is already a common occurrence, both among friends and via organized apps or websites.

During the lockdowns in Shanghai in 2022, for a period of time there was no delivery of food and people were not permitted to leave their apartment complexes for any reason. In order to cope, apartment complexes came together to order groceries in bulk from wholesalers, requiring a wholesale delivery truck to come and those in the residence to work to unload, repack and distribute groceries to the apartment complex. This is obviously an extreme version of group purchasing, but illustrates how Chinese consumers were able to adapt an existing online buying behaviour to adapt to an extreme situation.

On the next page we profile a host of startups who are enabling group buying to allow consumers to tap into bulk purchases and help to alleviate market inefficiencies in urban and rural areas globally.

- CityMall is a social e-commerce platform offering lifestyle and curated products through peer-to-peer referrals on WhatsApp. CityMall helps lower-tier cities in India experience online commerce by enabling neighbourhood community leaders to set up their virtual stores on WhatsApp. Community leaders sell products by aggregating orders from their network of customers using e-commerce tools and taking care of last-mile logistics; they earn through commission. Product categories include groceries, apparel, cosmetics and daily essentials at discounted prices.

- DealShare is a multi-category consumer products platform that targets rural and small-town consumers in India. It offers products across categories such as grocery, clothing, home, beauty and wellness, personal care and electronics. DealShare sources products locally and offers deep discounts and rewards to shoppers who buy in groups. It leverages demand aggregation of mass market products using social virality, also allowing users to share unique links for products or deals through WhatsApp to enable the group to access discounts.

- Gobillion is an Indian group-buying startup that was founded in 2021. Gobillon pioneers the 'Team Buy' model, through which customers can team up with friends and family to buy online together to save on their daily needs while building trust through community engagement. Gobillion enables consumers to find product deals and share them with their network of contacts, via messaging apps such as WhatsApp. Product prices decrease as more consumers join the deal.

- KitaBeli is an Indonesia-based social commerce platform founded in March 2020. KitaBeli allows users to share product and price information with their social circles and build teams to purchase these items at discounted prices. The platform uses a partner-based delivery network; network individuals earn commission for performing last-mile delivery. KitaBeli offers a wide range of products across daily essentials, CPG goods, fashion, beauty and electronics categories.

- Founded in 2010 and headquartered in Beijing, China, Lashou is a location-based social commerce platform that offers group-buying discounts on product categories such as beauty, health, food, travel and entertainment.

- Founded in 2018, Mall91 is an India-based full-stack community social commerce platform that uses the concept of group discount buying at a zip-code level. Mall91 enables commerce through video and voice, driven by referrals and group buying, offering locally manufactured products at discounted prices. The platform combines video-based shopping, a vernacular-voice recognition-based catalogue and WhatsApp-like chat-based checkout. Its product catalogue has 200,000 items under apparel, accessories and daily essentials across 15,000 SKUs, and the platform houses 15,000 product videos in eight Indian languages.

- Founded in 2020 in California, PowerBuy is a social commerce-as-a-service platform through which customers can earn discounts on products by influencing their peers, friends and family through social media to buy the same item, turning them into influencers for these e-commerce stores. PowerBuy also helps merchants add group-buying functionality to any of their product pages.

- ShopG is a social commerce platform through which users can place group orders with their friends to access discounts. It was founded in 2019 in Bangalore, India. Product categories include grocery, home décor, kitchen, beauty and personal care. ShopG has over 1,000 community leaders that work with regional brands for product sourcing, offering them access to remote places and helping ShopG build an engaging social platform.

Video commerce and livestreaming

Social commerce is being turbo charged by the advent of livestreaming which allows brands to directly merge content and commerce in a seamless platform and transaction. A host of new companies are providing shoppable videos and live videos for product discovery and purchase through social media channels, including the following.

- Founded in 2018, Bulbul is an India-based video shopping app that aims to make online shopping fun, engaging and social. Consumers can receive product information by watching videos and live events created by hosts, sellers and individuals in the Bulbul platform, rather than going to the product description pages. These videos help consumers discover products and make informed purchase decisions, and drive conversion. Bulbul caters to a 'shoppable videos' model that involves shopping through videos that showcase a brand or product within India's social commerce ecosystem.

- Founded in 2018, Buywith is a US-based online shopping livestream platform that helps brands, retailers and influencers to host live shopping events. Buywith enables brands to connect with social media influencers and scale their business by gaining access to a large community of shoppers. It also empowers influencers to broadcast their online shopping experiences with brands and retailers on any social media channel, to share with their followers and influence them to buy.

- CommentSold is a social commerce platform that helps businesses sell through social networking with affordable and innovative software solutions. Its live selling feature facilitates livestreaming via a mobile app and social media. CommentSold also helps create engaging video content for customers to watch, buy through and share; content creators can broadcast through a webstore, mobile app or social media.

- Founded in 2017 and headquartered in California, Firework is a video platform that offers short, vertical video technology for everyone. It facilitates selling in real time through high-quality, interactive livestreams. Firework also offers short and immersive shoppable videos that increase customer engagement and drive conversion of website visitors. Firework currently has a reach of over 250 million people globally who consume millions of short videos across hundreds of categories, according to the company.

- Founded in 2019, Glance is an Indian artificial intelligence (AI)-based software company that delivers personalized and live content across categories such as games, travel, entertainment, fitness, sports and news on the lock screens of smartphones. Glance is a 'screen zero' content delivery platform. Its short format videos can be shared through social media platforms and WhatsApp. Glance acquired Shop101, a social commerce platform, to integrate celebrity and influencer-led commerce on its platform in June 2021.

- Founded in 2016 in Canada, Livescale is a video platform that enables organizations to transform content and e-commerce into real-time shopping. Livescale empowers brands to build community through its live shopping technology that facilitates these brands to offer an immersive, engaging and seamless shopping experience. The company claims that it bridges the online–offline gap by changing the way brands build, engage and sell to their communities. It leverages the power of live shopping to innovators that help brands convert community to sales

- Founded in 2018, NTWRK is a US-based mobile-first video shopping platform that integrates entertainment and commerce, providing consumers access to products from known personalities, artists and brands. It offers daily excusive product drops, shoppable content from creators, virtual festivals and social distribution through its worldwide community of artists and fans/influencers, offering wide reach for brands and users.

- Shoploop is a mobile-based video shopping platform created by Google's in-house incubator, Area 120, that helps consumers to discover products in an engaging, informational and entertaining format. Shoploop uses short-video formats, focusing more on purchasing decisions than products themselves, to drive product discovery so that consumers need not go through product pages and descriptions. It facilitates brand-influencer partnerships and enable shoppers to shop directly from influencer videos. The platform currently focuses on beauty and personal care products.

- Simsim, founded in June 2019 in Delhi, is a video-based social commerce platform that sells fashion, beauty, electronics, health and wellness products. The platform uses videos to attract more customers, engage them in a more informative way and drive conversion. Simsim works with influencers, known as 'community opinion leaders', who create informative videos related to the products sold on the platform. Simsim shoppers can receive product information by watching these videos instead of reading product descriptions. YouTube acquired the platform in July 2021.

- Founded in 2020, US-based SPIN Live is an end-to-end platform that focuses on product discovery through live commerce. Spin Live enables creators to connect with their brands, stream live product videos and monetize their content. It integrates merchandising, checkout, payment and community into one seamless video experience. It also enables retailers to partner with influencers who can stream to their followers. Shoppers can watch live and purchase directly through the app.

- Founded in 2014, Switcher Studio is a US-based mobile video app that helps organizations to create multi-camera livestreaming videos by connecting to multiple iPhones and iPads. Switcher Studio's shoppable livestreams help businesses connect with viewers in real time, sell more products and expand their customer base. It also helps to broadcast and record vertical videos, offering better mobile viewing experience and enable direct social media sharing of video clips as promos and teasers.

Social payments integration

In order to enable seamless transaction companies are offering peer-to-peer digital payments that integrate social functionality such as text, voice and video. Some of these companies around the world include:

- Cassava Smartech is a diversified smartech group offering digital solutions in e-commerce, healthcare, finance, education and social payments to drive socioeconomic development in Africa. Cassava Social Payments is an integrated social payments platform that combines social chat and mobile payments in a single app. The platform enables customers to chat – via text, voice and video – with their friends and family, send money to them and pay for anything, on the go.

- Cash App is a financial platform that enable users to transfer money to one another using a smartphone app. It was founded in 2013 and is head-quartered in the US. Cash App lets users pay anyone instantly and receive money from peers. It also offers a customizable debit card facility for everyday spending and accessing discounts.

- Founded in 2011, US-based Chirpify helps to turn social media replies and comments into cash, helping businesses and consumers to buy, sell and pay in-stream on social media, according to the company. Chirpify enables brands to listen for triggers such as emojis, keywords, likes, mentions and hashtags on social media – including Instagram, Slack and Twitter – and provide cash or card-linked offers for their social actions. Brands can reply to people to collect and save their phone number or payment handles to enable automatic payment in future through Venmo or PayPal.

- Founded in 2009 and headquartered in California, Mfino offers mobile financial services, payments and commerce to enable digital transforma-tion in retail. Mfino's mobile wallet facilitates peer-to-peer payments through email, phone number or any social media messaging channels. It also helps to automate operations through Chatbots to reach more customers and offer a frictionless banking experience.

- Founded in 2015, Moneymailme is a money transfer and chat app that combines social interaction with sending and receiving money from others. Moneymailme enables the transfer of funds through social tech-nologies such as chat and video calls in a fast and secure way. It enables overseas transfer and offers multiple currency formats.

- Founded in 2019, US-based PaySplit is a social payments platform that enables influencers, content creators and artists to seamlessly transact with brands, agencies and audiences in a global payment ecosystem, removing the barriers for connection, according to the company. PaySplit links can be added to social media bios, enabling followers to accept and make payments.

- Founded in 2012, Social Media Gateways (SMG) is a US-based platform and service provider that offers digital transformation tools for businesses. One of its platforms, PaySoko, offers social payments and e-commerce solutions that connect merchants with customers, sponsors and service providers. The company claims to bridge the gap between customer engagement, payments and logistics, enabling people to engage and pay for goods and services. Its technology helps customers and businesses to transact securely with one another, irrespective of their geography and currencies.

Content and commerce will continue to be a virtuous cycle for brands and retailers that get it right. The product content leads to commerce conversion, and then more commerce will come with positive content that drives even more commerce.

Terence Ng, Senior Analyst, Coresight Research (2022)

TEN THINGS RETAILERS NEED TO KNOW ABOUT SOCIAL COMMERCE

1 Consumers across age groups are active on social media and an increasing number of these are turning to social media for shopping.

2 Social media creators are monetizing their fanbase with new technology and tools to incentivize shopping.

3 Livestreaming and social commerce festivals are growing – allowing for multiple brands to band together to drive consumer traffic and excitement.

4 Consolidation within the technology industry is rapidly changing the social commerce landscape, affecting retailer partnerships and strategies.

5 Gaming is becoming the new battleground for social commerce with the advent of the Metaverse and increase in in-game shopping opportunities.

6 Numerous emerging startups around the world are gaining popularity as they innovate new aspects of the social commerce landscape.

7 Content and commerce are becoming more and more blended, especially in the short-video area, driven not only by TikTok/Douyin but by emerging startups and increasing adoption of short video by established players.

8 Group buying is gaining speed around the world, building on its popularity in China and allowing users to band together for special offers and bulk purchases.

9 Numerous solutions exist for shoppable videos or livestreaming, allowing retailers to easily adapt to this new and growing format.

10 Social commerce is becoming easier to implement with new integrated payment solutions, removing a key barrier for both consumers and retailers.

People are missing the human connection in e-commerce. Social commerce brings people together and creates memories while shopping from people they trust and admire. People trust creators much more than companies. The next step in social commerce is when creators are the retailers.

Gil Elias, Founder of influencer commerce startup Nillio (2022)

KEY TAKEAWAYS: SOCIAL COMMERCE

Not only can brands build meaningful relationships with consumers through social media channels, but they also have the opportunity to glean insights about the content their target audiences crave and link this content directly to purchases. By implementing data analysis into digital content operations, brands can optimize their content to better resonate with consumers and achieve online marketing and sales objectives.

- Brands and retailers should look to leverage community-led engagement as a way of boosting the discovery phase of social commerce and drive authenticity.

- To avoid relinquishing valuable customer and conversion data to third-party channels, retail companies should navigate social interactions toward self-owned websites to collect data. Offering discount code-driven sign-ups is one way of encouraging social media users to complete the journey to brand sites and become customers.

- As shoppable- and live-video content integrations speak to consumers' increasing demand for more seamless online shopping experiences, we expect more retail companies to enter the livestreaming e-commerce space.

- Retail companies should develop a variety of influencer marketing strategies, including a multi-tiered approach – leveraging big-name influencers to micro-influencers. The lesser-known personalities could be powerful allies to brands with their authenticity and dedicated followers.

References

Business Wire (2022) Take-Two and Zynga to combine, bringing together best-in-class intellectual properties and a market-leading, diversified mobile publishing platform, to enhance positioning as a global leader in interactive entertainment, 10 January. www.businesswire.com/news/home/20220110005389/en/ (archived at perma.cc/F4YT-5DDL)

Elias, G (2022) Interview with the authors, July.

Ng, T (2022) Interview with the authors, July.

Peterson, M (2021) Apple now calls itself a gaming company fighting with Microsoft, Sony, AppleInsider, 29 October. https://appleinsider.com/articles/21/10/29/apple-now-calls-itself-a-gaming-company-fighting-with-microsoft-sony-nintendo (archived at perma.cc/YS4E-L3SU)

Redmond, W (2020) Microsoft to acquire ZeniMax Media and its game publisher Bethesda Softworks, Microsoft News Center, 21 September. https://news.microsoft.com/2020/09/21/microsoft-to-acquire-zenimax-media-and-its-game-publisher-bethesda-softworks/ (archived at perma.cc/4GKH-U4N6)

Redmond, W (2022) Microsoft to acquire Activision Blizzard to bring the joy and community of gaming to everyone, across every device, Microsoft News Center, 18 January. https://news.microsoft.com/2022/01/18/microsoft-to-acquire-activision-blizzard-to-bring-the-joy-and-community-of-gaming-to-everyone-across-every-device/ (archived at perma.cc/UM24-PT2U)

Stuart, K and Hern, A (2014) Minecraft sold: Microsoft buys Mojang for $2.5bn, *The Guardian*, 15 September. www.theguardian.com/technology/2014/sep/15/microsoft-buys-minecraft-creator-mojang-for-25bn (archived at perma.cc/2K8A-PSM3)

Verdu, M (2021) Expanding our games team with the acquisition of Night School Studio, Netflix, 28 September. https://about.netflix.com/en/news/expanding-our-games-team-with-the-acquisition-of-night-school-studio (archived at perma.cc/X3BT-9W5P)

Weinswig, D (2021) Retail-tech landscape: Social commerce, Coresight Research. https://coresight.com/research/retail-tech-landscape-social-commerce/ (archived at perma.cc/FV7V-S6G3)

Weinswig, D (2022) US social commerce survey 2022: Capitalizing on social media influence in retail, Coresight Research. https://coresight.com/research/us-social-commerce-survey-2022-capitalizing-on-social-media-influence-in-retail/ (archived at perma.cc/G529-MMFS)

07

Creating retail media to monetize consumer traffic

LEARNING OBJECTIVES

Retailers are increasingly seeking new ways to monetize their traffic and customer base, and retail media provides an ideal platform for this relatively new revenue stream. In this chapter we delve into the details of retail media, including:

- how changes in consumer privacy drove the retail media sector
- how retailers are rolling out media to connect with their consumers and increase their e-commerce margins
- what methods are producing the highest revenue conversion and monetization
- data mining and intelligence offered by retail media
- personalization methods created by retail media

The rise of retail media

Faced with ever-increasing competition and the slimmer margins that tend to come with expanded online sales, more retailers are turning to retail media to capitalize on burgeoning shopper data and create new revenue streams.

Retail media is an evolved way of advertising whereby brands utilize retailers' digital and physical channels to promote their products and spread awareness. These ads are often displayed in-store or featured on e-commerce sites – on the home, category, search results or product detail pages – as well as via external channels such as social media platforms Facebook and Instagram; retail media helps brands to boost their presence on the digital shelf.

Retailers are increasingly racing toward the $75 billion high-margin prize in retail media, according to Coresight's 2022 retail media market size estimates (Weinswig, 2022). Retail giants Amazon and Walmart disclosed that their global retail advertising revenue in 2021 was $32.1 billion and $2.1 billion, respectively (Weinswig, 2022). Adoption is on the rise – and retail media networks aren't just for retail giants anymore. Retailers of all sizes can use their first-party data to drive sales and bring in ad spend from their brand partners.

Retail media trends

We have identified five key retail media trends to watch going forward:

1 Retailers are launching retail media networks (RMNs) to generate incremental revenues. Retail giants Amazon and Walmart, specialty retailers Ulta Beauty and The Home Depot, and rapid-delivery companies Instacart and Gopuff have launched their own RMNs to monetize their retail data. RMNs allow retailers to add high-margin advertising business to their revenue streams.

2 Strategic partnerships enable retailers to show value to their brand partners. Retailers are entering into strategic partnerships with measurement providers, such as NielsenIQ, a global information services company, to measure media effectiveness and enable brand partners to optimize based on their return on investment (ROI) and return on advertising spend (ROAS).

3 Retail media allows brands to offer personalized promotions to customers. Consumers have come to expect personalization in discounts and rewards. Using retail media to offer personalization across promotions and recommendations in real time is likely to lead to an increase in sales and basket size.

4 Brands are using retail media to gain deeper insights into key metrics. Retail media enables brands and advertisers to close the loop and see the impact of their advertisements on real-time sales.

5 Retailers are investing in in-store digital advertising. Along with monetizing their digital store data, retailers are setting up in-store digital displays placed at strategic locations to engage with consumers. These interactive signages can be highly effective in driving conversion and add an extra level of complexity when measuring the overall attribution of media spend.

We believe that the relevance and popularity of retail media will continue to grow. This new business model is likely to become a mainstream revenue channel for retailers. We expect to see retailers enter into strategic partnerships with measurement providers to expand their retail media advertising revenues.

Why retail media?

More than ever, consumers are using digital channels for their day-to-day needs. However, changes in consumer privacy regulations have forced brands to re-evaluate the use of first-party data – the information that a company collects directly from its customers, prospects and users, either online or offline, through websites, apps, social media and surveys. Retailers own a significant share of first-party data that is crucial for brands and advertisers. Many are investing a share of their media dollars to reach shoppers through retailer-owned channels.

The drive to monetize shopper data and increase profit margins is attracting more retailers to start their own RMNs or affiliate with networks organized by companies that aggregate retail channels. An RMN is a digital advertising business that enables brands and advertising partners to buy advertising space across the retailer's properties or properties controlled by digital marketplaces or quick-commerce companies (see Figure 7.1).

FIGURE 7.1 Types of retail media networks

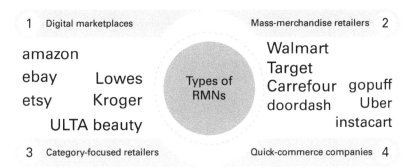

1   Digital marketplaces   Mass-merchandise retailers   2

amazon   Walmart
ebay   Lowes   Types of   Target
etsy   Kroger   RMNs   Carrefour   gopuff
                                            doordash   Uber
        ULTA beauty   instacart

3   Category-focused retailers   Quick-commerce companies   4

SOURCE Coresight Research

What is driving the adoption of retail media?

E-commerce growth acceleration

It is no surprise that we have witnessed significant growth in the overall e-commerce market, particularly coming out of the pandemic. The onset of the global pandemic in 2020 signalled a permanent shift in consumer behaviour. Every aspect of life moved behind a screen, from work to play and everything in between. As consumers adapted to shopping for anything and everything online, their expectations regarding digital experiences grew exponentially – and they continue to evolve. This paradigm shift in consumer behaviour is one of the critical factors responsible for the continued growth of the retail media industry.

The move away from third-party cookies ('the cookie apocalypse')

Tightening consumer privacy standards and the phase-out of third-party cookies and mobile identifier restrictions have transformed marketers' acquisition, retention and engagement with customers.

- Social media sites Facebook and Twitter removed third-party data from their advertising platforms in 2018 and 2019 respectively, due to privacy regulations restricting the use of third-party cookies. In August 2019, Twitter issued a public apology to its users for using personal information for advertising purposes.

- In 2019 Mozilla Firefox blocked thousands of web trackers by default, protecting users from many websites, analytics companies and advertisers that want to follow their paths across the web.

- Google announced plans to block third-party cookies from Google Chrome in 2020. The company plans to completely stop tracking customer interactions on its browser by 2023.

- In 2020 Apple released a major update to Safari Intelligent Tracking Prevention, the privacy feature that allows its Safari web browser to block cookies. The update ensured that no advertiser or website could use commonplace tracking technology and blocked all kinds of third-party cookies.

Advertisers recognize the imperative to adopt alternatives to the use of cookies as an advertising measurement tool. First-party data provides brands with unique information about customers, which helps them to improve their data-driven marketing initiatives. In a survey conducted by Coresight Research in November 2021, more than half of all US-based executives whose organizations use first-party data for marketing purposes reported that the efficient use of first-party data helps drive online sales – making this the topmost benefit (Weinswig, 2022).

Many retailers control a treasure trove of first-party data through their digital presence and opt-in loyalty programmes. Members willingly share preferences, feedback and contextual information. Using this consumer data from retailers provides an opportunity for brands to derive actionable insights that can have a positive impact on revenue.

Retailers are launching RMNs to generate incremental revenues

Although e-commerce businesses have grown over the last few years, structurally, they have variable costs and generate lower margins than brick-and-mortar retail channels. In addition to managing competitive pricing, online businesses incur additional variable overhead costs in the form of shipping costs and handling returns. Retailers have typically focused on customer retention and loyalty to drive revenue, often turning to the last mile to provide competitive offerings that meet consumer expectations for convenience and speed in fulfilment – leading to an increase in fulfilment costs.

Retailers must find a balance between increasing fulfilment capabilities while also generating higher margins each year. Furthermore, temporary forces such as labour shortages, rising product costs driven by inflation and supply chain issues increase the pressure on margins. RMNs ease these pressures on margins by allowing retailers to add high-margin advertising business to their revenue streams.

During its earnings release, Walmart CFO Brett Biggs said that the company's retail media arm, Walmart Connect+, helped the company to achieve high margins amid rising margin pressure on its e-commerce business. Biggs confirmed that the retailer plans to scale Walmart Connect+. He said, 'Walmart Connect+ advertising experienced robust sales growth this year with a strong pipeline of new advertisers and large growth opportunities ahead. We continue to make strong progress in some of our newer, higher-margin initiatives' (Weinswig, 2022).

RMNs not only offer new revenue channels but also help brands to analyse customers' shopping habits and buying patterns as they hold a vast amount of first-party data, all sourced from retailers' owned brick-and-mortar and digital ecosystems. With more precise targeting capabilities, first-party data-driven advertising may drive incremental purchases on retailers' own e-commerce stores and inform better decisions on media spend overall. First-party data offers advertisers and brands unique information about their customers, leading to better customer understanding. This insightful information can, in turn, help retailers to improve the accuracy and relevance of their messaging – leading to enhanced customer satisfaction as well as greater brand recognition. Where the first generation of RMN focused on generating margins, the new generation is now more focused on showing value to the brands that require the insights that inform their media decisions and rationalize their media spend.

Retailers offer brands multiple options to target and advertise to the right audience on their digital channels – through preferential placement of sponsored products, search engine optimization tools and by running various types of ads in search results and on product pages. Through these initiatives, retailers secure incremental advertising revenues. For these revenues to be sustainable and incremental, retailers need to make sure that they are able to show ROI to the brands and measure the impact of their ad spend.

Are these retail media networks successful? So far, the answer is a resounding yes. Below are a few examples from large retailers and how their RMNs are delivering value for the companies.

- Amazon announced that its global retail advertising segment generated revenues of $31.2 billion in 2021; revenues in the fourth quarter of 2021 grew by 32.0 per cent (Weinswig, 2022).
- During Walmart's earnings call the company disclosed that its global advertising revenue for 2021 was $2.1 billion (of which $1.6 billion was generated by the media business) (Weinswig, 2022). The company is planning to scale its high-margin retail media business and claims that it is an important factor for its growth.
- French supermarket chain Carrefour expects its retail media arm, Carrefour Links, to generate additional ROI of up to $223.5 million by 2026 (Weinswig, 2022).

Strategic partnerships enable retailers to show value to their brand partners

Not all retailers possess the resources, skills, tools or data sets needed to monitor, manage and analyse siloed customer data to create value for their brand partners. Technology providers such as NielsenIQ help retailers to set up their retail media business – from insights and analytics to activation, targeting and measurement.

These technology platforms often leverage AI to understand customer needs; align with brands on assortment and promotion; provide insights to optimize marketing and ad budgets; and connect customers with the right products at the right time and in a highly personalized manner.

Retail media intelligence platforms gather data such as customer profiles and shopping behaviour to identify retention, win-back and cross-selling opportunities. For a measurement provider such as NielsenIQ, this also extends to supply chain, inflation, market dynamics data – creating an end-to-end platform.

Innovative regional and specialty retailers are moving decisively to pursue strategic partnerships to build their retail media capabilities. One notable example is online grocer FreshDirect, which began collaborating with ciValue, now a NielsenIQ company, to improve its insight-sharing programme. FreshDirect will use the platform to gain insights into customer preferences and launch customer-centric marketing strategies. And Michaels, a US-based specialty retailer, partnered with global retail media technology provider Criteo. Criteo will enable Michaels to scale its retail media programme with new capabilities, such as sponsored products and display and off-site advertising.

Retail media allows brands to offer personalized promotions to customers

With retail media, advertisers can meet customers at the right time and at the right place. First-party retailer data allows brands to offer mass personalization at scale – communicating with individual customers and not stopping at customer segments. Delivering a connected personalized customer experience has become a 'must-have' for brands to remain relevant and ahead of the competition.

Personalization is extremely important for both brands and retailers – it helps to improve loyalty and increase sales. Through personalization, retailers help consumers to navigate choices at speed.

When it comes to discounts and rewards, customers have come to expect personalized offers and relevant rewards. Offering personalization across promotions and recommendations in real time typically leads to an increase in sales and basket size. It also attracts customers to try new products and encourages them to buy more, leading to a sales uplift.

Retailers need to invest in retail media intelligence platforms that allow them to predict, share, launch, analyse and manage offers across all channels in real time – as well as to scale their personalization programme and reduce the time required to initiate campaigns.

Brands use retail media to gain deeper insights into advertising key metrics

Retail media allows advertisers to measure the impact of their ad spend to the point of purchase, offering closed-loop measurement (the ability to measure the impact of campaign activity on in-store action) that enables brand advertisers to tie a media campaign to real sales data.

Global CPG brand Kraft Heinz used retail media to promote its 2021 'Leave it to Lunchables' ad campaign, which yielded more than 3.6 million impressions, according to the company. The ad campaign ran across multiple platforms, including display ads on recipe pages, digital circulars and in-store kiosks. According to Kraft Heinz Senior Shopper Marketing Manager Desiree Casey, 'It's just a great way for [the company] to reach those independent customers and to be able to provide equity in advertising against our brands, amplifying what we already have going on in the circular and bringing it to life online' (Weinswig, 2022).

For every campaign launched, brands can capture the click-through rate, spend, cost per click, sales and ROAS for each individual product. As an example, Walmart's demand-side platform, Walmart DSP (part of Walmart Connect+), delivered around 500 per cent ROAS for Société Bic (known as BIC), a French disposable consumer product manufacturer (Weinswig, 2022).

Retailers such as Amazon and Walmart have insightful first-party data, including consumer browsing and purchase data, which allows them to identify customers who make a purchase after seeing an ad. This ability to identify the right customers at the point of sale attracts brand advertisers. Retailers such as Kroger and Walmart merge in-store sales data to generate incremental value to advertisers by utilizing their first-party shopper data across traditional and digital channels.

Retail media provides brands with the following advertising benefits:

- rich first-party data foundation
- closed-loop retailer data to drive personalization
- clear measurement and campaign attribution
- actionable audience insights to inform merchandising decisions

Retailers are investing in in-store digital advertising

Amid pandemic-led lockdowns over the last two years, retailers have reinvented brick-and-mortar stores to become a key part of their omnichannel sales strategies. We expect retailers to increasingly leverage in-store digital ads to deepen their engagement with customers, using AI-driven technology and data to present personalized content to customers when they interact with digital screens.

In-store digital advertising allows brands to gain access to data and create focused advertising campaigns to reach customers when they are most likely to make a purchase decision – in the aisle and at the point of sale. Compelling in-store digital signage – alongside other omnichannel marketing strategies, such as digital marketing and shelf-placement – can be highly effective in driving conversion, making it an appealing concept for retailers.

Walmart began using digital screens for in-store advertising (Wal-Mart TV) in 1998. In 2006, it launched the Walmart Smart Network, which uses upgraded digital technology to deliver ads in stores. The company has installed more than 170,000 digital display screens across its 4,700 stores globally. In January 2022 Walmart piloted its newly designed digital displays at Store 4108 in Springdale, Arkansas. The screens offer contextual information about products and brands and are passively interactive – they display customer reviews when products are lifted from the shelves. The company has also placed QR codes throughout the store to enhance the in-store shopping experience.

Cooler Screens, a US-based digital in-store retail media company, has installed more than 10,000 screens across 700 retail locations in the US, enabling retailers and brands to display messages to their target audiences. The screens have sensors that can monitor the shopper and their activities – such as seeing the ads and selecting the products – enabling retailers to measure the effectiveness of the advertising campaign. Several startups, such as Freeosk, offer an ad network wherein brands can buy digital ad slots on each vending machine to encourage people to purchase their products.

Additionally, as part of their proximity marketing strategy, retailers can use mobile beacons to gather information about customer movements, send alerts to customers' phones to optimize and personalize the in-store experience. Retailers can pair beacon-based apps and proximity marketing software to capture the geographic location of the user and then deliver relevant content based on their immediate environment.

Target uses this technology to map routes for customers to help them locate products on an aisle-by-aisle basis. And beauty retailer Sephora uses beacon technology combined with push notifications to alert customers that they can claim a free 15-minute in-store makeover, for example.

CASE STUDY
Retail media and the grocery channel

Retail media has seen significant growth in the grocery channel during the past few years – accelerated by the pandemic and the quick rush to online grocery ordering for pickup or delivery. Rob Christian, Chief Strategy Officer at grocery e-commerce technology provider ShopHero Inc, told Coresight Research that CPG brands are raising their marketing budgets and are allocating 'brand new money' for the retail media landscape (Weinswig, 2021).

The grocery sector illustrates three key trends in retail media in the US grocery market:

- retailers' strategies to capitalize on the pandemic-driven e-commerce boom using retail media
- instacart's heavy investment in advertising services for CPG brands
- the impact of tightening online consumer privacy standards – and how this heightens the retail media opportunity

Retailers are capitalizing on the e-commerce boom using retail media

Over the past two years, many grocery retailers have launched retail media offerings, in some cases listing them as separate entities from their core retail segment. These include the largest players, such as Walmart, Kroger, Albertsons and Ahold Delhaize, as well as regional grocers like Wakefern, Hy-Vee and Southeastern Grocers. However, the pandemic-induced surge in online grocery shopping – with much of it happening on traditional grocers' websites – has increased the scale of the overall retail media opportunity, making grocers' websites more valuable as advertising properties and establishing their growing online audiences as important marketing assets.

Amazon, which spearheaded the retail media trend, has taken advantage of its massive audience: the online retailer offers preferential placement of 'sponsored products' and other promoted marketing on its website. This incremental advertising revenue has a high drop-through to the bottom line and has allowed Amazon to invest in price and service capabilities.

In March 2021 Kroger reported that its retail media business grew 135 per cent year over year in financial year (FY) 2021, with almost 1,300 brands using its Kroger Precision Marketing platform. This helped contribute $150 million in incremental operating profit to the company. The company projects its advertising business to grow nearly 30 per cent in FY 2022 (Weinswig, 2021) and sees the potential for a multibillion-dollar retail media business in the next few years.

Brands and retailers are not the only ones looking to capitalize on the retail media surge. A significant new category of third-party technology providers has emerged to help retailers set up their own media networks or help brands buy from those retail media networks. This space is highly fragmented and overlapping, and still expanding with new entrants.

Instacart is doubling down as an advertising platform for CPG brands

Instacart is an important player to watch as the US grocery sector turns its focus toward retail media. The pandemic spurred a surge in grocery delivery demand, catapulting Instacart from a luxury to almost an essential service. The company's substantial growth has made it a serious contender in grocery e-commerce alongside Walmart and Amazon.

Instacart has ambitions to grow into a significant advertising platform. In May 2020 Instacart launched a new advertising tool that CPG brands can use to promote their products on Instacart's website and app. The new self-service tool, called Featured Products, is based around keyword-targeted advertising campaigns and allows advertisers to bid on relevant keywords and then promote products related to those terms. Instacart's other ad formats, including coupons, promotions for free delivery and banner adverts, will remain a part of its managed advertising offering.

The company reportedly introduced more advertising placements after 2020 saw uptake of its Featured Products service triple and the number of advertisers on the platform quintuple. Coresight Research has identified from job advertisements posted by Instacart that the company is looking to grow its advertising revenue by five times over the next two to three years.

Instacart is also investing heavily in advertising expertise to strengthen its retail media team. In August 2021 Instacart appointed Fidji Simo as its new CEO, replacing its founder Apoorva Mehta. Before joining Instacart, Simo served as Vice President and Head of the Facebook app, and oversaw Facebook's mobile monetization strategy and advertising business. Instacart also appointed Carolyn Everson as President in the same month; like the new CEO, she spent more than a decade at Facebook and brings extensive experience in building advertising relationships. Over the past year, Instacart has also added two senior hires to its retail media business: Vice President of

Ad Sales Ryan Mayward, who joined from Amazon, and Vice President of Ads Engineering Vik Gupta, previously from Google.

As Instacart doubles down on retail media, other quick-commerce players will be watching closely and learning from its example – and a number of rivals are already pushing into retail media. As Instacart prepares for a possible public offering, the growth prospects in retail media could be an important focus for future investors. Retail media revenue can compensate if pandemic-driven demand in its core business fades, and can be supported by the addition of new features such as live video streams from influencers, conversational AI and augmented reality to unlock opportunities.

Tightening consumer privacy standards heighten the opportunity

Tightening consumer privacy standards have undercut longstanding digital marketing tools such as third-party cookies. These developments will hinder advertisers' insights into which consumers have been exposed to ads, as well as their ability to connect data to that of other channels.

Retail media fills this void: retailers' ability to access first-party data and close the loop by identifying those who make a purchase after seeing an ad makes it a compelling new channel for advertisers. Some retailers such as Walmart and Kroger aim to blend in-store sales into the picture as well, and they have the first-party shopper data across traditional and digital channels to do it.

We believe retail media will become a permanent and integral part of how grocery retailers generate revenue. Structural shifts in the advertising marketplace have created the opportunity for retailers to become highly effective channels for marketing investment. Since building out e-commerce capabilities consumes much of retailers' time and resources, monetizing their sites will be a priority – particularly as they look for a source of steady profits to offset their lower-margin e-commerce business.

The ultimate goal of retail media is to utilize this channel to have your customers purchase more from you, via providing timely, personalized and relevant purchase inspiration. While some retailers, particularly large multi-brand retailers, can generate significant new revenue streams from retail media, retailers should not lose sight of the ultimate goal of retail media: to sell more to your existing consumers.

Ken Fenyo, President, Research and Advisory, Coresight Research (2022)

TEN THINGS RETAILERS NEED TO KNOW ABOUT RETAIL MEDIA

1 Changes in privacy laws and norms are allowing retailers to be a primary holder of consumer data.

2 A number of large retailers have launched their own retail media networks to generate revenue from their consumer data and access.

3 Retailers can be a valuable source of data and a marketing channel for their brand partners.

4 Retail media is a powerful tool for delivering increased personalization to consumers.

5 Technology advancements are allowing for new solutions for in-retail advertising that can increase the value of retail media.

6 The grocery sector provides an illustrative example of the power of retail media.

7 Retail media not only provides a new revenue stream, but also allows the retailer to increase sales with existing consumers.

8 Enhancements in AI and data analysis increase the value of retail media networks and the data that they can provide to brands.

9 Retail media is an opportunity to provide a closed-loop advertising solution to brand partners, allowing for very accurate advertising spend tracking and ROI attribution.

10 Retailers of all sizes and types can take advantage of the retail media opportunity.

KEY TAKEAWAYS: RETAIL MEDIA

We believe retail media will increase in importance as consumers continue to shift their habits online. The advertising solution can be a win–win for all parties involved:

- Shoppers benefit from the personalized offers.

- Companies can experience increased brand awareness and higher return on their ad spend.

- Retailers can garner increased product sales and alternative revenue.

As more retailers join the retail media bandwagon, competition for advertising budgets will increase, underscoring the need to provide brands and advertisers with a good experience and greater return on their spending. Retailers should provide efficient workflows, greater access to data and more accurate measurement within their retail media solutions.

References

Fenyo, K (2022) Interview with the authors, July.

Weinswig, D (2021) Digital retail media: A new opportunity for US grocery, Coresight Research. https://coresight.com/research/digital-retail-media-a-new-opportunity-for-us-grocery/ (archived at perma.cc/BHE3-EHZ2)

Weinswig, D (2022) The evolution of retail media: Five trends to watch, Coresight Research. https://coresight.com/research/the-evolution-of-retail-media-five-trends-to-watch/ (archived at perma.cc/WK6K-G56S)

08

Supply chain

LEARNING OBJECTIVES

In this chapter we present:

- five strategies for brands and retailers to make sourcing more responsive and less susceptible to external pressures
- companies with innovative solutions for ensuring resilient and agile supply chain ecosystems
- how artificial intelligence can assist in sourcing
- profiles of technology innovators in the supply chain sector

The pandemic shock to supply chains

The events of 2020 warranted a close re-examination of sourcing strategies and prompted implementation of more robust supply chain approaches as consumer demand for some categories plunged while other categories saw a sharp increase. However, following the initial shock of the pandemic, 2021 and 2022 turned out to be markedly disruptive and challenges compounded: global supply chain disruptions were up 88 per cent year over year in 2021 – on top of a 67 per cent increase in disruption in 2020 (Mayer, 2022).

These statistics underscore the need to build further agility and resilience into supply chains and sourcing, to ensure businesses are as prepared as possible for impending uncertainties in the future.

Achieving agility and resilience in sourcing

While agility and resilience have long been at the heart of sourcing strategies, the pandemic exposed vulnerabilities in even the most well-planned supply chains.

For many companies, the disruptions that arose demanded companies to deal with several challenges at once, including the following:

- shutdowns of manufacturing/vendor facilities
- inventory pile-ups in stores, warehouses and distribution centres
- clogging of routes to market
- mass employee absenteeism – in 2021, labour events that disrupted supply chains globally were up 156 per cent year over year (Mayer, 2022)
- seesawing in consumer demand

Below, we present five ways that companies can build stronger sourcing processes, with examples from major retail players.

Consider costs and speed-to-market at each stage of sourcing

Companies are often focused on achieving cost savings through isolated sourcing proposals and speed-to-market by simply considering proximity of sourcing locations. However, by optimizing time across each stage of the sourcing chain, companies could reap incremental speed-to-market benefits.

In a 23 November 2021 earnings call, Gap Inc (2021) stated that it was factoring longer delays at ports when planning its product booking deadlines for 2022 so that it could ship most of its goods through ocean freight and receive them on time. It has also accelerated the use of digital product creation for Old Navy's fall orders, adding further speed and efficiency to sourcing.

Macy's underwent a significant supply chain overhaul through 2019. Its supply chain teams previously worked in brand silos specific to brands rather than product categories, with separate end-to-end processes for each brand, including transport and technology. For a retailer with such scale, centralizing operations was not only economical but also helped design teams to work more cohesively. For example, developing common fabrics and samples across brands can cut down approval times in the product development and innovation stage and save on shipping them together. Macy's achieved a 6 per cent uplift in the cost of goods in pilot programmes under the new centralized strategy and aims to achieve a 6–8 per cent decrease in the cost of goods by 2023 (Weinswig, 2022).

Increase control over the supply chain

Acquiring vendors or facilities at various stages of the supply chain helps brands and retailers to grow control over sourcing, gain improved visibility and have a greater say in operations of that stage.

Ahold Delhaize announced a supply chain overhaul in December 2019, which included creating an integrated self-distribution model, warehouse design innovations and an expansion of facility locations. As the pandemic elevated demand for essentials, the company recognized its supply chain transformation as more important than ever – matching investments on the demand forecasting and replenishment sides, too.

At the outbreak of the pandemic in 2020, Ahold Delhaize faced challenges in keeping up with the demand surge and had to shift from one main supplier to secondary and tertiary suppliers. The company even had to source products from vendors that specialized in bulk supply to business consumers, and break product down for retail consumer use, according to Chris Lewis, EVP of Ahold Delhaize's Retail Business Services (which is responsible for back-end innovation). Lewis stated in an August 2020 interview that 'having control of inventory across 18 distribution centres and 2,000 stores means that [Ahold Delhaize will] be better prepared for any spike in sales, from a hurricane or other natural disaster, for example' (Blair, 2020).

Prada is a firm believer in vertical integration. It believes that its control over its factories and supply chain has given the company a competitive advantage over its industry cohorts amid pandemic-led disruptions. At its Investor Day call on 18 November 2021, group management remarked that the company owns 23 manufacturing sites and has long-term relationships with strategic suppliers (Prada Group, 2021b). Prada's acquisition of 40 per cent of an Italian yarn supplier in June 2021 is likely part of its long-term strategy to continually tighten its supply chain control (Prada Group, 2021a).

Re-assess supply chains and invest in technologies

The pandemic and resulting disruptions have underscored the significant need for investment in supply chain technologies. Moving forward, retailers should turn to innovative technologies to grow visibility and improve efficiency.

UK-based online retailer Ocado has developed technology that can help to better predict inventory replenishment rates, achieve shorter supply chains and provide greater control over the sourcing process. In 2019 Ocado invested in vertical farming startup Jones Foods and partnered with 80 Acres Farms, an indoor farming company, which could eventually help Ocado grow produce closer to customer locations, cutting down sourcing efforts and transport times, as well as increasing product freshness.

Ocado stated on its 11 February 2020 earnings call that having larger-scale automation and predictability across its warehouses has helped it to remain efficient. Its robotic picking warehouses, automated vehicle routing and scalable last-mile technology have supplemented its efforts in sourcing, too (Weinswig, 2022).

Walmart announced its investment in indoor farming company Plenty on 25 January 2022 (Repko, 2022). Plenty's proprietary farming technology allows the cultivation of multiple crops on a single platform, in a shorter timeframe and with lower consumption of water and land compared to traditional farming, according to the company's press release. Walmart aims to cut time to market with its investment in Plenty.

Expedite communication and transparency

When the pandemic hit, companies had to respond quickly, internally and externally, to understand and act on surges in demand and shortages in supply. Expedited communication and greater transparency will be beneficial for retailers in improving response times and allowing them to take corrective action quickly in the future.

Tractor Supply has been re-evaluating its sourcing strategy over the past few years, according to Colin Yankee, the company's EVP and Chief Supply Chain Officer (Weinswig, 2022). This re-assessment has been driven by internal strategies, such as switching to a total landed cost model (final product costs plus associated shipping and logistics costs incurred in delivering goods to their final destination) from a total cost of ownership model (total landed cost plus costs to own the product, such as storage).

External factors have also had an impact – including tariff changes in 2018 prompting a switch from Chinese imports to making goods in the US or importing from Mexico. The company applied learnings from these changes to manage pandemic-driven disruptions. Tractor Supply is using a mix of structured and unstructured data to coordinate activities in its sourcing chain. One area of focus for the company has been to get earlier visibility into supplier production and transport, so it can be more reactive in case of disturbances and take corrective action across the rest of the supply chain.

Explore new supplier partnerships

While longstanding relationships with suppliers provide immense cost benefits to retailers, companies should maintain agility by establishing new relationships, too. Finding new suppliers helps companies be apprised of untapped resources for their products and maintain a directory they can leverage when necessary.

As trade fairs were cancelled globally in 2020 and much of part of 2021, several companies hosted digital events for supplier or vendor pitches to still be able to explore new partnerships:

- Meijer held a Localization Summit on 1 April 2021, to find suppliers of baby, beauty, grocery and personal care products in the US states that it operates in.

- Lowe's, Staples and Walmart held virtual pitch events in 2020 for small businesses and entrepreneurs to supply specific product categories.

Partnering with innovators for supply chain optimization

Brands and retailers should look to digital partners to help make their sourcing resistant to shocks yet flexible enough to respond quickly and effectively. These companies all came up with innovative solutions for ensuring resilient and agile supply chain ecosystems:

- Community Marketplace is a business-to-business marketplace launched by wholesale organic foods distributor United Natural Foods Inc (UNFI). Suppliers can use this platform to sell to UNFI's retailer clients and ship products directly to them. Retailers are able to identify local suppliers quickly and suppliers can find retailers to sell to without having to attend a physical trade fair – cutting the time it takes to source and vet suppliers.

- Fashwire is a global marketplace for fashion designers that offers insights into consumer buying patterns, allowing them to make better and quicker design and production decisions. Having up-to-date, actionable insights is key to developing resilient supply chains in a fast-changing market, such as apparel.

- Everstream Analytics is a supply chain risk analytics company. It uses predictive analytics to help supply chain and logistics specialists have better visibility across their supply chains and make informed decisions on potential disruptions.

Implications for brands and retailers

Retail players are likely to continue facing disruptions to their supply chain, with factors such as port congestion, inflation and the ongoing Russia–Ukraine conflict presenting major challenges. With the Covid-19 vaccine rollout at inconsistent stages across the world, retailers with international sourcing locations need to be prepared for hiccups in supply as well as fluctuations in demand.

We see the following implications for brands/retailers:

- Retailers should consider cost savings and speed-to-market through each stage of sourcing and not reserve the decisions to the end segments of the sourcing processes. Large firms will benefit from centralizing decisions while smaller firms should look to decentralization in their supply chain.

- Retailers should expand control over sourcing to be able to respond to demand variabilities quickly. Vertical integration and localizing supply are two ways they can achieve this.

- Retailers and brands should invest in technologies and digitalize the sourcing segment of their supply chains to be on par with the last-mile delivery aspect of their supply chain.

- Previous disruptions to sourcing will give retailers a journal of learnings that they can leverage. They should be quick to sift out relevant lessons and communicate swiftly with concerned parties to minimize ongoing disruptions.

- In times of interruption to supply chains, brands and retailers need to work evermore closely with suppliers and stress the importance of communication. Constant communication and partnership are key to creating win–win situations, even amid adversity.

- Brands and retailers are likely to look for technology that will assist them with identifying areas of risk and how to prepare for them. Technology that provides cost savings, speed, transparency and visibility across the sourcing and supply chain will stand to benefit in the ongoing re-assessment of sourcing strategies.

Artificial intelligence and the supply chain

Sourcing journeys involve multidirectional flows of data between various parties. Much of this data tends to be recorded manually or documented on paper and transferred to a data analysis software, and typically housed in data silos for specific business units. During these processes, valuable data could be lost, misrepresented or have errors incorporated, preventing companies from unlocking the full potential of their sourcing strategies. There is a need for robust data networks that support solutions with artificial intelligence (AI), machine learning (ML) and Internet of Things (IoT) technology. The first step to realizing the full value of digitalization is to assess and upgrade retailers' existing data networks.

Brands and retailers tend to work with a number of manufacturers, vendors and agents for their sourcing and procurement needs, equating to hundreds of suppliers spread across many geographies, each with varying degrees of scale, compliance and quality. Information and data moving between each of the parties and being captured in siloes tend to vary, as companies use different systems and software. This poses difficulties for sourcing and procurement teams in linking up and accessing data they need to act on. AI applications can help alleviate these challenges and make sourcing more efficient.

AI's ability to draw insights from distinct data sets enables sourcing teams to answer several questions that can help formulate their sourcing strategy, such as:

- Who needs what and when?
- How much will be spent?
- Which are the ideal suppliers?
- What are the costs and benefits of working with each supplier?
- How often do we buy?
- Where and when will the goods be delivered?

Artificial intelligence applications in sourcing

We highlight five key applications of AI in sourcing for the retail industry on the next few pages, as well as an example of an innovative technology company that is enabling these applications.

Supplier or vendor search

At this stage, the brand or retailer analyses consumer and industry needs, and communicates objectives to their sourcing teams. Sourcing specialists define the strategic sourcing scope and a procurement process plan, which establishes and documents the baseline for assessing efficiency. Once the company's strategic goals, target audiences and brand positioning are defined, the team looks for sources of supply, manufacturers or vendors, and submits and manages vendor requests.

Identifying the right set of suppliers that can deliver on these goals is a challenge, which gets further complicated for multi-category brands and retailers, and when sourcing from multiple suppliers for each product category.

An AI-enabled smart supplier search involves combining sourcing expertise with an AI-powered tool to enhance supplier identification. The technology can almost instantly skim through millions of suppliers and provide recommendations based on search criteria defined by the sourcing specialist. If the tool uses natural language processing (NLP), the specialist can enter the search criteria using plain language. With each iteration of terms input by the specialist, the NLP tool builds out its database further and gets trained to learn and deliver better results. A typical human search may look for suppliers in a familiar environment or industry, such as leather goods in retail, but an AI tool can search for suppliers in other industries that can provide the same or similar products or raw materials.

As an example, a manual search for vegan leather suppliers in a paper-based index will only be possible if the user uses the term 'vegan'. In an AI-based system, vegan leather suppliers can be tagged with alternate terms, such as 'non-animal' or 'plant-based', to deliver a wider range of search results.

AI INNOVATOR IN SEARCH

Founded in 2015, Scoutbee is an AI-driven supplier discovery platform that helps identify suppliers within days, rather than weeks or months (the typical timeline when performing a search unaided by AI). Users define their search criteria in the Scoutbee platform by providing the product name, process and other information.

According to Scoutbee, two critical information criteria that users must provide are keywords and known suppliers so that the engine can establish a baseline to learn from. After the criteria are defined and the engine runs, it generates a longlist of suppliers within three to five days for the user to examine and shortlist suppliers from whom they can then invite requests for information (RFIs).

Scoutbee serves the automotive, chemicals, energy, engineering, fast-moving consumer goods (FMCG) and pharmaceutical industries.

Spend analysis

Companies undertake cost-benefit analyses to identify the best suppliers, requiring an efficient spend classification system for comprehensive results. Manual spend classification or even semi-automated classification falls short of the depth that an AI-driven solution can offer.

Matching supplier names, spending, purchase frequency and contract information from earlier purchases can be a challenging process.

With an AI application, spend classification algorithms sift through line-item information and highlight keywords to link to spend categories by associating input variables, such as general ledger codes (codes assigned to financial entries in a firm's accounting ledger), contract information, purchase order numbers and supplier names, using NLP. ML is then used to classify the output into specific categories. This technology can drill down to a granular level within product descriptions, suppliers or accounting/budgeting line-items and capture detailed data.

Spend classification algorithms include various techniques, ranging from supervised learning (a human user teaches the programme to identify patterns in spending) to unsupervised learning (software is programmed to identify patterns without human intervention) and reinforcement learning (human users review the algorithm's classification decisions and reward or penalize it based on accuracy). Using spend classification algorithms reduces human error, increases efficiency and processing capacity, and frees up employee time to work on more creative tasks, such as strategy planning.

AI INNOVATOR IN SPEND ANALYSIS

Established in 2000, ProcurePort provides cloud-hosted e-procurement software and services to companies across the food and beverage, healthcare and manufacturing industries. ProcurePort uses a structured spend analysis process to clean and analyse spend data. The spend analysis platform imports data from Excel or other comma-limited file formats and cleans it by flagging duplicate or incomplete entries.

At the next step, it 'normalizes' supplier names – a process of using AI to group names that seem similar so that the user can choose the correct supplier names. The engine stores these variations so that it can refer to it for future spend analyses and also enhance its own analytics capabilities. The software then auto-categorizes the suppliers but also allows users to override the classification if there are errors, and then classifies spending based on the user inputs. Finally, the AI engine runs through the output to identify any missed categorizations and completes them.

Examining, formulating and storing documents

After sourcing teams shortlist suppliers based on an assessment of documents received – including RFIs or requests for proposal (RFPs), cost-saving evaluations and final negotiations – they place orders with the ideal suppliers. Sourcing teams will likely deal with several documents at this stage, such as supply contracts and purchase orders, which contain key information on product specifications, quantities, quality levels required, compliances regulations, subcontract policies and deadlines.

Ensuring contracts have the relevant language and terminology, maintaining unstructured contract databases and risk assessment can be challenges.

By utilizing AI, companies can save contracts in electronic format or convert scanned documents into text format with optical character recognition (OCR) for contract lifecycle management (CLM) systems to read and analyse them. NLP can help extricate useful information from these documents. Users train NLP models by establishing sample documents in the interface, with specific annotations on each element before running the programme on other contracts. Extracting important information and terms with NLP can assist firms in compliance, determining potential risks within contracts and highlighting items for review – helping them transition to sophisticated end-to-end sourcing systems.

AI INNOVATOR IN DOCUMENT STORAGE

Razor365 is a CLM application that automates the complete contracting process from requisitions to renewals and intermediate actions, including reviews, auto-drafting, negotiation, comparison, versioning, signing and execution. The platform uses AI to track deviations and map risks when various stakeholders make changes to drafts and flags them for review. The platform also uses AI to summarize billing or fulfilment obligations to communicate them to relevant teams.

Production monitoring

Quality control and compliance monitoring must take place regularly to ensure that production is proceeding according to agreements and to spot and solve issues as they occur. Brands and retailers can have inspection teams carry out some of these activities or appoint an agent to manage them. Suppliers' quality control specialists or agents will need to submit documents certifying quality and compliance at various stages of the production, from sampling to packaging.

Quality control and compliance monitoring – crucial processes to reduce inefficiencies and deliver quality, low cost and speed-to-market – still largely rely on archaic, manual, paper-based processes on spreadsheets. This leaves global supply chains mostly disconnected and prone to lack of visibility, inefficiency, inaccuracy and risk.

Automated compliance monitoring and inspection, and real-time data analysis and sharing can help promote transparency and equip firms to better prepare for and handle disruptions. AI programmes can be developed to detect anomalies in production and identify areas open to potential human error or interference that could lead to a lack of compliance.

AI INNOVATOR IN PRODUCTION MONITORING

Founded in 2015, the Inspectorio platform digitalizes the quality control and compliance monitoring processes within the apparel, accessories and footwear supply chain using mobile, web and AI technologies. The platform employs AI to analyse data that has been entered into the system for predictive and prescriptive capability. This includes:

- *Defect prediction*: Inspectorio is able to predict the stages of the supply chain where potential product failures or defects will occur, based on data collected. While risk assessment has typically been dependent on the experience and knowledge of a single human inspector, Inspectorio transfers this function to an application that leverages a large amount of data analysed through AI.

- *Risk assessment*: Inspectorio can identify the probability of a production site not meeting the quality standards of a particular buyer, and the potential future performance of that production facility, based on its historic performance. This allows large companies that typically need to inspect thousands of facilities to decide which ones require direct inspections and which can be trusted for self-assessment.

- *Fraudulent behaviour monitoring*: Inspectorio's technology can predict fraudulent behaviour by inspectors, according to inspection results and how inspections are performed, by studying factors such as the time per inspection and how inspection results have been revised during the process. The platform can also analyse the historical performance of a facility and flag the risk of inspectors obscuring or falsifying inspection results.

Shipping to destination markets and making payments

Sourcing teams track the movement of shipped goods and need to be able to apprise relevant teams if there are roadblocks. They also need to ensure that necessary documents are sent by the supplier and shipper to receive the goods at the destination port or warehouse. For imports, there are additional documents necessary, such as bills of lading/airway bills, import licences, packing lists, letters of credit and certificates of origin. Once these documents are received, the accounts payable team then have to provide instructions to release payments, based on the payment terms agreed – whether through direct settlement, via a bank or escrow.

Managing multiple documents, communicating the right information in a timely manner, and making payments on time can be a challenge for retailers. Moreover, reviewing and processing invoices is a largely manual effort and is time-consuming. Without stringent checks in place, there is also a high risk of processing fraudulent invoices.

AI algorithms can read, extract and input data from documents received to improve communication with stakeholders across the supply chain.

AI INNOVATOR FOR DOCUMENT PROCESSING

Founded in 2017, Rossum automates document-based communication between parties. The platform offers an AI-based document processing gateway that collects, processes and communicates documents to relevant parties. It uses computer vision to quickly read invoices, packing lists, bills of lading and other documents, and cognitive intelligence that mimics the human brain to capture data. It then provides intuitive assistance to users to help them validate and rectify the data. The platform connects with the companies' as well as senders' IT systems to automate document communication. It also includes tools to manage document traffic and generate analytics. For the automated communication to take place smoothly, accurate data capture is key and Rossum's machine learning algorithms learn and improve each time they capture data, and human users either correct the data or use what was captured.

The implications of AI in sourcing for brands and retailers

Supply chains have increasingly come under the spotlight as pandemic-led disruptions have exposed their vulnerabilities, leading companies to undertake a strategic overhaul of their sourcing operations. As retailers and brands need to work with numerous suppliers scattered internationally, each with varying degrees of scale, compliance and quality, managing sourcing processes is incredibly complex.

Data captured between each of the parties is largely stored in siloes, blocking opportunities for sourcing and procurement teams to leverage unified insights and take efficient actions. AI can help alleviate these challenges and make sourcing more efficient. Implications of this for retailers include:

- Retailers need to leverage AI across multiple functions within the retail value chain to be able to derive economic cost savings and achieve revenue growth.

- Integrating repetitive functions with AI platforms will help reduce room for error, predict risk instances and prescribe corrective actions.

- Cutting out manual processes frees up time for personnel to spend on analysing processes, managing disruptions and exploring strategies for efficiency.

- Building out processes with AI-based applications that integrate well across functions and platforms will help companies to grow toward a digitalized, cohesive supply chain and increase visibility across processes.

The pandemic has shone the spotlight on the supreme importance of supply chains, which carry the retailer's most important asset (their inventory) for distribution to consumers. Instability around the world could persist for an extended period, and supply chains will remain a major focus for retailers.

John Harmon, Senior Retail/Technology Analyst, Coresight Research (2022)

TEN THINGS RETAILERS NEED TO KNOW ABOUT SUPPLY CHAIN

1 Supply chain challenges will continue for the foreseeable future – every retailer needs to continually re-assess their supply chain.

2 Cost and speed-to-market are the two most critical aspects of every supply chain.

3 Most retailers are seeking ways to strengthen control over their supply chain.

4 New technologies are making supply chain innovations possible for the first time.

5 AI has become a powerful tool in supply chain optimization.

6 Enhanced forecasting enabled by AI and machine learning allows businesses to make better decisions to reduce inventory wastage and optimize sales of high demand items.

7 AI can help solve problems for companies that have data stored in silos, and helps reduce supply chain complexity.

8 Investments in AI in sourcing can increase efficiencies by reducing spending and increasing revenue opportunities.

9 Retailers should partner with innovators to take advantage of new technology advancements leading to more efficient and less disruptive supply chains.

10 With an outlook for increased inflation and increased international uncertainty, retailers need to assess their supply chain for potential problems and proactively make changes to reduce bumps along the road in the future.

KEY TAKEAWAYS: SUPPLY CHAIN OPTIMIZATION

We recommend five strategies for global brands and retailers to improve sourcing agility and resilience:

• Consider costs and speed-to-market at each stage of sourcing. Companies are often focused on isolated sourcing proposals and proximity of sourcing locations. However, by optimizing time across each stage of the sourcing chain, companies could reap incremental speed-to-market benefits.

- Increase control over the supply chain. Acquiring vendors or facilities at various stages of the supply chain helps brands and retailers to grow control over sourcing, gain improved visibility and have a greater say in operations of that stage.

- Re-assess supply chains and invest in technologies. The pandemic and resulting disruptions have underscored the significant need for investment in supply chain technologies. Moving forward, retailers should turn to innovative technologies to grow visibility and improve efficiency.

- Expedite communication and transparency. When the pandemic hit, companies had to respond quickly, internally and externally, to understand and act on surges in demand and shortages in supply. Expedited communication and greater transparency will be beneficial for retailers in improving response times and take corrective action quickly in the future.

- Explore new supplier partnerships, and consider adding vendors to augment the use of AI in the sourcing process. While longstanding relationships with suppliers provide immense cost benefits to retailers, companies should maintain agility by establishing new relationships, too. Finding new suppliers helps companies be apprised of untapped resources for their products and maintain a directory they can leverage when necessary.

References

Blair, A (2020) How agile sourcing kept ahold supply chains moving when covid struck, Retail Touchpoints, 24 August. www.retailtouchpoints.com/topics/supply-chain-sourcing/how-agile-sourcing-kept-ahold-supply-chains-moving-when-covid-struck (archived at perma.cc/X4MP-DG8E)

Gap Inc (2021) Gap Inc reports third quarter results, 23 November. www.gapinc.com/en-us/articles/2021/11/gap-inc-reports-third-quarter-results (archived at perma.cc/6NRB-G23V)

Harmon, J (2022) Interview with the authors, July.

Mayer, M (2022) Supply chain disruptions up 88% in 2021, Supply & Demand Chain Executive, 20 January. www.sdcexec.com/sourcing-procurement/procurement-software/news/22005891/resilinc-supply-chain-disruptions-up-88-in-2021 (archived at perma.cc/HXU3-VREN)

Prada Group (2021a) Prada Group and Ermenegildo Zegna Group acquire the majority stake in Filati Biagioli Modesto SPA, 22 June. www.pradagroup.com/en/news-media/press-releases-documents/2021/21-06-22-acquisition-filati-biagioli-modesto.html (archived at perma.cc/HV4X-AG6C)

Prada Group (2021b) Prada Group hosts a capital markets day, 18 November. www.pradagroup.com/en/news-media/press-releases-documents/2021/21-11-18-prada-group-hosts-a-capital-markets-day.html (archived at perma.cc/S6ZZ-AABZ)

Repko, M (2022) Walmart makes an investment in vertical farming start-up Plenty, CNBC, 25 January. www.cnbc.com/2022/01/25/walmart-makes-an-investment-in-vertical-farming-start-up-plenty.html (archived at perma.cc/52TM-BKDS)

Weinswig, D (2022) Achieving agility and resilience in sourcing: Five strategies for brands and retailers, Coresight Research. https://coresight.com/research/achieving-agility-and-resilience-in-sourcing-five-strategies-for-brands-and-retailers/ (archived at perma.cc/2G28-7KYJ)

09

To NFT or not?

WHAT IS AN NFT?

NFTs (non-fungible tokens) are non-exchangeable units of data stored on an indelible record of transactions (blockchain). NFTs have skyrocketed in popularity along with pandemic-fuelled interest in blockchain and cryptocurrencies, allowing for authenticity, security, verification and protection of digital assets. Because of their ability to protect and verify ownership, NFTs can represent any type of digital asset.

The NFT digital collectible market

The ability to protect and verify ownership enables virtual games built on blockchain technology to set up in-world economies not hindered by third-party delays or transaction costs. These features provide blockchain games and virtual worlds with the opportunity to establish functioning in-game economies, leading brands and retailers to begin minting and selling NFTs as individual pieces and collections as they look to expand their businesses, strengthen brand names and increase their customer base and loyalty.

Since the first NFT was minted in 2014, a number of brands, both in the physical world and existing only in the Metaverse, have generated millions of dollars in sales with NFT collections. Their ability to create scarcity and drive demand demonstrates large potential for selling digital goods and services in virtual worlds. NFTs have complex technologies that allow for superior verification of ownership, authenticity of products and distinctiveness throughout the Metaverse. Despite dealing with fraud, many solutions are being developed to support high-volume NFT trade, which is necessary for commerce in virtual worlds. NFT technologies are crucial for establishing functioning in-world economies.

Many retailers have released NFT collections to raise brand awareness and begin selling digital products in the Metaverse. Brands may also tie NFTs to physical products, allowing customers to see a verified record of transactions for a product they are purchasing, improving authenticity and loyalty. As the Metaverse continues to evolve, brands will develop innovative strategies to strengthen their brand name and raise awareness.

Over the next few decades, if the Metaverse does evolve to become an extension of the real world, NFTs will comprise the basis of in-world economics and could represent every unique digital asset in virtual worlds and on blockchains. The NFT market is set to grow from $35 billion in 2022 to $80 billion by 2025, representing a CAGR of 31.7 per cent, according to financial services firm Jefferies Group (Canny, 2022a).

LEARNING OBJECTIVES

In this chapter we will take a deep dive into NFTs specifically, including:

- a look into the background of NFTs

- advantages of NFTs

- details about the technology underlying NFTs

- what retailers should know about NFTs

- examples of NFTs released by brands and retailers

Background: The development of NFTs

One of the main reasons for the recent growing popularity of NFTs, other than their scarcity, is that many notable brands, celebrities and retailers began generating staggering NFT sales during the Covid-19 pandemic. Even before the pandemic accelerated a shift to virtual life, however, NFT technology had been developing steadily.

Blockchain technology was first introduced in 2009, when Bitcoin's creator, Satoshi Nakamoto, mined the 'Genesis Block'. Bitcoin, the first major blockchain, did not directly support unique tokens with non-fungible hashes until 2014, when the Counterparty platform introduced XCP (its own currency built on Bitcoin) as well as standards (known as token standards) for smart contracts in blockchain, which is crucial for smoothly transferring and verifying NFT transactions and ownership. Smart contracts are lines of code written into blockchain that automatically execute contracts when pre-existing conditions are met. Newly minted NFTs will be native to a specific blockchain, with different smart contract features establishing their rules for transfer.

Below is a brief timeline of important events in recent NFT history leading up their explosion in popularity and establishment as the backbone of commerce in virtual worlds.

2012	• Coloured coins are created on the Bitcoin blockchain. Similar to NFTs, these repurposed Bitcoins are coded with metadata to represent other assets such as stocks, bonds or commodities.
2014	• The first-ever NFT, a colourful animated octagon, is minted by Kevin McCoy in May 2014. It later sells for $1.4 million at an auction in June 2021.
	• Counterparty, 'Bitcoin 2.0' (a peer-to-peer decentralized financial platform for trading Bitcoin NFTs) is launched. The protocol allows users to write smart contracts into blockchain.
2015	• In April, arcade game *Spells of Genesis* becomes the first gaming company to feature in-game assets based on a blockchain.
2017	• One of the first blockchain-based virtual games, *CryptoKitties*, is released, allowing users to adopt, train and raise cats, which are represented by NFTs.
	• CryptoPunks, which have sold for hundreds of millions of dollars due to their historical significance and scarcity, comprise the first NFT collection launched on Ethereum (consisting of 10,000 unique pieces).

Advantages of NFTs in the Metaverse

As users spend more hours in the Metaverse, they will likely become more invested in their digital personas, customizing their avatars with unique accessories, attire and cosmetics – represented by NFTs. As each digital asset is unique, users prescribe them with value and can sell them in an NFT marketplace or virtual world as they would in the real world. NFTs allow for interoperability, with users free to bring their assets and avatars between virtual worlds.

NFTs benefit from the strengths of blockchain, upon which they are based. In-game payments for blockchain-based virtual worlds and transactions of digital assets are not subject to third-party delays; they are instant, verified and secure; and they provide the purchaser with a verified record of products' transaction history, improving authenticity. Because of these features, NFTs can represent all types of digital assets, and economies within worlds are free to thrive without interference or delay experienced in today's world of centralized finance with fiat currencies.

Due to their complexity and digital nature, however, critics say that prices are overinflated, and NFTs are fraudulent. In fact, in January 2022, the largest NFT marketplace, OpenSea, stated that 80 per cent of NFT sales were 'plagiarized works, fake collections, and spam' (OpenSea, 2022). Despite the risks of conducting transactions in a market fraught with fake products, we believe that NFTs are important for retailers to build a virtual presence.

Protecting ownership, distinctiveness and documenting authenticity

The Metaverse will likely become a fully functioning economy and fully formed universe. Because virtual and augmented renderings of practically any real-world object can be created or copied very easily in a virtual setting, it is crucial for users to protect the originality of virtual avatars, establish ownership of digital assets of all types and values, and ensure the authenticity of virtual products. Without the scarcity that drives NFT demand, it is difficult, if not impossible, to lay the groundwork for active in-world economies that function much like markets in the real world.

By tying assets to NFTs through digital certificates, NFT meta data and transaction history, and social media announcements, platforms are able to protect ownership as users build inventories of digital assets (from avatar makeup, accessories and clothing to land parcels, to essentially anything). Every node in a blockchain maintains a record of transactions, so ownership can only be disrupted if all the nodes are disrupted.

On 8 February 2022, cross-world avatar platform *Ready Player Me*, developed by Wolf3D, released avatars featuring various CryptoPunks NFTs. Owners of the original CryptoPunks NFTs will have the exclusive opportunity to use these avatars in various virtual world platforms, but no other users will. The distinctiveness of these 10,000 avatars, tied to the original collection, is protected.

Interoperability

Although many virtual worlds currently exist separately from one another, NFT technology is crucial for bridging the gap between these worlds and creating a truly uniform Metaverse, where users are able to bring their digital assets (other than land) and avatars from environment to environment – a prerequisite for introducing customers to digital lifestyles.

This concept is known as interoperability and is extremely important to the Metaverse's success, because users will want to take their virtual assets and explore different immersive environments and virtual worlds that each have their own unique offerings. Without an interoperable ecosystem, users are confined to one Metaverse and are unable to interact with acquaintances in other universes without setting up an entirely new digital identity and so losing digital assets. Without NFT technology protecting and verifying ownership on blockchain, a digital asset only has value in its native game.

Currently, interoperability mainly applies to virtual worlds based on the same blockchain – for example, *Decentraland* and *The Sandbox* are, in theory, interoperable because they are both built on Ethereum. In the future, advances in technology will make cross-chain communication possible, where separate blockchains send and receive information and data – enabling NFTs constructed on different blockchains to be interoperable. Games not based on a blockchain, such as *Fortnite* and *Roblox*, have created large and thriving ecosystems with their own protections of digital assets, but they run on different technology. Without significant technological development, assets from these non-blockchain worlds would lose value in other environments.

The underlying technologies behind NFTs

Blockchain

Blockchain comprises three layers. Layer 3 covers blockchain-based applications and games (virtual worlds) that feature cross-chain implementation for different Mainnet blockchains (primary public blockchain) to send and receive data. Layers 1 and 2 are key infrastructure for NFTs, as we discuss below.

NFTs IN LAYER 1

Layer 1 is the underlying blockchain architecture, the first or original platform, such as the Ethereum or Bitcoin Mainnet.

Layer 1 blockchains released more recently may have more technological capacity, similar to Layer 2 protocols; for example, Flow, released in 2020 by *CryptoKitties* creator Dapper Labs, is fast, decentralized and friendly for developers. Many Metaverse games are based on Flow. As of January 2022, however, roughly 80 per cent of NFTs still trade on Layer 1 protocol Ethereum, according to JPMorgan (Canny, 2022b).

In older Layer 1 infrastructure, blockchains are typically somewhere between somewhat centralized and performing at a high level but not highly secure (for a larger number of users), and decentralized and secure but slow.

Fees for blockchain transactions, called gas fees, in older Layer 1 blockchain protocols also tend to run higher, as the technology is less developed. This means that conducting commerce and trade with low-value and high-volume NFTs is more difficult, as there is a hefty transaction cost associated with each transfer. Gas fees will vary greatly amongst blockchain, but users must make them to compensate for the energy required to put the transaction on blockchain; these fees also go to the miners as rewards.

NFTs IN LAYER 2

Layer 2 comprises scaling solutions and protocols that are built on top of Layer 1 infrastructure, often utilizing off-chain transactions to improve speed, efficiency and cost. Due to high fees and scalability issues, many of the older Layer 1 blockchain protocols are adding second layers in the form of scalability solutions and sidechains, which are built on top of the original blockchain.

Layer 2 protocols, including multi-chain, are mostly in development to address scalability issues, with many handling transactions in a sidechain (separate blockchain running parallel to the main one) to improve speed and reduce fees. In blockchain platforms that have introduced Layer 2 protocols, transactions take place on the second protocol, but related data and proof (verification) of those transactions are stored in the original Layer 1 blockchain platform, which is used to verify that transactions are processed correctly on Layer 2.

The first Layer 2 protocol for Ethereum, Immutable X, was created specifically with NFTs in mind, as it offers massive scalability, instant and secure trades, and zero gas fees. By partnering with blockchain solution provider StarkWare, the platform allows massive batch trades to take place off-chain;

those transactions are then put on-chain (onto the Ethereum Mainnet) in a single transaction with one gas fee, which Immutable covers. Immutable recently raised $200 million in an investment from Tencent and *The Sandbox* owner Animoca Brands to expand globally and build its blockchain gaming ecosystem (Betz, 2022).

Many other scaling solutions specifically designed to smoothen NFT trade exist and are in development for today's top blockchains.

CRYPTOGRAPHIC HASHES

Cryptographic hash functions, which are important for all NFTs, are algorithms or mathematical formulas that take arbitrary amounts of data about the digital asset and convert them into a string of enciphered text called the hash value, or encryption. This hash value represents the NFT, and it can be used to verify the owner, serving in place of a password and making the NFT non-exchangeable.

Strong hash functions should be 'collision-free' to ensure security, meaning that no two inputs (string of characters) produce the same output so it is near-impossible to guess the input value. Using cryptocurrencies as payment increases security even further, with transactions being recorded across every block in the distributed ledger.

TOKEN STANDARDS FOR SMART CONTRACTS

In Ethereum and many other blockchains, smart contracts are lines of code, or computer programmes, written directly into blockchain that automate the execution of contracts once pre-existing conditions are met; they enable parties to be certain that a transaction has taken place immediately, rather than experiencing third-party delays and transaction costs. In other words, smart contracts are responsible for handling and securing transfers of NFTs, and verifying ownership on blockchain.

When a new token is created, whether fungible or not, it is issued with a token standard, which defines the rules that smart contracts must follow for how that token (or later tokens minted in the same denomination if it is a currency/coin) is transferred and how records of transfers are stored on blockchain. These standards also ensure that tokens of new projects remain compatible with existing blockchains. ERC-20 is one of the most popular token standards on the Ethereum blockchain, defining rules for fungible tokens such as virtual currencies. ERC-721 is the most popular standard for NFTs such as digital artwork or music.

Although NFTs and cryptocurrencies are based on the same technology, NFTs operate on specific standards, whereas tokens in any denomination of a cryptocurrency are issued on standards for fungible tokens.

Most blockchains will have technology similar to token standards. Newer Layer 1 protocols such as Solana, released in 2020, feature slightly different systems. Each account created in the Solana chain has a unique address and is owned by a programme, which enables minting, transferring and burning. The mint address for a particular token determines fungibility.

What retailers should know about NFTs

Businesses looking to sell digital products as NFTs and tie real-world products to NFTs have several options for blockchains and marketplaces to use, each with slightly different features to consider. Table 9.1 from DappRadar shows the top five NFT marketplaces not confined to a specific gaming environment or brand (for NFTs of all types), where transaction fees are charged and vary by marketplace (the marketplace's income), and gas fees are variable based on time of transaction and blockchain that was used.

Notable brands and retailer NFT examples

Many retailers from different industries have partnered with NFT platforms, marketplaces and blockchains to mint and sell NFT collections. As NFTs can

TABLE 9.1 NFT marketplace characteristics

Marketplace	Volume* ($b)	Blockchain	Fees and gas
OpenSea	23.50	Ethereum, Polygon	2.5% transaction fee + Ethereum gas
LooksRare	18.20	Ethereum	2.0% transaction fee + Ethereum gas
Magic Eden	0.74	Solana	2.0% transaction fee + Solana gas
Solanart	0.64	Solana	3.0% transaction fee + creator's fee + Solana gas
AtomicMarket	0.39	Wax	2.0% transaction fee + creator's fee + Wax gas

SOURCE Coresight Research, Dapp Radar
NOTE * Volume as of 15 March 2022

come to represent any type of digital asset that trades on a blockchain, brands have engaged in innovative strategies to capitalize on the benefits of NFT scarcity and security.

This is where brands and retailers can really be creative and innovate to create compelling marketing and technology campaigns that develop meaningful connections with their customers. Below, we present examples of unique NFT-related offerings from notable brands operating in various sectors.

NIKE (APPAREL)

Nike is heavily involved in building a Metaverse presence, filing patents to pair physical goods and NFTs and for the sale of downloadable goods, and creating a virtual headquarters, Nikeland, in the *Roblox* Metaverse.

In December 2021 Nike acquired RTFKT, a digital apparel company that mints virtual sneakers, clothing, accessories and avatars as NFTs for users to customize their virtual and digital lives. RTFKT has released its CloneX collection of unique avatars for users to take across the Metaverse as identities. The collection is one of the top 10 highest-selling NFT collections (total sales), and its mysterious Nike-branded MNLTH collection, a levitating box that 'seems to be sentient', is also in the top 30, according to NFT data aggregator CryptoSlam.

In collaboration with University of Oregon alum and designer Tinker Hatfield, Nike also released Oregon Duck-branded limited-edition Nike Air Max 1 sneakers, paired with 'Ducks of a Feather' NFTs, worth about $2,800 at time of auction according to Ducks of a Feather (Carrillo, 2022). With these moves, Nike has positioned itself well to be a big player in avatar accessorizing and augmented-reality fashion.

CLINIQUE (COSMETICS)

Estée Lauder's first set of NFTs was minted in 2021 for Clinique, its venerable beauty brand. Clinique held a competition for its Smart Rewards loyalty members, who would each share stories of optimism and hopes for the future. Judges selected three winners who were awarded an NFT each, named 'MetaOptimist', and were digital representations of their flagship products, Moisture Surge 100H and Almost Lipstick Black Honey. The goal of the campaign was not to generate millions in additional sales from NFTs, but to increase interaction and loyalty, giving customers a platform to tell a story.

Clinique partnered with Layer 2 Ethereum protocol Polygon and promises to deliver customers authentic and interconnected real-time experiences by continuing to leverage its NFT marketplace for unique and immersive offerings.

Leading up to Christmas 2021, Mattel, the manufacturer of iconic toy car brand, Hot Wheels, released toy car NFTs as part of a unique strategy to increase exclusivity and market certain hot wheels paired with NFTs as valuable collectibles that appreciate in value over time, according to statements from the company. Mattel released 40 limited-edition Hot Wheels designs along with animated cars depicted driving, starting at $15 each. Each product came with either four or 10 NFTs, with various levels of exclusivity. Over 5,000 (5 per cent chance for any customer) of these NFTs were also redeemable for physical versions, blurring the lines between real and virtual and increasing the company's customer base.

Partnering with Wax Blockchain, Mattel is also giving customers the opportunity to buy, sell and propose trades of the collectible Hot Wheels in the Wax NFT marketplace, while also showcasing their inventories on social media. The global marketplace allows users to track rarity with comprehensive ownership records.

Implications of NFTs for retailers

Although NFTs are complex technologies – which, in their early days, have experienced issues with fraud – they have huge long-term potential as they may eventually come to represent every type of asset.

By tying both real and virtual assets to NFTs, blockchain is able to provide superior verification of ownership and authenticity than assets have in the real world, as there is a record of every transaction being stored in each block. Smart contracts, which are essential for NFTs, allow both parties in transactions to be immediately certain the transaction has occurred, without incurring costs or delays through third parties. Because NFTs are non-exchangeable, protect ownership and execute transactions automatically, they enable decentralized in-world economies to thrive. Many organizations are building solutions to support high-volume NFT trading in these virtual world economies.

Each NFT minted, per its token standard, will come to represent a specific digital asset, whether it be an avatar or digital clothing, accessories, cosmetics, etc. This means they will be important in enabling users to protect the distinctiveness of their digital personas. Many NFTs are also constructed on the same blockchain, making the interoperability of assets between different virtual worlds theoretically possible.

Many retailers have partnered with blockchains, NFT platforms and blockchain projects to mint NFT collections that have generated hundreds of millions of dollars in sales. However, we believe that retailers with stronger brands, as opposed to multi-brand retailers, will have larger opportunities to leverage NFT-related technologies, as single brands can be more recognizable and provide higher levels of product interaction and experience for customers.

INTERVIEW

Scott Eneje, Co-Founder of Yandi Digital Solutions (2022)

Scott Eneje is a Lagos-based NFT creator and investor. He has been on the forefront of NFT development since the market started to grow. He is a co-founder of the team that recently minted their own collection of NFTs called Alkebulan Tribe Comic and Gaming NFT – Genesis Series.

Over time, Scott quickly progressed from just being an NFT investor, to a co-creator of NFTs. He has also expanded his interest and approach to include virtual real estate, which he sees as the future of NFTs. The key lesson that Scott has taken away from his work in the NFT space is the importance of an engaged and committed community. He cautions that it is not just the size of the community that matters, but also the level of commitment and engagement in comparison to just a mass number of people within the community.

In the world of NFTs, there are different types of investors (buyers of NFT collections are referred to as investors), and although many projects go in with the hopes to sell out their pieces, a majority of projects are built on the basis of a growing utility and introduction of multiple products. Creators who intend to build a community around an ever-growing product space are affected by the large group of investors known as flippers. These type of investors are motivated by fear of missing out (FOMO), but end up having negative impacts on projects with long-term visions and value.

Another group of investors are collectors/holders. These are investors who are interested in utilities, values, long-term projects and advancements. These investors seek projects that can keep growing to maximize profits rather than just buy and sell at any margin that is slightly above purchase price.

Creators of NFTs must understand what types of investors they want in their community and actively engage with that class of investors.

Scott and his partners were able to create their own dedicated community by focusing on education. In Africa in particular (and around the world), many people in the NFT space are seeking to enhance their wealth. In order to educate their community on how to increase financial strength and value through Crypto and NFT portfolios, Scott and his partners started hosting weekly seminars which they promoted in their Discord group. They had around 150 people join their first session, 800 people at their second session and by the time the third session came around they had thousands of people joining, and that exponential growth trajectory has continued, with over 18,000 people on their Discord now. By providing educational opportunities that directly benefit their community, they were able to rapidly grow their community group and win their trust and commitment.

Scott believes that the key to creating value through your NFTs is to focus on rarity (this is often the attractiveness and uniqueness of each individual NFT so that the NFTs are not close replications of each other), documentation of founders, uniqueness of the projects and art, high-level engagement and interest for holders. The combination of focusing on the quality of the NFTs in the collection along with engagement of the community are the two most important values for creators and holders in the sector.

Scott plans to continue to expand his presence in the virtual real estate sector. He envisions this sector changing rapidly, especially as new platforms are offering virtual real estate such as Other Deeds by The Other side (owned by the Bored Ape Yacht Club), *Decentraland* and *The Sandbox*. He believes that the virtual retail world will become even more valuable than it is now – with virtual stores, where people can shop with their avatars, try on clothes, buy them virtually and then have them shipped to their home in the real world.

Scott believes that the NFT and Metaverse market is about to change very quickly, and that this will happen sooner than most people think. He also understands that there may be some wait-time as he expects the hardware technology space to still take about 5–10 years to catch up with the software that helps facilitate the development and general adoption of the Metaverse. Once the hardware catches up, the Metaverse will accelerate quickly.

Scott has the following advice for retailers as they evaluate their Metaverse strategy:

- The first thing you should do: make sure you have the right information. There is still not a great deal of in-depth understanding in the industry, and it's critical that you have the right understanding and information in order to develop your strategy.

- Start growing your digital community. Community is the most critical piece of your Metaverse strategy and it takes time to build a real community.

- Engage your customer base digitally. Consumers need to be interacting with you and your products – they must become a major part of the decisions in order to feel like a community.

- Start building out communities around your collections. Let the community guide your NFT collections and development, listen to their views and ensure they love the narrative of that product more than you do – they are the ones who create the FOMOs that the NFT space depends on. Don't just find a random community and start building a collection, the collection should attract people who are like-minded.

- The key for retailers to unlock the value in the Metaverse is to create their community, engage their community, understand their community and develop what they own and build for their community.

TEN THINGS RETAILERS NEED TO KNOW ABOUT NFTs

1 NFTs allow consumers to express their individuality in virtual worlds via digital items, fashion and collectibles.

2 NFTs provide a community for holders – spanning online and offline events and community projects.

3 The Metaverse ecosystem is rapidly developing – retailers should carefully evaluate their partners, platforms and marketplaces to ensure they are in line with industry developments and their consumers' preferences.

4 A number of brands and retailers, ranging from luxury to streetwear to CPG companies, are launching NFTs – there have been no major failures at this point – allowing early adopters to build experience and credibility.

5 There are numerous opportunities for NFTs to revolutionize the concept of ownership going forward – retailers should understand how this is evolving and determine how it can impact their business.

6   NFTs provide a new revenue opportunity for brands and retailers as they can now sell digital items in games or virtual worlds, as well as NFT collectibles.

7   Brands and retailers are utilizing NFTs to drive offline revenue as well – whether by creating physical products tied to NFTs, enabling e-commerce in the Metaverse, providing special privileges to NFT holders or using NFTs to drive consumer traffic to offline stores.

8   Brands and retailers should engage the NFT community by hiring people who have a deep understanding of the community, partnering with like-minded creators and aligning with technology innovators enabling NFT development.

9   Retailers are investing in virtual real estate to build digital stores and experiences in the Metaverse.

10   The time to experiment with NFTs is now – brands and retailers are being rewarded by customers for being early adopters – don't miss out.

KEY TAKEAWAYS: NFTs FOR RETAILERS

Regardless of your outlook for the future of NFTs and its ability to continue to generate high prices for specific works of digital art, one thing is clear: NFTs are here to stay and retailers should be finding ways to start engaging with NFTs now.

To date we have not seen one failed retailer-launched NFT, showcasing how accepting the NFT community is to new entrants and highlighting how entering early can benefit brands and retailers.

As retailers evaluate their NFT strategy, they should keep the followings things in mind:

- NFTs are in their infancy; much will change in the future, and change will happen fast.
- The key to success with NFTs is connecting with your community. Make sure to identify who your community is, and how you can connect with them in a meaningful way.
- Brands and retailers are already entering the NFT space and making investments and partnerships with emerging technologies.
- NFTs can be a new revenue channel for retailers by selling NFTs, digital collectibles and integrating with physical location and products.

References

Betz, B (2022) NFT platform Immutable raises $200m at $2.5b valuation, CoinDesk, 7 March. www.coindesk.com/business/2022/03/07/nft-platform-immutable-raises-200m-at-a-25b-valuation/ (archived at perma.cc/D9WB-53D4)

Canny, W (2022a) Jefferies sees the NFT market reaching more than $80b in value by 2025, CoinDesk, 20 January. www.coindesk.com/business/2022/01/20/jefferies-sees-the-nft-market-reaching-more-than-80-billion-in-value-by-2025/ (archived at perma.cc/6ZUC-3M5Q)

Canny, W (2022b) JPMorgan says Ethereum is losing NFT market share to Solana, CoinDesk, 19 January. www.coindesk.com/business/2022/01/19/jpmorgan-says-ethereum-is-losing-nft-market-share-to-solana/ (archived at perma.cc/7PAM-HBF5)

Carrillo, A (2022) Nike's special edition 'Flying Formation' Air Max 1 shoe comes with NFTs, Input, 18 February. www.inputmag.com/style/tinker-hatfield-nike-air-max-1-flying-formation-nfts-ducks-of-a-feather-oregon-university-auction (archived at perma.cc/CKG5-QTXB)

Eneje, S (2022) Interview with the authors, July.

OpenSea (2022) However, we've recently seen misuse of this feature increase exponentially. Over 80% of the items created with this tool were plagiarized works, fake collections, and spam, Twitter. twitter.com/opensea/status/1486843204062236676 (archived at perma.cc/TN4M-B4RG)

10

Bringing blockchain to retail

WHAT IS BLOCKCHAIN?

Blockchain enables brands and retailers to engage in Metaverse commerce and improve product tracking, authentication and overall security for consumers. Blockchain is a system in which a shared record of transactions made in cryptocurrencies is maintained across several computers working together to form a decentralized peer-to-peer network.

LEARNING OBJECTIVES

In this chapter we look at how retailers can and should bring blockchain into the retail environment – ranging from inventory management to supply chain optimization, and how these changes can increase revenue and decrease operating costs. We discuss:

- how blockchain forms the basis of the Metaverse
- the history and technological infrastructure of blockchains
- what brands and retailers should know about blockchain
- examples of how retailers are utilizing blockchain in their operations

Metaverse and blockchain

To be truly decentralized, Metaverse platforms should be built on blockchains, which provide security, transparency and anonymity. Because of these features, users are free to explore the Metaverse without fear of privacy breaches, manipulation of their data or judgement. Self-expression is likely to flourish in the Metaverse as users from all over the world explore interests and hobbies not feasible in the real world for any number of reasons.

With blockchain technology, there are no third-party transaction costs or delays, and both buyers and sellers can be immediately certain transactions have taken place. Taking power away from centralized institutions and distributing it among blockchain increases transparency and trust for consumers. Because a record of transactions is stored on every block, control of information is not restricted to a single entity, meaning blockchains are decentralized; a hacker would have to change every single block to corrupt or steal data, a virtually impossible task.

In the Metaverse, a new decentralized and anonymous universe, people are free to enjoy experiences with limitless possibility without fear of manipulation or privacy breaches. The possibilities for self-expression are virtually endless. As such, commercial opportunities to take advantage of trends that are likely to emerge from self-expression will be plentiful.

The Metaverse will likely be a synchronous environment, meaning users have instantaneous communication with businesses and brands that, in the real world, could operate thousands of miles away. Blockchain, along with cryptocurrencies, enables seamless cross-border payments not hindered by exchange rates or additional delays from multiple banks involved with transactions.

There are many other benefits of blockchain, including speed, trust, reduced costs, improved privacy, cross-border flow, control and anonymity. Virtual worlds based on blockchain will enjoy all of these benefits, and as a result trade between businesses and customers is free to flourish, unlike in today's world of centralized finance, fiat (government) currencies and third parties (banks).

Blockchain and transactions

Blockchain transactions are surging, and many robust solutions built on original blockchains are being constructed to support high volumes of in-game transactions. Records of transactions are distributed across all systems in a blockchain, meaning control is decentralized. In virtual worlds, where digital products can be created with minimal cost and resold without degradation, transparency and security of blockchain will be crucial.

Blockchain provides anonymity in the Metaverse, as transactions are only known by wallet addresses. It also allows for economies within virtual worlds to be faster and more efficient in transactions, unlocking active cross-border and high-volume trade. Because transactions are verified by peers and recorded across multiple points in blockchain, privacy and data security in the Metaverse will be superior to current platforms such as social media. Decentralization will help to enable access and improve transparency in virtual worlds, which, by nature, will be difficult to navigate, teeming with avatars, products, worlds and virtual offerings.

Providing anonymity to enable self-expression

Environments constructed on blockchain technology will be completely anonymous – all transactions are tied to wallet addresses, rather than anything linking to a real-world identity. Unless a user wishes others to know their real-world identities, they are free to explore the Metaverse and customize their avatars in ways they may not in the real world or on social media due to fear of judgement. Users are free to explore interests with anonymity, engaging with brands globally that they may not shop with in the real world. Blockchain also enables instant payments and transactions between parties that are located far away from one another in the real world.

For example, an anonymous user purchased a $450,000 plot of land in *The Sandbox*'s Snoopverse, Snoop Dogg's Metaverse where he will host concerts and interact with fans (Weinswig, 2022). As Snoop Dogg's brand is heavily influenced by cannabis, the user who purchased this plot may want to remain anonymous for reputational purposes. Plots of land in *The Sandbox* are represented by NFTs and traded on the Ethereum blockchain.

Users may also customize avatars to explore different lifestyles and environments than they would in the real world. For example, history buffs can explore vintage worlds, which simulate various time periods throughout history, and science fiction fans can enjoy alien worlds and virtual space exploration. Without revealing identities, avatars are free to explore different worlds and environments from the comfort of their homes, building interests they never knew they had and exploring immersive offerings accessible to anyone which, in the real world, would be unfeasible to take part in for whatever reason.

Decentralization for protection of ownership, transparency and privacy

Blockchain provides users with an immutable record of transactions for history of ownership and creation of assets. No single entity, such as a bank, is responsible for managing ledgers of transactions. Because records are stored on each 'block', or each system, in blockchain, all blocks would have to be compromised to corrupt data, meaning that ownership of assets is verified and secured. As users become more invested in their digital lives, they will want to protect ownership of virtual assets such as land spaces, apparel, avatars and any unique items they acquire. In virtual environments not built on blockchain, users may have limited and unique items stolen, with no guarantee of recovery.

In a virtual setting, users of all kinds, whether well intentioned or not, will be creating virtual products and reselling products at virtually no cost with no degradation, requesting payment in cryptocurrencies. The transparency that blockchain provides will help users to navigate the clutter of the Metaverse, giving everyone access to product history and data at any time so that they can ensure what they are buying is authentic.

One of the biggest issues with social media, currently the most popular use of the 'Web 2.0' (non-interactive 2D web), is security. Platforms such as Facebook, Instagram, Twitter and YouTube have access to large amounts of data, and customers have become concerned that their security and privacy is compromised. Because there are multiple worlds, theoretically all interoperable with one another, built on different technologies and blockchain platforms, the Metaverse is decentralized; no one entity will have the power to effect large-scale changes or manipulate users by amassing large amounts of data on them. As we mentioned above, transactions are also anonymous, tied only to crypto wallets.

Blockchain's underlying technology

Blockchain technology had been in development for decades, but was first introduced in 2009, when Bitcoin's creator Satoshi Nakamoto mined the 'Genesis Block'. Since then, many blockchain solutions and platforms with varying technological features and capabilities have been released to support a global vision of decentralized finance with few barriers for conducting transactions and trade.

The underlying infrastructure of blockchain technology is complex, with many moving parts, but the decentralization it creates is key to enabling seamless and instant transfers and transactions between businesses and customers.

Blockchain layers

Blockchain comprises three main technological layers, each building on top of the previous layer (see Table 10.1).

Blocks, miners and nodes

Data blocks, which link together in a chain to form blockchain, can each be thought of as individual pages on a ledger. Blocks are composed of several components, including the header and the body. Blockchain miners, who can be anyone, download and install special programmes on their computers to mine blocks that are added to the chain; these programmes also enable their systems to securely communicate with one another. Once a computer installs such a programme, it becomes a node in blockchain.

In simple words, the header is the portion of the block that contains information and data about the block itself, including the following:

- *Hash*: Each subsequently created block contains the hash, or algorithm used for encryption of data, of the previous block.

TABLE 10.1 Blockchain layers

		Description	Examples
Layer 1	→	The underlying blockchain architect, the first or original platform, the Mainnet (primary public blockchain)	Ethereum, Bitcoin, Solana
Layer 2	→	Scaling solutions and protocols that are built on top of Layer 1 infrastructure, often utilizing off-chain transactions to improve speed, efficiency and cost	Polygon, Immutable X, Ronin
Layer 3	→	Blockchain-based applications and games (virtual worlds) that may feature cross-chain implementation for different Mainnet blockchains to send and receive data	*Decentraland, The Sandbox, Axie Infinity*

SOURCE Coresight Research

- *Nonce*: Miners must calculate a 'number only used once' to create a new block and add it to the chain.
- *Time stamp*: The time stamp contains complete information about date, hours, etc.
- *Merkle root*: Each transaction on blockchain comes with a hash, and these hashes are linked in a tree-like structure, called the 'Merkle tree'. The Merkle root refers to the base hash that all the transactions are based on (individual hashes are hashed again then merged with one another to create the hash for the entire block).

Every individual block body stores a limited number of transactions in an ordered list (the Merkle tree). Because each block is connected to another by storing the hash of the previous block, records of transactions cannot be altered unless the hash of a block and all the subsequent hashes of following blocks are changed as well. These features help to make blockchain immutable.

Public ledger and peer-to-peer network

The ledger, as it relates to blockchains, is a publicly available record of transactions that maintains the identities of parties securely and anonymously, along with a comprehensive record of genuine transactions that have executed between participants and cryptocurrency balances. Blockchain is a type of public ledger, where pages are represented by individual blocks.

Network participants, or nodes (systems running blockchain's software), are responsible for authenticating and verifying transaction details. Select participants, or full nodes, maintain copies of the entire ledger on their devices. Because of this distribution, no single authority has total control over the ledger, and transactions are verified solely on the basis of available funds (in cryptocurrency). In today's world of centralized finance, banks are responsible for maintaining this record, and the public has no access.

In a peer-to-peer (P2P) network, every node is equal to one another. They are each responsible for the same workload, no individual node has privileges, and there is no primary administrator or device in the network. The network also comes together to enable shared resources and assets, such as network bandwidth and storage capacity.

In a client–server network, one could download (receive) a file (asset) from a webpage, where the downloader is the client, and the website is the server. In a P2P network, users download (receive) the file (asset) and receive bits and pieces of it from other systems that already have the file or portions of it while simultaneously uploading the same file to other devices requesting it.

FIGURE 10.1 Client–server network vs peer-to-peer network

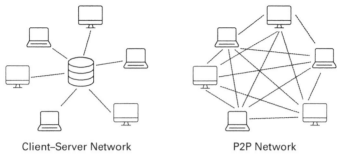

Client–Server Network   P2P Network

SOURCE Coresight Research

Consensus mechanisms

Consensus mechanisms, which vary by blockchain platform, are processes used by blockchains to reach agreements on data values in the network; they correlate directly to efficiency and differentiate each blockchain. In other words, these protocols are in place to ensure all nodes are in sync and agree on a transaction, adding it to blockchain. They are also responsible for increasing security and authenticity of ownership by ensuring each transaction added to blockchain is legitimate.

Bitcoin, Ethereum and Solana are three of the most popular blockchains; in general, the earlier a blockchain was released, the older and less efficient the mechanism. Each consensus mechanism has its own benefits, but the largest trade-off seems to be between security and efficiency. In virtual worlds, digital asset trade will likely be higher volume than commerce in the physical world. Depending on what a business may want, many different blockchains could provide solutions.

Keys and wallets

To transact on blockchain, users need to set up a cryptocurrency wallet that supports tokens such as Ethereum, Bitcoin and Solana. Examples of wallets include Coinbase Wallet, Exodus and MetaMask.

A public key allows users to receive transactions (either NFTs or cryptocurrency transfers). The wallet address is a hashed version of this public key, meaning that users can share it freely. For example, creators may share their address for donations. With the public key, which may or may not be tied to identity (users' choice), anyone can also see who the owner of an asset or crypto funds is, improving transparency.

However, the owner of those assets or funds must have the private key, located in a crypto wallet, to gain access. The private key serves as a password, and can come in many formats, such as a 256-character long code. Regardless of format, the number is massive. Encryption and receiving access is a three-step process:

- A transaction sent to a user is encrypted with the public key, and can only be decrypted with the corresponding private key (the two are created together).

- A digital signature is generated through combining the correct private key with the encrypted data.

- Nodes automatically check and authenticate the transaction; any unauthenticated transaction is rejected.

Joining blockchain-based virtual games

To fully take advantage of decentralized in-world economies with instant and verified transactions, accessible to anyone in the world, retailers and brands may look to consider establishing a presence in a blockchain world. In these virtual games, brands can purchase secure land spaces, offer highly customized experiences only bounded by imagination and sell zero-cost digital products as NFTs.

Examples of retailers using blockchain technologies in virtual environments

Luxury brands are highly involved in the Metaverse, launching NFTs as digital assets to capitalize on the exclusivity and scarcity that they provide. Leveraging blockchain, NFTs provide a completely secure public record of ownership for limited-edition collections and rare items, driving levels of exclusivity and demand not possible with physical products.

In addition to minting NFT collections, luxury brand Gucci has collaborated with a few different platforms, including *The Sandbox*, *Fortnite* and *Roblox*, and created virtual stores and experiences for customers. Gucci has purchased land in *The Sandbox* (based on Ethereum) for an immersive Gen Z world, which will likely follow the same principals as its previous 'Gucci

Garden' in *Roblox*, where users were given a customizable androgynous avatar. Gucci's goal was to spark self-expression and enable creativity that connects users to their childhoods and imagination. Through its new world, Gucci has the opportunity to expand its customer base to curious *The Sandbox* users who do not have access to Gucci stores in the real world or who do not currently shop with the brand.

In September 2021, France-based luxury retailer Christian Dior SE, or Dior, partnered with cross-platform avatar tool Ready Player Me to bring its customized looks for avatars to travel across more than 1,000 virtual worlds and applications. Although creators such as Dior are not required to tokenize the avatars they design for trade on blockchains, Ready Player Me offers the opportunity for them to do so, increasing monetization opportunities and protecting creators' work (Weinswig, 2022).

Dior has created multiple immersive environments inspired by its brand where anonymous users are free to customize their avatar in line with Dior's offerings. Offering these avatars as NFTs allows users to maintain their identities securely across the Metaverse on blockchain, increasing customer loyalty and potentially providing Dior with 'free' brand recognition and marketing on other platforms.

Implications for retailers

The anonymity provided by blockchain allows users to fully express themselves by exploring offerings from brands and retailers operating in different parts of the world, and by developing new interests.

As there are many virtual worlds that will likely all be interoperable, no one entity will have the ability to manipulate users based on data; this is one of the biggest concerns users have of popular Web 2.0 platforms, such as social media. The decentralized nature of blockchains, and the worlds constructed on them, helps to alleviate these concerns.

What retailers should know

As blockchain provides so many benefits for consumers over traditional centralized finance, businesses and retailers, whether they want to fully establish a presence in the Metaverse or not, should be looking to incorporate blockchain-related technologies as soon as they can.

Benefits of blockchain outside of the Metaverse

Transactions for any type of asset, whether digital, physical or both (some products are tied to NFTs), can be executed on blockchain, allowing retailers to utilize the technology whether they have a store or offering within the Metaverse or not.

Through a publicly viewable ledger of immutable transactions, transactions and payments are instant and ownership is verified. Such a system is much more powerful than today's world of centralized finance, where parties must rely on banks to accurately manage transactions, dealing with third-party delays and fees. Blockchains could therefore significantly increase cross-border trade and in-world economic activity. The technology is essential to support the trade volume of in-world economies, as businesses can offer the same experience to consumers from all over the world, expanding their customer bases and enabling access not possible in the real world.

For retailers and brands, blockchain offers benefits in product quality and supply chain improvement, inventory management, loyalty programmes and payment channels.

- *Product quality and supply chain*: If an item or product (in the supply chain or after sale to a customer) is found to be defective, blockchain records enable retailers to track the product and see where the fault occurred, then find other defective products. This also helps retailers to highlight weaknesses in supply chains by identifying issues with certain manufacturers or batches.

- *Inventory management*: Blockchain will allow retailers to have better control over their inventories, improving efficiency to decrease inventory costs and increase customer fulfilment. Assets such as product units and orders can be tokenized and represented on blockchain, giving retailers the ability to track every stage. Blockchain tracks vast amounts of data and is a valuable and trustworthy source for forecasting demand.

- *Customer loyalty*: Customers can be given 'loyalty tokens' rather than reward points. Tokens would never expire and could be interoperable on multiple blockchain platforms. This would increase freedom for customers in how they spend their rewards points. Tokens also eliminate the need to develop a costly loyalty system, as blockchain already contains an immutable history of transactions, a record of loyalty.

- *Improved payment channels*: Traditional payment providers take far too long to settle transactions. Transactions in blockchain are as fast as exchanging cash in real life, with no intermediaries to slow the process and charge fees. In centralized finance, as central banks have control to mandate liquidity requirements, they have influence over commercial banks. Blockchain eliminates this centralized control.

INTERVIEW
Zachary Rubin, Founder, Go Arena (2022)

Zachary is an entrepreneur and inventor in the Metaverse space, where he has been at the forefront of accelerating adoption of crypto payments, NFT marketing and Metaverse business model innovation. Zachary has always been passionate about technology and was schooled in engineering and industrial design. Zachary has focused on research into robot walking mechanisms and self-driving cars. He also created a startup that took core technologies and placed them into a fitness context with GoArena and sold his crypto payment company – Pollen NFT – to Crossmint.

Zachary sees the blockchain as a tool to address market inefficiencies, generally through the use of a distributed ledger. The Metaverse can be thought of as this technology's creative playground, as exemplified by the popularity of NFTs and gaming. However, there are many other ways in which brands can utilize the Metaverse. He is excited about the prospects for innovation in the following areas:

- *Product legitimacy*: Fake or unauthorized goods continue to be a problem for brands, especially in markets such as China where manufacturers are so sophisticated in manufacturing goods that even the brands themselves have a difficult time telling the difference between an authorized and unauthorized product. NFTs enable manufacturers to attach a digital signature to the item on a distributed ledger that is sold along with the product. Since the NFT is attached to blockchain, consumers can have confidence that the goods they have purchased is authentic and authorized.

- *Ticketing*: The ticketing market is rife with inefficiencies, where sellers are not always able to control the distribution of their tickets, providing opportunities for middlemen to intervene and increase ticket prices well above the intention of the artist and venue. Consumers also have to worry about whether they are getting sold a fake ticket. Artists and promoters could use NFTs to assign a ceiling value or secondary sales 'tax' to a ticket to ensure that ticketing for their concerts is accessible, transparent and authentic. By using NFTs to enforce rules on secondary sellers, artists and promoters can ensure that their intentions are honoured.

- *Tokens*: Tokens created on blockchain will allow for the authenticity of ownership for a host of financial and legal properties, including stocks, real estate deeds and intellectual property. Adding this layer of transparency and trust will make the exchange of these goods safer, and will create a digital asset that bridges the gap between ownership and regulation.

Although the concept of decentralization is a core tenet of the Metaverse, Zachary also sees this as an impediment to the widespread consumer acceptance of many aspects of the Metaverse. In the current environment, even something as basic as creating a wallet to make and accept crypto payments can be a rather large hurdle for the average consumer. In addition to the number of steps required for setting up the wallet, many consumers are concerned about security and fraud, which makes widespread consumer acceptance more difficult. Zachary expects that, over time, the Metaverse/Web 3.0 landscape will develop in much the same way as Web 2.0, where certain companies quickly gained scale and acceptance by making things easy for consumers, such as Amazon for e-commerce, Facebook for social media and Google for search.

Zachary has the following advice for retailers as they establish their own Metaverse strategies:

- *Keep an eye on the trends*. The market is changing so quickly that the way that consumers engage with the technology is shifting every three months. It's imperative that retailers keep a close eye on these trends to make sure they are up to date with the market and consumer acceptance.

- *Focus on community*. Companies often focus too much on the technology, and not on the community. The technology is just a means to an end. What consumers really want is a way to connect and engage with others via shared digital experiences.

- *Hire the right people*. It's critical that companies have employees or consultants that understand these communities and want to connect with them. Find someone who is entrenched in platforms such as Discord or Twitter and understands the subculture within the crypto world. Look for mentally young people who are natural participants or creators in online communities.

TEN THINGS RETAILERS NEED TO KNOW ABOUT BLOCKCHAIN

1 Retailers are using blockchain technology to improve customer satisfaction, authenticity and operational efficiency.

2 Blockchain allows retailers to benefit from a decentralized peer-to-peer network for security, transparency and authenticity.

3 Blockchain provides a seamless cross-border payment solution for retailers, unhindered by currencies.

4 Brands are engaging with blockchain to establish virtual stores, customize avatars and create immersive environments.

5 Blockchain offers retailers benefits in product quality and supply chain improvement, inventory management, loyalty programmes and payment channels.

6 Retailers are increasingly accepting cryptocurrency as a payment option.

7 Market inefficiencies can be addressed utilizing blockchain.

8 The technology and infrastructure are changing very rapidly – retailers should ensure that they stay current on blockchain trends.

9 Customer loyalty programmes can be enhanced with the use of blockchain.

10 Blockchain can attract new customers around the world, especially those already immersed in the Metaverse community.

KEY TAKEAWAYS: BLOCKCHAIN

Blockchain technologies support high-volume digital asset trade, protect ownership and provide authenticity. In a digital sense, where products are easy to create and resell, these features are crucial for functioning in-world economies. For retailers and brands, blockchain offers benefits in product quality and supply chain improvement, inventory management, loyalty programmes and payment channels.

Blockchain will empower businesses to conduct seamless transactions with customers from every part of the globe, and as every asset may eventually come to be represented as an NFT traded on blockchain, it will be crucial for retailers to begin familiarizing themselves with the technology.

Key takeaways from this chapter include:

- Blockchain is a new way of conducting financial transactions that is independent of traditional banks and intermediaries, thus opening up payment options to customers around the world in a single currency.
- Blockchain is the building block upon which the Metaverse is based, and retailers should start to develop their blockchain strategies in tandem.
- Industries that tap into rarity and exclusivity, such as luxury and streetwear, have been early adopters of blockchain and the Metaverse, tapping into their strengths in marketing exclusivity and limited-edition products.
- Blockchain adoption enables retailers to operate in multiple virtual worlds, allowing for the sale of virtual items, customizable avatars and even real estate purchases, to create brand stores or experience in virtual worlds.
- Blockchain also provides opportunities to create efficiencies in areas such as inventory management, supply chain improvement and loyalty programmes.

References

Rubin, Z (2022) Interview with the authors, July.

Weinswig, D. (2022) Building blocks of the Metaverse: Blockchain, Coresight Research. https://coresight.com/research/building-blocks-of-the-Metaverse-blockchain/ (archived at perma.cc/6Q7T-XRLB)

11

Digital payments on the rise

LEARNING OBJECTIVES

In this chapter we cover the key points of the shifting payment infrastructure in retail, including:

- the increasing use of social media for retail inspiration and shopping
- high friction in online checkouts leading to high cart abandonment rates
- one-click checkout technology powering more conversions
- retailers shifting toward a decentralized model
- highlighting global digital payment innovators leading change in the sector
- the increase in the number of retailers accepting cryptocurrency
- trends in payments in the Metaverse

The rise of alternative payment methods

Pandemic-induced growth in e-commerce sales has led to increased focus among brands and retailers on developing their payment infrastructure. And digital payment services are of paramount importance in the customer experience journey, impacting sales conversion and brand loyalty.

The digital payments industry spans a broad range of solutions, from checkout experiences and fraud prevention solutions to digital wallets and cryptocurrency. Fuelled by increasing e-commerce penetration, the global transaction value for digital payments is set to increase from $7.86 trillion in 2022 to $10.7 trillion in 2025 – a CAGR of 10.9 per cent (Statista, 2022).

Consumers are increasingly exploring the benefits of various alternative payment methods (APMs) when shopping online, amid advances in payment technology and increased engagement with innovative shopping channels. Young, tech-savvy generations – Gen Zers and Millennials – are leading the APMs adoption charge.

A Coresight Research survey of consumers in the US and Canada, conducted in March 2022, found that higher proportions of Gen Zers and Millennials used digital wallets, prepaid cards and buy now, pay later (BNPL) in the 12 months prior to the survey than the proportions of respondents overall (Weinswig, 2022).

Below, we explore consumer adoption of two of the most technologically innovative APMs: digital wallets and BNPL.

Digital wallets

Consumers continue to adopt digital wallets, such as Apple Pay and PayPal, as they are convenient, accessible and secure, allowing shoppers to skip entering shipping and payment information when shopping online. Juniper Research estimates that the value of mobile wallet transactions globally will exceed to $12 trillion by 2026, up from $7.5 trillion in 2022 (Smith, 2022).

Buy now, pay later

While BNPL companies such as Affirm and Afterpay gained popularity during the pandemic, the Coresight Research survey shows continued momentum in consumer interest, even as pandemic effects subside: among the American and Canadian consumers who are either interested in BNPL or are already regular or occasional users of this APM, more than half expect to maintain or increase their frequency of BNPL usage in the next year (Weinswig, 2022).

BNPL is becoming increasingly popular due to the immediate affordability granted through payment plans amid the highest inflation in four decades. Retailers should look to implement BNPL options to enhance their payment infrastructure and attract shoppers.

The role of social media in shopping

Consumers continue to discover retail inspiration when browsing online, including on social media. Retailers that make it easy for consumers to seamlessly pay for products they are interested in can convert inspiration to sales quickly on the same platform.

However, while plenty of shoppers research or discover products while browsing on social media, 75 per cent of respondents in Coresight's survey reported that they abandon purchases at least sometimes (Weinswig, 2022). Among that subset of respondents, the top reasons for giving up on making a purchase via social media are:

1   It is easier to buy elsewhere (41 per cent).

2   The page jumps to another website (34 per cent).

3   The user does not trust shopping on social media (31 per cent).

4   There is a lack of built-in payment functionality on the site (24 per cent).

Retailers should focus their resources on creating a more seamless checkout experience on the social media channels consumers use most, as social media shoppers tend to shop more frequently than others: Coresight's survey found that of the respondents who browse products on social media, almost half (45 per cent) do so once a week. Among those frequent browsers, more than half make a purchase via social media at least once a month (Weinswig, 2022).

High online cart-abandonment rates at checkout

Around 70 per cent of online shopping carts in the US are abandoned (Baymard Institute, 2022) – indicating that retailers are failing to convert a high number of consumers who are on their website and interested in their offerings.

Three of the biggest friction points leading consumers to abandon carts are:

• *Checkout is time-consuming*: Checking out on many retailers' websites can take a long time due to high complexity, redirection to different websites and lengthy entry of shipping and payment information. This results in consumers thinking they would be better off using a channel with a quicker checkout system that stores shipping and payment information, such as Amazon, to buy their desired product.

• *Distrust of fraud protection*: Many consumers lack trust in websites' fraud protection, especially when using a new checkout software they are not familiar with. Furthermore, the online checkout process varies greatly between retailers, increasing the likelihood of shoppers feeling uncomfortable with a new checkout experience.

- *Lack of APMs*: Consumers may prefer to shop with retailers that accept APMs such as digital wallets, BNPL and cryptocurrency. Upon seeing that their preferred payment method is unavailable, a consumer may choose a shop that does accept APMs.

To improve online conversion rates, retailers can work with retail technology providers to integrate their checkout solutions, removing friction points in the checkout process and enhancing the consumer convenience.

Applications of one-click checkout technology

One-click checkout technology is revolutionizing the payment space and enabling retailers to provide a quick and easy checkout experience. By using safely stored, pre-entered shipping and payment information, one-click checkout allows customers to checkout securely and quickly, impacting e-commerce, payment infrastructure and retail discovery:

- *E-commerce*: One-click checkout technology enables a frictionless checkout experience that decreases cart abandonment by reducing third-party website usage and removing the time required to enter shipping and payment information.
- *Payment infrastructure*: The back-end function of one-click checkout technology utilizes several digital integrations, including with payment gateways and processors, to provide a seamless payment process.
- *Retail discovery*: By closing the gap between browsing and buying, one-click checkout technology bolsters the importance and use of digital platforms that consumers use as a point of retail inspiration and discovery. Retailers can work with retail technology providers to embed one-click checkout in their sales channels, allowing consumers to quickly check out at the point of discovery rather than being redirected to a different website.

Retailers should assess whether their current payment infrastructure is optimized to enable high-quality checkout experiences for their shoppers – and implement technologies where necessary.

> The proliferation of payment providers and other vendors (such as for fraud detection) is making integration more difficult for retailers. New services such as buy now, pay later look likely to add even more complexity.
>
> Paul Anthony, Co-Founder of Primer (2022)

CASE STUDY
Bolt

Bolt is a checkout-technology company that enables retailers to provide their customers with a one-click checkout experience when shopping. The company was founded in 2014 by Ryan Breslow and is currently led by CEO Maju Kuruvilla and headquartered in San Francisco, California.

By facilitating a quick and easy one-click checkout experience, the company aims to narrow the gap between browsing and buying by removing friction in the online checkout process, including the need to memorize and fill out usernames, passwords and payment information, and giving shoppers their preferred method of payment. In doing so, Bolt assists retailers in enhancing their online checkout process and lowering checkout abandonment rates.

Value proposition for retailers and consumers

For retailers:

- Enables 47 per cent higher conversion rates (Kuruvilla n.d.), by removing friction points during the checkout process to facilitate a quicker end-to-end online shopping journey that narrows the gap between browsing and buying.

- Increases store account creation and ownership of first-party data, which merchants can utilize to recognize their shoppers and create personalized shopping experiences that lead to higher lifetime value (LTV) and shopper loyalty.

- Utilizes a headless approach to building one-click checkout options on a variety of digital surfaces, providing the flexibility to tie into different platforms and architecture.

For consumers:

- Enables convenient and quick online checkout by removing the need to memorize and repeatedly enter usernames, passwords and payment information.

- Grants the ability to use alternative forms of payment instead of the traditional debit or credit card, including digital wallets, BNPL and cryptocurrency (with the planned acquisition of Wyre) – allowing consumers to use the payment method most convenient to them when checking out.

- Provides fraud protection, which assures consumers of the security behind their digital transactions, as well as real-time tracking capabilities and dashboards that enable users to stay on top of their orders.

Moving toward decentralized commerce

Previously, e-commerce required a centralized authority, such as Amazon or eBay, that aggregates supply and demand channels within a marketplace to facilitate transactions between buyers and sellers. While this system facilitates transactions where parties can easily trust one another, a centralized system makes it hard for many mid-market and enterprise merchants to run their own independent e-commerce business without integrating into large marketplaces.

Advances in blockchain technology and cryptocurrency are supporting the decentralization of online retail through peer-to-peer computer systems and digital tokens. Additionally, the irreversible and secure nature of blockchain technology fosters an environment of mutual trust.

Headless e-commerce

Headless e-commerce architecture is advancing retail's shift to decentralized commerce by deconstructing the components of large, centralized marketplaces. Headless commerce means that the front-end code (head) is decoupled from back-end commerce functionality, which handles tasks such as merchandising and payment processing, enabling quick and easy front-end updates without interfering with the back end.

Key benefits of headless e-commerce architecture include increased flexibility and scalability, and shortened launch and website-update times.

Many of these technical issues can be alleviated through the implementation of a headless structure, which moves away from a single code base and bolsters retailers' operational efficiency and ability to scale. We believe that many retailers will need to – and will continue to – make the shift to a decentralized model for their e-commerce design architecture.

Acceptance of cryptocurrency as payment

The global pandemic and its impact on financial markets and technological advancement brought renewed interest in the application of cryptocurrency as a form of payment in the retail world. According to a Pew Research Center survey, about 16 per cent of the American public is already investing, trading or using cryptocurrency (Perrin, 2021), indicating that many Americans have become familiar with or are already using cryptocurrency in some form, meaning retailers should weigh the benefits of accepting cryptocurrency at their establishments.

Another sign of the growing interest in cryptocurrency transactions are the increasing number of blockchain wallets being created. According to data from Blockchain.com (2022), a cryptocurrency financial services company, the total number of unique wallets on their site was 82.8 million on 16 May 2022, up from 46.9 million at the onset of the pandemic in 2020 – a 77 per cent year-over-two-year increase.

Meanwhile, many retail and foodservice companies, including The Home Depot, Starbucks and Whole Foods, have started accepting cryptocurrency in some form, while others are expressing interest in doing so – 80 per cent of merchants in both the retail and grocery, and luxury goods sectors stated that they were open to receiving cryptocurrency payments, according to a survey conducted in the fourth quarter of 2021, by Worldpay and Crypto.com (2022).

Accepting cryptocurrency payments can bring in new customers, along with other benefits. A 2020 study commissioned by BitPay, a leading provider of Bitcoin and cryptocurrency payment services, found that 40 per cent of customers who pay with cryptocurrency are new customers to a company, and customer purchase amounts are usually double those of credit card users (Forrester Consulting, 2020).

As digital shopping grows in popularity, more consumers are turning to cryptocurrency as a payment method. We expect this trend to continue, driving retailers to advance their payment infrastructure to accept cryptocurrency, so as not to be left behind in a growing retail trend.

Global digital payment innovators

We are always meeting new startups addressing problems such as payments, and we have personally met more than 40 of these that are tapping into growing trends in the payment industry, across areas such as:

- buy now, pay later
- checkout experiences
- cross-border payment solutions
- cryptocurrency and digital assets
- digital wallets
- payment gateways and processors

- payments-linked loyalty/reward services
- risk management and fraud prevention
- subscription management solutions

Payment trends in retail

We believe that all of these innovations in the payment sector are being driven by the following two trends:

1 *Cryptocurrencies are on the rise as the Metaverse expands*
   Coupled with the decentralized nature of blockchain, the expansion of the Metaverse is leading to a rise in digital asset ownership and the use of cryptocurrencies as a payment method, which is not going unnoticed by retail's major players. Amazon will reportedly launch its own cryptocurrency in 2022, which will enable payments using 'Amazon Crypto Token' for purchases on its website. Furthermore, Google formed a partnership with digital asset marketplace Bakkt in late 2021 to pave the way for crypto acceptance in its Google Play app.

2 *Inflationary pressures are fuelling deferred payment demand*
   We expect payment for purchases with tailored and flexible BNPL plans – even for small-ticket items – to be one of the fastest growing payment trends in 2022. BNPL saw major popularity during the pandemic, which can be attributed to increased e-commerce shopping as well as surges in unemployment and uncertain financial conditions. This demand has persisted, and will likely increase amid inflationary pressures: during Cyber Week (23–29 November 2021) alone, the use of BNPL jumped by 29 per cent year over year (Doniger, 2021).

We expect more retailers to introduce BNPL services as a payment method to keep up with demand and boost sales – BNPL can deliver 20–30 per cent higher conversion rates for merchants and 30–50 per cent higher average ticket sales, according to Deirdre Cohen, SVP and Head of Acquiring at Visa (Weinswig, 2022).

The payment retail tech landscape by category

We are constantly meeting and evaluating retail tech companies, and we are seeing the layout of the payments landscape emerge in the last few years.

Below are the key categories of innovation we are seeing in the payment space.

- *BNPL*: Companies are enabling consumers to split payments into smaller chunks and pay in installments following a schedule plan, usually for free.

- *Checkout experiences*: Companies are focused on delivering user-friendliness for checkout experiences, including one-click, contactless and automated checkout solutions.

- *Cross-border payment solutions*: Companies are helping businesses to send and receive money overseas and support payments in global currencies.

- *Cryptocurrency and digital assets*: Companies are enabling merchants to accept payments in digital currencies and companies with marketplaces for trading digital currencies and assets.

- *Digital wallets*: Companies are enabling digital payment methods, including peer-to-peer payment via a QR code or phone number.

- *Payment gateways and processors*: Companies are enabling merchants to accept payments from different networks and providing API integrations for e-commerce websites.

- *Payment-linked loyalty/rewards*: Companies are providing payment-linked loyalty programmes that incentivize purchases by linking consumers' loyalty cards to mobile apps and awarding loyalty points for payments.

- *Risk management and fraud prevention*: Companies are offering security, fraud prevention, account authentication and chargeback management solutions through analytics, ultimately helping merchants to maximize revenue.

Figure 11.1 lays out some of the startups in each of the payment categories.

Web 3.0 payments

In recent years, many new and highly technical payment methods for retailers, brands and businesses have emerged to increase efficiency, reduce costs and help unlock trade barriers. As consumers continue their shift toward a digital life, payment systems and solutions are evolving at a rapid pace – and

FIGURE 11.1 The digital payment ecosystem

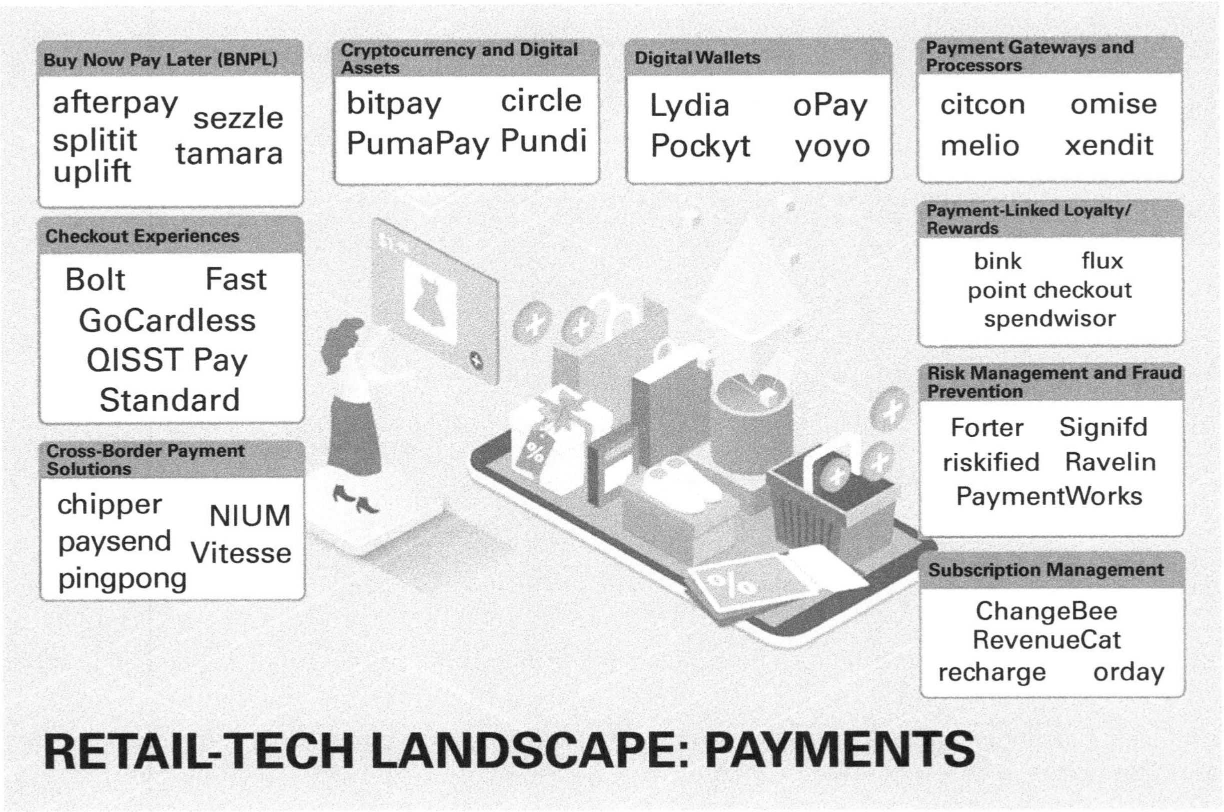

RETAIL-TECH LANDSCAPE: PAYMENTS

Buy Now Pay Later (BNPL)
afterpay   sezzle
splitit   tamara
uplift

Checkout Experiences
Bolt   Fast
GoCardless
QISST Pay
Standard

Cross-Border Payment Solutions
chipper   NIUM
paysend   Vitesse
pingpong

Cryptocurrency and Digital Assets
bitpay   circle
PumaPay Pundi

Digital Wallets
Lydia   oPay
Pockyt   yoyo

Payment Gateways and Processors
citcon   omise
melio   xendit

Payment-Linked Loyalty/ Rewards
bink   flux
point checkout
spendwisor

Risk Management and Fraud Prevention
Forter   Signifd
riskified Ravelin
PaymentWorks

Subscription Management
ChangeBee
RevenueCat
recharge   orday

SOURCE Coresight Research

have been accelerated by the emergence of the Metaverse and Web 3.0. Unless Metaverse and virtual economy payment infrastructure is secure, fast and reliable, retailers and brands will be less likely to use it as a new channel for sales and customer interaction.

Blockchain is a distributed ledger that will power cryptocurrencies (the currency of the Metaverse) and digital assets such as NFTs. However, the payment channels and methods by which transactions are completed and funds are received can vary significantly by blockchain and payment solution, and are crucial components of Metaverse infrastructure. Without speed and reliability, the potential of joining a virtual economy and ecosystem, accessing customers from distant corners of the world seamlessly, is diminished.

Metaverse-specific crypto tokens, such as *Decentraland*'s MANA or *The Sandbox*'s SAND, used as currency and for payments by users on the platforms and in respective marketplaces, can also be used to gauge financial health. Metaverse tokens have not been immune to the price crash of cryptocurrencies, but, with little interoperability (transferability of assets between platforms), their individual prices should not matter, as payment processors allow for immediate conversion to fiat currencies.

Whether Web 3.0 technologies, such as cryptocurrencies and NFTs, are adopted rapidly in the near term or slowly over the course of decades, Metaverse and digital activities continue to increase on a global basis, as does access to Metaverse-related technologies. It will be essential for brands and retailers to incorporate efficient payment systems that allow them to adequately handle the increase in customers that Web 3.0's connectivity will bring.

Components of Metaverse payments

Metaverse payments require multiple components, with the most essential being:

- blockchain, NFTs and cryptocurrencies to achieve decentralization
- digital wallets to send/receive funds and hold assets
- crypto payment gateways to process digital transfers and funds (for businesses, brands and retailers)

We explore each in detail on the following two pages.

BLOCKCHAIN, NFTs AND CRYPTOCURRENCIES

Blockchain is a system in which multiple nodes (computers) work together to form a peer-to-peer network which is responsible for maintaining a ledger of digital transactions; this is similar to a bank's ledger, but no one entity has control to manipulate or change transactions, making the system decentralized.

Cryptocurrencies and NFTs, which will eventually come to represent all Metaverse assets and unique products, are powered by blockchain and are essential for establishing in-world Metaverse economies.

Despite the ongoing volatility in NFT prices, transaction volume is somewhat steady and still spikes on days in which popular collections are released. As the world continues to move toward Web 3.0 and retailers find new and innovative ways to utilize blockchain's security, verification and efficiency through NFT-related strategies, blockchain systems are becoming more and more important for supporting increased transaction volume.

Within each virtual world, users and customers will pay for assets and virtual products (held in the form of NFTs) for their avatars and personal virtual spaces by using the world's cryptocurrency token.

DIGITAL WALLETS

Cryptocurrency and digital wallets, such as Coinbase Wallet, NFT, and Metaverse-specific wallets, such as MetaMask and Meta Pay, BlockFi and Crypto.com, will be crucial for payments in the Metaverse. Both users and creators as well as smaller businesses, retailers and brands will use these wallets as a means to store cryptocurrency funds and NFTs, engaging in direct trade with customers within virtual worlds. In addition, exclusive access to NFTs is available in the wallets, along with the private and public keys to send, receive and unlock cryptocurrency payments.

Meta Platforms, one of Web 3.0's earliest pioneers, announced in June 2022 that it was developing a digital wallet, Meta Pay, specifically for customers to tie to their digital identities and purchase virtual assets and digital products. Similar to MetaMask, Meta Pay will focus on two important aspects of virtual economies: securing digital ownership and providing easily accessible digital assets.

Using crypto wallets, retailers, businesses and customers can enjoy the benefits of blockchain, including security, immutability, immediate transfer and anonymity, which allow trade within virtual worlds and economies to flourish. However, while blockchains are generally secure, wallets and companies operating those wallets are not necessarily reliable and may be prone to breaches and hacks. It is important for retailers to choose a wallet that has sufficient safeguards against theft of funds and potential breaches of data. BlockFi Wallet, for example, does not operate with its own token and has opened itself up for federal regulation; as a result, it has not yet reported a significant theft (though it has had a data breach).

Given the volatility in cryptocurrencies, it is understandable that many retailers and brands are still hesitant to adopt these technologies. To help remove the barriers to digital trade and entering virtual worlds, fintech giants such as MasterCard have filed patents for virtual credit and debit cards in the Metaverse, and Visa and Amex are not far behind in Metaverse-related consulting. It may soon be possible for retailers to access a larger customer base through the Metaverse without adopting crypto, although they would not enjoy any of blockchain's benefits.

CRYPTO PAYMENT GATEWAYS

There are many reputable crypto payment gateways (processors) currently on the market, including BitPay, Coinbase, CoinGate, Crypto.com and Flexa, as well as processors focusing on Metaverse payments, such as MoonPay.

Businesses could use wallets to send and receive funds from customers, but payment gateways remove the extra work of exchanging currencies and managing multiple wallets across various platforms and applications. The customer makes a crypto payment in the Metaverse, in-store or on mobile. The amount paid is equivalent to the crypto's fair market value (in fiat currency) at the time. The gateway immediately converts the cryptocurrency payment into the currency of choice, and the money is deposited into the payee's account in intervals (decided by contract).

CASE STUDY
MoonPay

Many crypto payment gateways are actively growing their partnership ecosystem to support mass adoption of cryptocurrencies. In particular, MoonPay, founded in 2018, has employed a number of Web 3.0 - and Metaverse-specific initiatives.

Focused on widespread Metaverse use and NFT adoption, MoonPay allows customers to purchase NFTs and cryptocurrencies with credit and debit cards and with Apple Pay and Google Pay, providing a link between the physical and virtual worlds and removing some of the barriers to cryptocurrency and NFT trading.

In April 2022, MoonPay, serving as a ramp provider (bridge from fiat to cryptocurrency), announced a partnership with Metaverse-specific wallet MetaMask, simplifying the process of trading and selling digital assets and tokens and making cryptocurrency payments. Available in more than 150 countries, MoonPay is significantly increasing MetaMask's utility and global user base. MoonPay also offers ramp services for users in Solana-backed Metaverse platform *Star Atlas*.

MoonPay is also the official payment processor of *FaZe Clan*, a gaming and esports organization whose members create engaging content and compete in hundreds of immersive multiplayer games, including *Call of Duty*, *Counterstrike*, *Fortnite* and *Rocket League*. Top *FaZe Clan* gamers are extremely influential, setting trends within platforms; they are already in-game and real-world celebrities. MoonPay will serve *FaZe Clan*'s digital marketplace, and the two will work together to create NFT-related products and content that stimulates growth in virtual-world economies.

Metaverse payment solutions and channels

Many individual Metaverse projects, such as *Decentraland*, *The Sandbox* and *Star Atlas*, depending on the blockchain they use, already feature in-world payment solutions. Any brand or retailer that has opened a storefront or sold virtual products to avatars within these platforms has taken advantage of these payment solutions.

While wallets and payment gateways provide retailers, businesses and customers with the means to send, receive and hold digital assets and currencies, the payment solutions and channels can vary significantly by each NFT or digital asset marketplace, and often sacrifice speed and efficiency for security. Mainnet blockchains, such as Ethereum and Bitcoin, never suffer from large hacks, but many blockchain payment channels are often more centralized, meaning control is less distributed in the network.

Layer 2 blockchains are scaling solutions and protocols that are built on top of Mainnet blockchains (such as Ethereum, Bitcoin, Cardano, etc.); they incorporate the Mainnet's security and help improve speed, efficiency and scalability. Sidechains, similar to Layer 2 solutions, are separate blockchain networks with their own security mechanisms that run parallel to the Mainnet; they are also being developed as scaling and speed solutions. Layer 2 and sidechain projects will typically have their own cryptocurrency token and ecosystem of projects and platforms.

There are already hundreds of Layer 2 projects and sidechains for multiple blockchains. We discuss three notable examples for Metaverse payments below.

Immutable X

Immutable X is a Layer 2 blockchain solution developed specifically to support higher-volume NFT trade in the Ethereum Mainnet. It has its own token, IMX, which has a market capitalization of over $150 million as of 27 July 2022, according to CoinMarketCap (2022a). Despite the ongoing cryptocurrency price crash, Immutable X is still investing heavily in developing its ecosystem – it announced a $500 million developer fund on 17 June 2022 (Weinswig, 2022).

To improve scalability, speed and efficiency, Immutable X employs zero-knowledge (ZK) rollups – when blockchain solutions group a large number of transactions together, validate transactions and data with a third party off-chain (in Immutable X's case, infrastructure provider StarkWare), and produce a single cryptographic hash for all the transactions, rather than a hash for each transaction. Immutable X covers the associated gas fee, which can vary based on network congestion and energy consumption, after moving the batch of transactions back onto the Mainnet blockchain. However, in using a third party (a much less decentralized system), Immutable X sacrifices security for efficiency.

Immutable X has partnered with short-video social platform TikTok in the past to mint and sell NFTs of top TikTok moments, featuring six culturally relevant moments from top creators, including Nike's digital fashion division, RTFKT. Additionally, gaming retailer GameStop is working with Immutable X to create its NFT marketplace for gaming collectibles.

Polygon

Polygon is a Layer 2 solution for all tokens built on the Ethereum standard; it has a market capitalization of over $4 billion as of 27 June 2022, according to CoinMarketCap (2022b).

MANA and SAND, of *Decentraland* and *The Sandbox*, respectively, are tokens built on the ERC-20 token standard, backed by the Ethereum blockchain. However, because *Decentraland* and *The Sandbox* have integrated

Polygon technology, users of both these platforms can enjoy Polygon's efficiency and speed using its token, MATIC.

Developers building on Polygon's proof-of-stake blockchain are able to build Ethereum-based decentralized applications as sidechains with the use of ZK rollups. Polygon technology also employs plasma chains – bundling a number of transactions into their own block on top of the Mainnet architecture and hashing it in a single submission. To support payments in blockchain-based games, Polygon also employs 'optimistic rollups', which are similar to plasma chains but for smart contract scalability (crucial for digital asset trade).

Polygon claims that these Layer 2 technologies make its proof-of-stake system 99.95 per cent more efficient than traditional proof-of-work blockchains such as Ethereum (though Ethereum is undergoing a merge with another blockchain to switch to this mechanism and will soon be as efficient on its own). Again, however, sidechains and rollups are more centralized and thus prone to hacks.

Many fashion brands have recognized Polygon as a go-to blockchain for carbon-neutral NFTs:

- Luxury brand Dolce & Gabbana, active in NFT markets, minted a collection through a partnership with digital asset place UNXD and Polygon, which fetched $6 million for the brand (Weinswig, 2022).
- Department store Macy's partnered with Sweets NFT Marketplace and Polygon to sell $9,500 NFTs inspired by Macy's Thanksgiving Day Parade.
- Sportswear brand Adidas and luxury brand Prada collaborated on an NFT collection minted on the Polygon blockchain; the collection was designed as a reward for Adidas NFT holders.
- Meta announced in May 2022 that NFTs would be coming to Instagram for creators and brands to sell digital products via a partnership with Polygon, citing its scalability and carbon-neutral footprint.

Arbitrum

Another Layer 2 blockchain solution that has been making headlines recently is Arbitrum, which is built on the Ethereum blockchain. Arbitrum utilizes a sidechain that processes transactions with the Ethereum token, meaning that it does not need a native token for its own ecosystem of developers and projects. Like Polygon, Arbitrum also uses optimistic rollups, which, as opposed to ZK rollups, do not validate transactions before batching them together (transaction verification can be disputed and resolved at a later point).

Horse racing-based Metaverse platform Game of Silks announced a partnership with Arbitrum in April 2022, integrating its payments technology to improve gameplay in its in-game economy. Game of Silks chose Arbitrum for its significant ability to scale the Ethereum blockchain.

Technology platform Request Finance employs Arbitrum technology to provide crypto invoicing, payroll and expenses, allowing businesses, brands and retailers to manage, view and pay all their crypto invoices in one place. Thousands of Web 3.0 startups and companies are beginning to use the service to pay suppliers, employees and contributors in crypto – an important concept as the Metaverse develops.

The future for Metaverse payments

Blockchain and cryptocurrencies provide efficiency, speed and security, representing the backbone of Metaverse payments and allowing virtual economies to be completely decentralized. There are many other technological components to digital payments in the virtual world, including payment gateways and digital wallets. Retailers and brands can begin using, exploring and testing these technologies even before entering a Metaverse platform to sell virtual products, services and experiences to customers. This would enable them to take advantage of an increasing number of digital customers who are becoming more and more connected as the Metaverse and its underlying technologies evolve.

Sidechains and Layer 2 solutions for payments in the Metaverse may improve efficiency, speed and scalability but will often sacrifice security. As payment technology improves and developers invest in finding better systems and mechanics, this trade-off will likely disappear.

Understanding payment solutions and underlying technologies is crucial for brands and retailers looking to take advantage of blockchain's massive potential; although it is still in its earliest days and suffering from volatility and scepticism, the technology over the next five to 10 years is set to improve significantly.

> The logjam of US payments tied to credit cards is finally starting to break up a little with the advent of BNPL and cryptocurrencies, and consumers could possibly enjoy more flexibility (and lower fees) in the future.
>
> John Harmon, Senior Retail/Technology Analyst, Coresight Research (2022)

TEN THINGS RETAILERS NEED TO KNOW ABOUT DIGITAL PAYMENTS

1 Younger consumers are increasingly demanding alternative payment methods such as BNPL and digital wallets.

2 One-click checkout reduces the number of abandoned shopping carts.

3 Consumers are discovering products on social media, but without a seamless payment option from social to purchase, many will abandon the transaction.

4 Accepting cryptocurrency can attract new customers.

5 As digital wallets become more user friendly, consumers will increasingly use blockchain and crypto payment options.

6 Luxury brands and fashion retailers are experimenting with carbon-neutral blockchain solutions.

7 Retailers should expect increased flexibility in the digital payment sector in the future.

8 Cross-border payments continue to get easier, paving the way for expanded customer bases for e-commerce platforms.

9 Retailers need to be continuously simplifying the payment experience for their customers.

10 The advancement of new technologies from QR codes to mobile to contactless payment will continue to transform the payment industry.

KEY TAKEAWAYS: DIGITAL PAYMENTS

As consumers continue to spend more online, the need for innovative, convenient and safe checkout solutions is increasing. And as the Metaverse continues to increase in popularity, there will be increased pressure for retailers to innovate their payment solutions. Key takeaways from this chapter include:

- Consumers are increasingly seeking ease and convenience at the checkout, and looking for solutions that do not require them to input their payment information every time.

- The use of alternative payment options is increasing, especially BNPL, which has been shown to increase conversion rates and average transaction values.

- A number of payment innovators are offering solutions for retailers to enhance their payment options.

- The Metaverse is opening new payment options for retailers as they expand into selling digital items and partnering with virtual worlds.

- The payment landscape is poised for rapid technological change over the next five to 10 years.

References

Anthony, P (2022) Interview with the authors.

Baymard Institute (2022) 48 cart abandonment rate statistics 2022, Baymard Institute. https://baymard.com/lists/cart-abandonment-rate (archived at perma. cc/FNB5-R9VD)

Blockchain.com (2022) Blockchain.com wallets. www.blockchain.com/charts/ my-wallet-n-users (archived at perma.cc/YZ8V-Z87P)

CoinMarketCap (2022a) Immutable X to USD chart. http://coinmarketcap.com/ currencies/immutable-x/ (archived at perma.cc/AH8U-3PVV)

CoinMarketCap (2022b) Polygon to USD chart. http://coinmarketcap.com/ currencies/polygon/ (archived at perma.cc/Z6KT-FE7E)

Crypto.com (2022) Both merchants and consumers are eager to mainstream crypto payments. http://crypto.com/company-news/both-merchants-consumers-are-eager-to-mainstream-crypto-payments (archived at perma.cc/625Y-3CWC)

Doniger, A (2021) Buy now pay later boom shows no signs of slowing this holiday season, CNBC, 4 December. www.cnbc.com/2021/12/04/buy-now-pay-later-boom-shows-no-signs-of-slowing-this-holiday-season.html (archived at perma. cc/H4ZQ-SEKJ)

Forrester Consulting (2020) The total economic impact of accepting Bitcoin using BitPay, BitPay. http://bitpay.com/resources/forrester-report-says-bitpay-adds-new-sales-and-2x-aov/ (archived at perma.cc/XZ5W-AXX2)

Harmon, J (2022) Interview with the authors, July.

Kuruvilla, M. (n.d.) Fearlessly building Bolt's one-click checkout, Bolt. www.bolt. com/blog/building-bolt-one-click-checkout (archived at perma.cc/UW4P-EE75)

Perrin, A (2021) 16% of Americans say they have ever invested in, traded or used cryptocurrency, Pew Research Center. www.pewresearch.org/fact-tank/2021/11/11/16-of-americans-say-they-have-ever-invested-in-traded-or-used-cryptocurrency/ (archived at perma.cc/7AAL-BT6D)

Smith, S (2022) Digital wallets transaction value to grow by 60% by 2026 globally, as PayPal and Alipay top competitor leaderboard, Juniper Research. www. juniperresearch.com/pressreleases/digital-wallets-transaction-value-to-grow-by-60 (archived at perma.cc/H2SE-2S7F)

Statista (2022) Digital payments. www.statista.com/outlook/dmo/fintech/digital-payments/worldwide (archived at perma.cc/45SM-T2ND)

Weinswig, D (2022) Building blocks of the Metaverse: Payments, Coresight Research. https://coresight.com/research/building-blocks-of-the-Metaverse-payments/ (archived at perma.cc/UU5H-ZK56)

12

Monetizing retail data while maintaining customer trust

LEARNING OBJECTIVES

In this chapter we will provide case studies of data monetization best practices and review use cases that benefit the retailer while keeping customer needs top of mind. We cover a range of data-related topics, including:

- retail data types and uses
- artificial intelligence and retail data
- data integration for personalization, inventory management, experiential retail and pricing rationalization
- data privacy limitations
- data sharing practices
- best practices and examples of retail data utilization

The role of data in a retail organization

Data should be the lifeblood of retail since it carries essential information that retailers can use to get to know and engage their customers better, and remove friction from shopping, checkout and delivery experiences. Much of this data is unfortunately stored in unconnected silos and retailers are, therefore, missing out on key data insights.

The retail industry is steadily becoming more competitive, which is largely due to:

- the steady encroachment of e-commerce, which is led by data-centric e-commerce companies that face lower entry barriers
- major technology investments among large retailers, particularly mass marketers such as Target and Walmart, who are making and benefiting from cloud computing and AI
- global competition in retail due to the advent of cross-border shipping and the emergence of technology-fuelled e-commerce companies
- wide swings in category demand during the pandemic, which favours retailers with advanced supply-chain management
- an increasingly flexible customer base, with little tolerance for friction and low switching costs among online platforms

FIGURE 12.1   The traditional retailer-centric omnichannel retail model

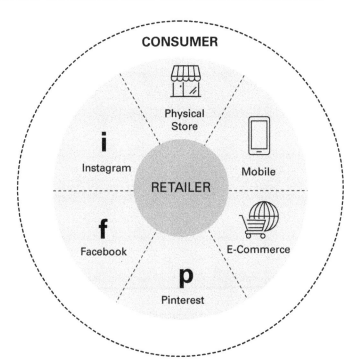

SOURCE Coresight Research

A retailer-centric vs customer-centric market

For decades, retail has centred on the physical store, with additional channels such as online commerce, social media and smartphone apps essentially 'bolted on' to the existing brick-and-mortar model, as depicted in Figure 12.1. This model is known as omnichannel retail – referring to the connected, but still siloed, channels that the consumer uses to communicate with the retailer.

Retailers that have emerged more recently than their longstanding traditional counterparts, such as Alibaba, Amazon and JD.com, have looked to reconfigure retail by putting the consumer at the centre. Whereas the retailer occupies the key location in Figure 12.1, new retail models centre on the customer, as shown in Figure 12.2. Alibaba refers to this model as New Retail and it is known as Boundaryless Retail by JD.com.

New Retail seamlessly merges the online and offline worlds, powered by data. It leverages data for developing new products and services, optimizing the supply chain, crafting marketing messages, managing operations, running IT and e-commerce systems and developing consumer insights. AI is the tool that links all of these functions.

FIGURE 12.2 The new, consumer-centric retail model

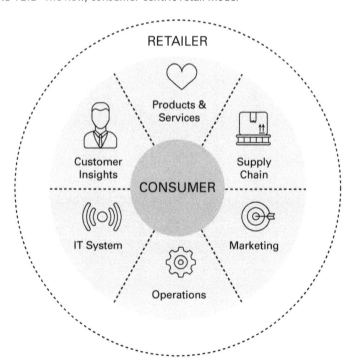

SOURCE Coresight Research

Retailers struggle to integrate their data

Retailers have access to multiple sources of data, much of which is confined to silos, which host different, unconnected types of data, impeding retailers from seeing the big picture. Figure 12.3 illustrates the different types of data that retailers can benefit from, including internal data such as transactions and external data such as product reviews and social media postings. Much of this data is unstructured in form. Figure 12.3 also highlights the insights that retailers may be missing from the lack of data connections.

Each type of data has its own unique limitations and only represents one piece of a retailer's data puzzle:

- *Transaction data*: This type of data shows what customers have already purchased, yet it contains no information on what they are interested in buying.
- *In-store data*: This data can offer a great deal of information on customer activity inside the store: including store areas visited by a consumer, their dwell time and items they picked up but did not purchase (for example, those left in a dressing room), as well as hot spots of dwell activity inside the store. However, retailers face the challenge of turning this raw data into the appropriate actionable insights. Although the potential to collect and leverage this data exists, not all retailers do so.

FIGURE 12.3   Retailers' data sources and potential insights

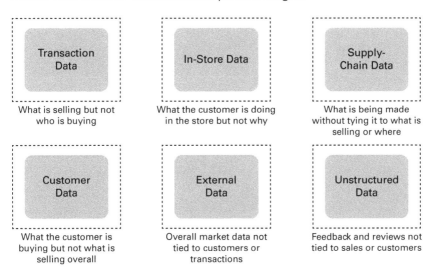

SOURCE Coresight Research

- *Supply chain data*: This data represents the 'what, when and where' of inventory, spanning from the manufacturer to the warehouse to the retailer, and sending demand and assortment information in the opposite direction. However, it does not reflect what consumers are actually purchasing and where.

- *Customer data*: This data is very powerful, particularly when part of a customer relationship management platform, as it can be analysed to predict what a customer is interested in buying, though it doesn't give a full picture of aggregate demand.

- *External data*: There is a wealth of data found in weather patterns and predictions, as well as calendar features such as upcoming holidays and local events, although it does not tie directly to what the consumer is actually buying.

- *Unstructured data*: There is additional external data in unstructured text format, such as product reviews and social media posts, which can be mined to determine general trends and feedback on individual products.

Artificial intelligence: New data relationships and actionable insights

The strengths of AI and ML, a subset of AI technology, include its ability to identify patterns and find relationships between disparate data sources – making both AI and ML useful in leveraging siloed data. AI connects disparate data sources to generate analytics and interpret words, voices and images.

The main strengths of AI are its applications as three types of ML analytics:

- Descriptive: What happened?
- Predictive: What will happen?
- Prescriptive: What should we do about it?

AI's ability to find insights in disparate data sets enables retailers to create a comprehensive view on their data, answering questions including:

- What are retailers selling (the full cart)?
- Who is buying?
- Where are consumers buying?
- How much are consumers paying?

- What is driving consumers to buy?
- Are consumers happy with their purchases?
- Where does a retailer stand versus its competitors?

Leveraging this data creates actionable insights for retailers and employees, such as on driving demand and conversion, pricing product effectively, configuring assortment and its location over time, and how to improve supply chain efficiency.

The Coresight CORE framework

To help to identify the opportunities for data and AI in retail, Coresight Research developed its proprietary CORE framework, as illustrated in Figure 12.4.

We discuss examples of AI in retail through the lens of the CORE framework.

FIGURE 12.4 The Coresight Research CORE framework

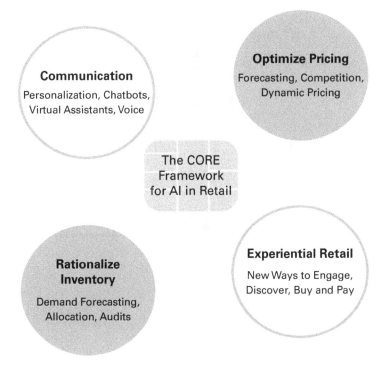

Communication
Personalization, Chatbots, Virtual Assistants, Voice

Optimize Pricing
Forecasting, Competition, Dynamic Pricing

The CORE Framework for AI in Retail

Rationalize Inventory
Demand Forecasting, Allocation, Audits

Experiential Retail
New Ways to Engage, Discover, Buy and Pay

SOURCE Coresight Research

C: Communication

AI's strengths in pattern recognition and finding connections in data have enabled new means of communication with computers, leading to the use of virtual assistants, chatbots, voice shopping and visual search functions in retail. AI-enabled means of communication are complementary: NLP combined with speech recognition inside an intelligent assistant enables a device to converse and respond to voice input.

- *Personalization*: AI can leverage customer data to build a profile of the consumer, which can be used to craft personalized product recommendations, home page views, emails and other marketing materials.

- *Chatbots*: This technology enables retailers to offer an around-the-clock response to simple customer inquiries. The value of chatbots is multiplied when they are able to access customer information and purchase history. This enables them to respond to a simple but sophisticated inquiry such as, 'I would like to return the blue sweater that I bought last month', which requires an understanding of products, their characteristics and customer data.

- *Virtual assistants*: Most major global technology companies have used AI to develop their own intelligent assistants, including Amazon's Echo, Apple's Siri, Microsoft's Cortana and many others.

- *Voice shopping*: This category leverages both intelligent-assistant and chatbot technology to enable consumers to receive a verbal shopping experience that is equivalent to online. It frees consumers from having to log on to their PCs or phones to shop, and also assists visually impaired consumers.

- *Visual search*: This technology leverages the strength of AI in image recognition and also requires intelligence to understand types of products, colours and styles. The goal is the 'holy grail' of retail, in which a consumer can take a photo of an item in a magazine, on a runway or on the street and be able to find and purchase that item, or a near-identical substitute.

Some examples of how retailers are using data and AI for communication, according to company reports, include:

- 1-800-Flowers is offering an intelligence personal assistant to provide support to phone calls.

- Chipolte is using customer insights to develop and promote its loyalty programme.
- Kohls is using ML to make predictions used in media buying and copywriting.
- H&M is using data to offer 'Style With' product recommendations.
- Macy's chatbot offer real-time responses about inventory, merchandise and orders through its website.
- Wayfair's visual search offering enables customers to submit photos of items they are interested in and find similar items on Wayfair.

O: Optimize pricing

The analytical functions of AI enable the technology to be used for forecasts and analyses, which can change dynamically.

- *Forecasting*: ML offers several tools for creating forecast models including regressions, time series and binary models. These models can incorporate internal and external variables to forecast the variables necessary to manage a retailer's business.
- *Competition*: AI's ability to analyse structured and unstructured data (such as text) can be applied to gain insights on competitor's product information and pricing data, as well as a retailer's own reviews and comments on social media to build profiles for developing new-product or pricing strategies.
- *Dynamic pricing*: Similar to the above, the automation capabilities of AI enable systems to constantly monitor competitors' prices and demand inputs, and set prices appropriately.

R: Rationalize inventory

ML excels in analysis and prediction, which makes it a useful tool in forecasting demand, product allocation and for conducting audits. Retailers can use these analytical methods to enhance supply chains and inventory management in the following ways:

- *Demand forecasting*: This method incorporates variables such as historical demand, consumer trends, weather forecasts, calendar events and other data to estimate product demand.

- *Inventory allocation*: Based on a demand forecast and using the same variables, retailers can create forecasts of demand by store or geography, online or offline, to position inventory at the optimal location.

- *Assortment allocation*: Again, based on a demand forecast and other data, retailers can determine the optimal quantities of products in a particular store or location.

- *Order management*: Software can determine the most efficient route for processing an order, online or offline, or shipping from the store or warehouse or via drop-shipping.

- *Warehouse management*: Demand and item-level forecasts can be used to determine the optimal placement of items within a warehouse to minimize fulfilment times.

Some examples of how retailers are using AI to rationalize inventory, according to company reports, include:

- Autozone is using AI to forecast inventory and replenishment demand in its distribution centres.

- Fedex's Surround platform enhances supply-chain visibility with near-real-time analytics.

- Lululemon uses intelligent sourcing to route orders through its distribution network.

- Walgreens Boots Alliance uses analytics to make daily forecasts on millions of items sold at the store level.

E: Experiential retail

The concept of New Retail refers to a seamless fusion of online shopping, offline shopping and logistics. Retailers can use AI to make the online and offline shopping processes seem unified and seamless. Other technologies, such as augmented reality and virtual reality and livestreaming, can provide a virtual experience of visiting a physical store or mall.

Retailers can leverage New Retail concepts in the following ways:

- *New ways to discover*: Wayfinder robots can guide customers to products within the store, and employee tablets can leverage customer data to make relevant, personalized product recommendations.

- *New ways to pay*: Self-service and checkout terminals leverage customer and product data, which retailers can use to inform consumer profiles through AI analysis. Self-service payment and information points also provide self-reliant customers with a better experience by expediting their journey through the store. Computer vision ensures the accuracy of the self-checkout process.

- *New ways to engage*: Livestreaming combines internet video with shopping to provide the thrill of live entertainment and scarce merchandise, broadcast from a store or a mall. Retailers can integrate AI into livestreaming to target content better and personalize livestream recommendations for consumers. Retailers can also utilize AI-powered virtual hosts for their livestreams to supplement their influencer-led sessions.

- *Blend online and offline*: In New Retail, a shopping journey can start online and end in the store, or vice versa. Consumers can shop online and pick up in store, or shop in a store and have their products delivered.

- *Logistics*: Automated warehouses and fulfilment centres leverage AI-powered computer vision technology and analytics to enable robots to navigate autonomously through the facilities. Moreover, retailers can leverage robotic vehicles, which use AI-fuelled computer vision and analytics to guide autonomous delivery vehicles to deliver products to consumers.

Some examples of how AI can be used to realize experiential retail concepts, according to company reports, include:

- 7-Eleven is installing self-checkout terminals nationwide in Japan as part of a government mandate to automate all convenience stores by 2025 in light of the country's labour shortage.

- Kroger's Chefbot, an AI-powered Twitter tool, makes recipe suggestions based on the food that the consumer has purchased.

- Lowe's AI-fuelled robot, LoweBot, answers spoken questions and guides customers in-store.

- Nike uses AI to offer in-store experiences that blend the physical and mobile worlds for Nike app users.

Implications for brands/retailers

AI can be used to find actionable, unseen insights from retailers' data that is otherwise largely trapped in silos. This can help retailers to improve consumer engagement, offer more relevant and personalized communication, run retail operations more efficiently and remove friction in shopping, checkout and payment to offer a seamless New Retail experience. Specifically:

- Brands and retailers can benefit from the strengths of AI and data in engaging consumers more and communicating with them in a more personalized manner.
- Brands and retailers can use AI and data to make their operations more efficient, particularly in terms of supply chains.
- Offering a seamless New Retail-inspired environment unlocks customers' demand for shopping whenever and wherever they want, and also reduces points of friction that cause cart abandonment.

Implications for real estate firms

- Real estate firms can use data and AI to engage and communicate with consumers in a personalized manner.
- Real estate firms can also reconfigure their properties to support New Retail, including providing the technology infrastructure for seamless commerce and creating space for automated fulfilment.

Implications for technology vendors

- There are opportunities for technology vendors to develop AI and data tools throughout the value chain, from software infrastructure to tools and apps.
- There are many opportunities for developers to create new apps that build on this strong technology foundation in ways previously unimagined.
- Livestreaming remains in its infancy, and there are many opportunities to enhance the technology through AI, as well invent new ways to leverage it across retail.

Using retail data to provide personalized marketing and services

Brands and retailers must recognize value exchange as a key component when they deliver personalized marketing efforts to consumers. Powering our insights is the analysis of findings from three Coresight Research surveys – two sent to consumers, and one to brands and retailers, in the US and the UK (consumer personalization survey – 5,014 US and UK consumers; retailer personalization survey – 260 US and UK brands and retailers; consumer privacy survey – 1,002 US and UK consumers) (Weinswig, 2022).

Brands and retailers must recognize value exchange as a key component when they deliver personalized marketing efforts to consumers. It is important that they understand their customers' preferences and deliver a consistent experience no matter when and where they choose to shop. While privacy regulations and controls seem like obstacles to accruing data, consumers are willing to share personal information if there is value to be gained. Now is the time for retailers to tap into loyalty programmes, predictive analysis and machine learning to meet the customer at every moment in the purchasing cycle.

Personalization in marketing can bring numerous benefits to brands and retailers, including increased customer lifetime value, stronger customer loyalty and increased market share. To optimize the effectiveness of personalization strategies, brands and retailers must understand consumer preferences and behaviour in order to choose the right channel. The key to building trust with consumer data is to provide next-generation marketing personalization that helps shoppers with product discovery and creates a seamless experience across channels.

Consumers also place data privacy top of their agendas and pay strong attention to how their data is being used. Brands and retailers must be respectful and transparent in their marketing personalization efforts when it comes to data privacy, in order to build consumer trust. New policies governing privacy – such as Google's and Apple's privacy updates in 2021 – offer retail companies an opportunity to rethink their approach to acquiring consumer data, and to use it in a way that makes shopping feel more personal without compromising data privacy.

It has never been more important for retailers and brands to adapt quickly to the changing preferences and behaviours of consumers, who now shop across a variety of platforms, devices and geographies. Customers are increasingly seeking tailored experiences and expect value back for sharing their data with brands and retailers.

The importance of personalization and its effective execution: Perceptions of consumers vs brands/retailers

Personalization can bring in extra dollars for brands and retailers, as more than two-thirds (71 per cent) of consumers surveyed in the Coresight personalization survey said they will shop more often with companies that personalize the experience (Weinswig, 2022).

Brands and retailers can deliver personalization to customers in the following ways:

- creating a consistent shopping experience across desktop, in-store and mobile sites, as well as through email
- offering products and experiences that align with the shopper's purchase patterns and browsing preferences
- adopting personalized pricing and promotional strategies such as coupon codes to reward consumers' loyalty

Another interesting finding from the Coresight personalization survey is that consumers think brands and retailers are not doing enough when it comes to personalization: 71 per cent of brands and retailers think they excel in marketing personalization, but only 34 per cent of consumers think the same (Weinswig, 2022).

Both consumers and brands/retailers think that fulfilment is a key area for improving personalization. With the Covid-19 pandemic having driven heightened fulfilment expectations among consumers, brands and retailers can gain a competitive edge by using inventory/delivery notifications as another way of connecting to customers as part of their orchestrated marketing strategy.

Key marketing channels: Email and mobile texts present opportunity

While consumers, retailers and brands agree that websites are the most important channel for personalized marketing, they diverge when it comes to other channels. Most notably, almost one-third of consumers cited email as the most important channel – tying in top spot with websites – but less than 10 per cent of brands and retailers reported the same (Weinswig, 2022). Despite the penetration of social media into our daily lives (a channel that ranked in the top three for both consumers and brands and retailers), email still represents a very important marketing channel that retailers and brands must not ignore.

Both consumers and retailers consider mobile texts and mobile apps among the top channels for personalized marketing. Although not a new tactic, personalized SMS marketing can provide an effective way to reach consumers while ensuring communications are relevant and timely.

Loyalty programmes: Providing data for brands and value for consumers

Loyalty programmes remain a popular choice for many consumers: 53 per cent of consumers from Coresight's consumer personalization survey said that they had joined a loyalty programme of at least one or more brand/retailer (Weinswig, 2022).

However, consumers need to be offered value in exchange for sharing their data with brands and retailers – and cost-saving incentives such as offers and discounts proved to be key reasons for joining a loyalty programme among consumers in our survey. If done well, loyalty programmes can be instrumental in helping brands and retailers drive customer lifetime value and ultimately increase overall company performance.

Not surprisingly, shoppers' age plays a role in determining motivators to join a rewards programme. While younger shoppers cited insider offers and VIP discounts as their motivators to join a loyalty programme, older shoppers are more value-conscious, reporting that price breaks and discounts are the primary reasons for joining a loyalty programme. Younger shoppers are also more likely to value exclusivity and access to events than other age cohorts. Retailers and brands should therefore tailor loyalty perks according to age demographics.

Some retailers and brands offer shoppers a full range of advantages to all loyalty members but showcase certain benefits to specific shoppers. For instance, Sephora's membership programme, Beauty Insider, offers consumers points based on purchase levels, as well as tier-based savings and lower shipping costs, which appeal to more mature shoppers. On the other hand, perks such as access to events and product samples are promoted to younger customers, personalizing sample recommendations based on each shopper's purchasing history. Adidas' Creators Club membership, which includes a tiered loyalty programme, has perks that not only include discounts but also rewards such as free premium access to the Adidas training and running apps when consumers reach a certain loyalty tier.

Personalization tactics: Lower-revenue retailers and brands lag behind

Nearly all retailers and brands – 98 per cent of the retailers in Coresight's retailer personalization survey (Weinswig, 2022) – are using personalization tactics of some sort, with the three most prevalent being the following:

- predictive personalization (cited by 50 per cent of brands and retailers in Coresight's survey) – the ability to predict preferences and actions of users based on their past online behaviours and then customize current and future communications via the right channel at the right time

- email send-time optimization (47 per cent) – a feature that enables marketers to send emails at the most optimal time to each recipient, based on when they are most likely to engage
- buyer journey-based personalization (44 per cent) – a tactic that caters to individual buyers' entire shopping journey, from discovery to point of purchase

Predictably, retailers and brands with higher revenues are better prepared: Coresight's retailer personalization survey indicates that US brands with revenues of $500 million or more are quicker to embrace more advanced forms of personalization and predictive analytics compared to smaller companies. Organizations generating under $500 million annually should start looking into personalization tactics that could help them better leverage shoppers' data.

There was a similar pattern among UK brands and retailers: those with revenue of less than £600 million (around $800 million) demonstrated a considerably lower usage of personalization tactics compared to those with higher revenues, and at the same time rely on targeted discounts/offers as a personalization tactic.

Apart from leveraging personalization tactics, most brands and retailers are also tailoring communications to customers according to their local region or recent behaviours. From the Coresight survey, 79 per cent of retailers and brands say they tailor communication to customers' online web visits, followed by 78 per cent that tailor to local region and 70 per cent that tailor to social media behaviours.

Consumer concerns around data privacy

The majority of consumers (96 per cent) are at least slightly concerned about data protection, according to Coresight's privacy survey (Weinswig, 2022).

The primary reasons for this concern include a lack of control over personal data, news of security/privacy breaches and seeing more ads that pertain to customers' personal behaviours. While the consumer privacy survey found that 36 per cent of consumers feel positive about sharing personal data to brands and retailers to receive better personalized experiences, consumers remain concerned about companies giving their data to third parties – cited by 13 per cent of survey respondents as a top concern. Brands and retailers therefore need to assure they are putting consumers' data to legitimate use. At the same time, this reinforces the importance of value exchange: consumers are willing to share personal data to brands and retailers if they perceive value in doing so.

Despite the concerns that consumers have around privacy and data protection, they are still willing to share their personal information with retailers and brands for value in return. For example, from Coresight's consumer privacy survey, 69 per cent of consumers said they would be willing to share their birthday with retailers and brands they trust. Brands and retailers should collect this data and build it into their personalization efforts.

The Coresight privacy survey found the following two trends:

- Higher proportions of consumers report willingness to share generic, less-sensitive personal information with retailers and brands (new or trusted) – such as their name, gender and email address – than the proportions willing to share sensitive data such as their home address and phone number.

- There was a 7–10 per cent difference in consumer willingness to share personal data with a trusted retailer/brand compared to a new retailer/brand, across all types of data.

This should serve as a wake-up call for retailers and brands to build marketing and data collection strategies that rely on information customers voluntarily provide. With new policies such as Google and Apple privacy updates limiting current data collection methods, now is the time for retailers and brands to pivot to machine learning, data collection and predictive analysis. Interestingly from Coresight's retailer personalization survey, 69 per cent of retailers and brands think user privacy updates from Google brought them a positive impact on personalization marketing strategies, while 65 per cent thought the same for user privacy updates from Apple.

Implications for brands and retailers

Personalized marketing uses data to create customized experiences for shoppers which can lead to better engagement, increased conversions and higher sales. This can only be done if retailers and brands elevate their efforts to meet consumers' expectations for custom content and experiences, and treat personalization as a strategic priority. The ways retailers and brands can do so include leveraging loyalty programmes, advanced personalization tactics and making the best use of personal data in order to create value exchange with consumers.

- Brands and retailers need to leverage personalization tactics to curate better offers for shoppers.

- Retailers and brands should re-examine where their personalization efforts are placed to more closely align with shoppers' platform and communication preferences.

- Shoppers are willing to share personal information in exchange for value, such as tailored offerings and purchasing incentives (including discounts).

- Promotions should not be the only tool for cultivating loyalty. Brands and retailers should place more focus on delivering customers the right content through the right channel at the right time.

- Data privacy is important to consumers but is not an obstacle to knowing a shopper's preferences. Consumers in fact are willing to share personal data which retailers and brands should use to their advantage.

The role of data sharing

While the role of data in all aspects of merchandising is increasingly important, in many cases, retailers are unable to allocate resources to these areas. As a result, they increasingly rely on their vendor base to understand and monitor sales and supply chain data, bring marketplace insights and recommend changes to assortment, allocation and inventory.

Several vendors that we spoke with noted that they have seen a steady progression towards increased data sharing over the last 10 years. They believe that this was initially driven by retailer cost cutting, which eliminated the internal resources dedicated to analytics. As one vendor noted, 'Ten years ago, they [retailers] had teams internally to analyse the data in depth, but as they cut costs, that is shifting to the vendor.'

There are distinct benefits for sharing data with vendors to accomplish these goals. Several of the retailers that we interviewed noted that they rely on their vendor partners to monitor inventory levels on individual SKUs and to bring them new ideas. 'An educated vendor is the best partner,' said one senior manager at a large apparel specialty retailer that uses SPS Commerce solutions.

The impact of collaboration on retailers' and vendors' revenues

Over the past two years, retailers have gained efficiencies in business operations through improved collaboration. Increased inventory efficiency – from both inventory optimization and the reduction of out-of-stocks – can have a direct and measurable impact on overall revenue.

Coresight Research surveyed 89 retailers who stated that their data collaboration had improved over the last two years (Weinswig, 2020). Respondents were asked to select the financial impact of improved collaboration across the following options: out-of-stock reduction, reduction of costs, sales increase, profit increase and an increase in shopper engagement or loyalty.

For retailers, reduced out-of-stocks is critical to improving inventory efficiency, and with fewer out-of-stock items, retailers can increase their revenue. 51.7 per cent of retailers that stated their collaboration had improved over the past two years noted that their revenues increased more than 4 per cent as a result of improved out-of-stocks and 54.5 per cent reported a similar sales impact from increased shopper engagement.

The retailers we spoke to that are sharing sales and inventory data with their vendor partners cited multiple examples of tangible benefits from their data-sharing programmes. Below, we summarize the most commonly cited examples:

- **Inventory turnover**: Vendors with SKU-level and store-level data are using that data to identify slow-moving SKUs, suggest tweaks to the promotion plan to move items that are not selling in a particular location and spot inventory build-up that needs to be addressed. Retailers cited significant benefits in reduced costs from out-of-stocks and overstocks.

- **Returns**: POS and inventory data provides visibility into consumer returns, helping both retailers and vendors investigate high-return-rate items and quickly make changes to combat this.

- **Shopper experience**: When inventory levels and out-of-stocks improve, so does the shopping experience.

Disparities in data sharing

Despite the well-established benefits that we have outlined, there are still some retailers that are reluctant to share some or all of their data, although this is no longer the norm.

As these programmes have continued to mature, retailers and vendors are sharing data more. One vendor that we spoke with estimated that 75 per cent of its retailer partners shared data with it at a frequency and granularity that enabled them to generate actionable insights on a regular basis (Weinswig, 2021). The frequency and granularity of data shared varies significantly by category and country, and even within categories.

Many vendors told us that the impact of sharing data with retailers was evident: when vendors had more data to analyse, they could more frequently generate ideas for retailers to achieve higher inventory efficiency. One retailer shared that some of its vendors would call on a weekly basis and say, 'This store is out of stock on this one widget.' In addition, several interviewees noted that more of retailers' internal resources were directed toward those accounts because they delivered better sales results.

Reasons for limited sharing

In cases where retailers are reluctant to share data, three common reasons emerged:

- *Own portals*: In our interviews, we found that retailers that have their own data portals are often unable to make the investment necessary to make data available to vendors with the appropriate controls. Several of the retailers that we interviewed overcame this issue by transitioning their data-sharing programmes to an external third party. This offloaded the operations and staffing of this function entirely.

- *Cultural resistance*: In this case, retailers are generally concerned that the data would be used against them. One vendor noted that this is a very common concern at the outset of data sharing but that this tends to dissipate over time as the retailer and vendor begin to mutually benefit from data sharing.

- *Capability*: Some interviewees noted that they do not receive data from smaller retailers that lack the capability to harness the data. Given the importance of data, this is becoming less common, although it exists where the retail market is highly fragmented. Engaging a third party to manage the programme is one solution.

Shifting to an external provider

As retailers are seeking to reduce costs, more are shifting their data-sharing programmes to external providers. We spoke with retailers that shifted from an internal-vendor data-sharing programme to one managed by an external provider. They offered the following advice:

- *Select a provider of high quality*: Retailers noted that data accuracy is critically important. If a merchant is also using an internal system, ensure that the data within the two systems are updated with similar frequency, or ensure that both merchants and vendors understand the differences in the data sets. Timeliness and accuracy of data are critical.

- *Leverage an industry leader*: Retailers that shifted from internally generated data sharing to an external platform noted that most of their vendors benefited from the move because it involved a shift to a standard platform that they used with other retail accounts. This streamlined the vendors' work and made it easier to give the retailer relevant industry insights.

- *Stop direct sharing*: One of the key benefits of moving to an external provider is removing the workload from a retailer's internal staff. Key to transitioning vendors to the new system is ensuring that they do not revert to merchants for the data. One retailer noted that this took some time, but now, they do not get requests for data from vendors to their merchants.

- *Address a shift to pay-to-play*: One retailer that we spoke with said that it saw initial resistance from vendors because they were shifting from a free to a paid system. They noted that this primarily came from smaller vendors that were not already using the external data provider or that were doing a small amount of business. In this case, the retailer addressed the concern by offering a sponsored programme for smaller vendors.

Best practices for data vendors

Both vendors and retailers that we spoke with highlighted the significant benefits that data sharing provides. Vendors that have invested in leveraging data discussed significant impacts for both the brand and the retailer. However, building trust with the retailer is critical to realizing those benefits. There are a number of best practices to follow to build trust and maximize gains when sharing data:

- *Be transparent about results*: One vendor noted that it is important to not sugar-coat historical results if they were not favourable. Exploring why the results were not good and the adjustments to be made does more to build credibility, while trying to make the numbers look better than they really are only diminishes trust and credibility.

- *Bring the data into conversations*: Vendors should be reviewing data weekly and identifying new opportunities at the very least on a monthly basis, although several larger vendors mentioned identifying opportunities for improvement across their portfolio weekly.
- *Identify new ideas and opportunities*: The key to success is to continually identify new opportunities for the retailer.

Key retail data sharing insights

As the retail environment remains challenging, retailers and vendors are increasingly collaborating to drive mutual benefit. We observed a global trend of retailers and vendors implementing strong data-sharing programmes.

Retailers are increasingly looking to their vendor partners to regularly monitor their data and suggest improvements to allocation and inventory. As a result, vendors are building their data-analysis capabilities. One vendor that we spoke with estimated that 75 per cent of its retailer partners shared data with it at a sufficient level that it could derive actionable insights on a regular basis.

We found that improved collaboration through data sharing yields measurable impacts to revenues as well as increased customer satisfaction and improved inventory positions. Our view is that data sharing will continue to advance, and the most sophisticated retailers will expand their data-sharing programmes to drive better business outcomes.

> AI allows you to see customer trends much more quickly than previous data analytics. At Tractor Supply we have a significant strategic asset in the 27 million customers in our Neighbor's Club Loyalty programme. To analyse this powerful consumer data in real time at the individual level, it is critical to have machine learning and artificial intelligence to understand it and boil it down into tactics that can be executed at the retail level.
> Letitia Webster, SVP of E-commerce, Omnichannel, Master Data Management, Tractor Supply (2022)

TEN THINGS RETAILERS NEED TO KNOW ABOUT DATA

1 Data is the foundation of next generation retail, allowing a customer-focused omnichannel retail environment to flourish.

2 Advances in data analytics such as AI and ML are enabling retailers to make more informed decisions on pricing, inventory allocation, order management and supply chain optimization.

3 Retail data enhances the customer experience by increasing personalization and improving customer communication with smart data, chatbots and enhanced search.

4 Data is powering improved consumer experiences with innovations such as wayfinding, enhanced product education and information, self-checkout and integrated offline/online experiences.

5 Retail data allows the retailer to provide a more personalized experience for the consumer – which has been shown to improve customer satisfaction and is being increasingly demanded by consumers.

6 Retailers now have an opportunity to monetize all of the data that they are collecting.

7 Coresight Research estimates that retailers can generate 0.1 per cent–1.0 per cent of total sales in data revenue (Weinswig, 2021).

8 Data sharing is becoming more common – allowing retailers to integrate data with suppliers and realize enhanced efficiencies.

9 As data becomes more complex, AI and ML are necessary to process and understand this large volume of data.

10 Data is the key to unlocking new revenue opportunities, and maximizing the revenue potential of a retailer's underlying business.

KEY TAKEAWAYS: IMPROVING RETAIL DATA PRACTICES

- New customer-centric models of retail increase the need for enhanced retail data usage and analytics.

- Personalization is one of the most sought-after uses for retail data. Using AI is an effective tool to enhance personalization.

- Data sharing with vendors and merchants is proving to be an effective way for retailers to enhance their data utilization, although retailers must shed some of their preconceived notions about data sharing.

- Excellence in retail data usage, with care taken to protect consumer privacy, can lead to enhanced customer loyalty and satisfaction.

- The Coresight SCORE framework provides a methodology for companies to assess their data needs: S: smarter customer engagement, C: communication, O: optimize pricing, R: rationalize inventory, E: experiential retail.

References

Webster, L (2022) Interview with the authors, July.

Weinswig, D (2020) Measuring the value of retail data sharing and analytics, Coresight Research. https://coresight.com/research/measuring-the-value-of-retail-data-sharing-and-analytics/ (archived at perma.cc/RM9B-AV6A)

Weinswig, D (2021) RetailTech: What do data and AI mean for retail? Coresight Research. https://coresight.com/research/retailtech-what-do-data-and-ai-mean-for-retail/ (archived at perma.cc/4HL2-NTL8)

Weinswig, D (2022) Retail personalization in 2022: Balancing trust, data collection and privacy, Coresight Research. https://coresight.com/research/retail-personalization-in-2022-balancing-trust-data-collection-and-privacy/ (archived at perma.cc/92QB-XKUH)

13

Enhancing consumer loyalty

LEARNING OBJECTIVES

In this chapter we examine best practices for loyalty programmes and how retailers can leverage data to drive growth, as well as several emerging trends in the implementation of such programmes. We cover:

- the types of loyalty programmes
- loyalty programme best practices
- key trends in loyalty programmes, with retailer examples
- using technology to innovate loyalty programmes
- a sampling of global innovators in the loyalty segment
- insights from an industry insider on building excellence in customer loyalty

Loyalty programmes: An overview

Retailers are paying closer attention to developing and fine-tuning their loyalty programme strategies. The pandemic has seen consumers favour reduced shopping trips, convenience and low prices, threatening their loyalty to previously preferred retailers. According to a McKinsey report, 78 per cent of US consumers have switched stores, brands or the way they shop due to the pandemic (Brown et al, 2022).

Loyalty programmes present opportunities for retailers to re-attract lost customers as well as retain customers. The value of loyal customers is that they typically spend more, and are more likely to promote the brand to others. According to management consulting firm AT Kearney (2018), it costs five to 25 times more to acquire a new customer than to retain an

TABLE 13.1 Two types of loyalty programmes

	Proprietary	Coalition
Concept	Points earned and redeemed within the business	Points earned and redeemed through multiple partners
Advantages to retailers	Full ownership of consumer data Easier to develop brand loyalty	Broader consumer base Lower fixed costs
Disadvantages to retailers	Narrower consumer base	Limited control of consumer data

SOURCE Coresight Research

existing one, indicating how crucial it is for retailers to get their loyalty programmes right.

Loyalty programmes provide another channel for retailers to engage with consumers and differentiate themselves from the competition through enhanced customer experiences. A well-designed loyalty programme can go a long way in helping retailers to gain a larger share of wallet and increase customer retention, and the data harvested through such programmes provide retailers with insights into their customers and can power personalization in marketing and promotions.

Types of loyalty programmes: Proprietary vs coalition

There are two types of loyalty programmes in the retail sector: proprietary and coalition. Retailers need to assess their strategic goals and consumer preferences before determining which type to implement.

PROPRIETARY PROGRAMMES

These programmes aim to focus on the company's core business and build a personal connection with customers. Retailers have full control of the programme's operation and marketing, as well as full ownership of customer data, allowing them to create a more consistent experience across channels and offer more customized solutions for consumers. This is intended to build emotional connections with shoppers, who are then more likely to promote the business to others.

Examples of loyalty programmes of this type include Family Mart's membership programme, IKEA Family, Sephora Beauty Insiders and Starbucks Rewards.

COALITION PROGRAMMES

These programmes are consolidated single platforms that benefit several companies. In addition to some retailers, airlines (frequent flyer programmes) and co-branded credit cards often adopt this kind of loyalty programme. It is easier and faster for consumers to earn points compared to proprietary programmes since coalition programmes offer a wider assortment of incentives built around low-, medium- and high-frequency shopping partners. Moreover, the lower-cost structure of coalition programmes versus individual programmes enables retailers to pass those savings on to the customer with more attractive incentives.

From a retailer perspective, these programmes do not require heavy investment in their development and management, as they are not bespoke. However, companies have limited access to consumer data, and it is difficult to differentiate themselves from competitors, presenting challenges in driving customer loyalty. Examples of coalition programmes include Matas, Star Alliance and Upromise.

Leveraging consumer data: Personalized promotion and rewards

Fully 78 per cent of US online shoppers are more likely to shop with brands that provide better personalized experiences, according to a study from digital marketing company Avionos (2019). By analysing consumers' shopping behaviours using technologies such as artificial intelligence, companies can create specific promotions and rewards that resonate with their customers and therefore drive return on investment. For example, based on historical purchasing behaviour, the Starbucks Rewards programme offers discounts for customers on the beverage that they often order, as well as birthday rewards.

Loyalty programme best practices to improve customer experience

Loyalty programmes help retailers to elevate the customer experience if implemented effectively. Brands must therefore identify consumer pain points in the process of joining and using the programme in order to mitigate the risk of deterring sign-ups. We examine some best practice for retailers in offering loyalty programmes in Figure 13.1.

FIGURE 13.1 Loyalty programmes: best practice

Recogniton	• Advertise the loyalty program on all channels • Encourage customer referrals

Registration	• Make it easy to enroll on all channels • Clearly state the privacy rules of the programme

Reward and Redemption	• Offer relevant rewards and personalized offers • Provide real-time account activity and redemption information

SOURCE Coresight research

RECOGNITION

Retailers should promote their loyalty programme on both offline and online channels:

- Loyalty programme banners and signages should be highly visible in the brick-and-mortar store, and sales associates should be trained to pitch the programme to every customer.

- Offering a signup bonus or instant reward is the quickest way to attract customers to join the programme.

- Existing members can be incentivized to promote the loyalty programme by offering rewards for referrals.

- Retailers should announce the launch of their programme over email to existing subscribers, as well as on social media and through their official website to attract new customers.

REGISTRATION

Programme enrolment should be quick and easy for consumers, whether it is done online or offline. With data privacy being a priority for many consumers, it is important that retailers request only necessary information and inform consumers how they will use that information.

REWARDS AND REDEMPTION

As all loyalty programmes offer rewards, it is key for each retailer to differentiate itself in some way from its competitors. Rewards should be relevant and resonate with the brand's target consumers. Offering tiered membership and providing personalized offers also make loyal customers feel more appreciated.

Ensuring that rewards are reasonably attainable is important. According to a report from digital marketing solutions provider Merkle (formerly HelloWorld), top complaints for loyalty programmes include the long time it takes to earn a reward and the short expiration of reward points; retailers should offer achievable targets that keep loyalty programme members engaged on a regular basis, as well as rewards that would appeal to consumers and are redeemable in a reasonable timeframe (HelloWorld, 2019).

In addition, consumers expect a seamless reward accrual and redemption process. As part of this, retailers should provide loyalty programme members with real-time account information such as a record of purchase history and rewards earned.

Key trends in retail loyalty programmes

Retailers are evolving their loyalty programmes to better meet consumer expectations, such as through implementing upgrades and offering premium membership tiers. Below, we discuss key trends that we are seeing in the loyalty programme market.

PREMIUM MEMBERSHIP ON THE RISE, BUT TIERED LOYALTY PROGRAMMES WILL CONTINUE TO BE POPULAR

Premium loyalty programmes are those for which customers have to pay a fee in exchange for access to exclusive discounts, and according to loyalty programme specialist Clarus Commerce, these programmes usually target the top 20 per cent of a retailer's customers (Caporaso, 2018).

The key driver behind a consumer's decision to join a premium loyalty programme is a clear recognition of value that the programme offers. According to Clarus Commerce's 2020 Premium Loyalty Data Study (2020), 70 per cent of consumers would join a premium loyalty programme if a preferred retailer offered one and the benefits were valuable. Moreover, almost 70 per cent of premium loyalty programme members in the US indicated that they would join another premium loyalty programme in 2020.

The same study found that strong premium loyalty programmes can be effective in warding off competition. Around 87 per cent of consumers who are satisfied with the benefits offered by a paid loyalty programme of their favourite retailers will likely choose that retailer over a competitor even if the latter offers a lower price, according to the study (Clarus Commerce, 2020). Such consumers are also more likely to recommend the brand to their families and friends.

More retailers are offering paid membership options that provide a superior experience for customers. With access to better and exclusive benefits, paid members tend to be more committed to the brand and engage more frequently. According to a McKinsey survey on loyalty programmes, paid loyalty programme members are 60 per cent more likely to spend more on a brand after subscribing, while free loyalty programme members are only 30 per cent more likely to increase spending on the brand (Boudet et al, 2020). The membership fee also provides an additional stream of income for retailers to fund the programme's operating budget.

However, it is also advantageous for retailers to offer a free programme for the other 80 per cent of their customer base. A free loyalty programme enables a low barrier to entry, which makes it easier for retailers to acquire new members. However, basic/free programmes can fail to provide sufficient benefits that are deemed valuable enough by consumers or drive true engagement among members. Offering a clear path for members to access greater benefits is a way to overcome this challenge – and this can be done through tiered loyalty programmes.

Tier-based programmes encourage customers to increase spending and engagement so as to reach the next level or avoiding dropping to a lower level; customers are prepared to keep spending to avoid losing valued privileges. Tiered loyalty programmes should aim to create more targeted experiences through segmentation and targeted communication. These programmes typically keep customers engaged over a longer period of time and give members that reach a new tier a sense of achievement, encouraging them to keep aiming for the next level.

Beauty retailers Sephora and Ulta Beauty are examples of retailers that run tiered loyalty programmes, which we outline in Figure 13.2.

LOYALTY PROGRAMMES ARE INCREASINGLY BEING INTEGRATED INTO MOBILE APPS

Mobile apps are an effective tool for driving user engagement and enhancing the customer experience, as retailers can send push notifications of promotions and personalized marketing to customers.

Retailers can boost omnichannel shopping via mobile apps by utilizing mobile location functionality to offer information and promotions regarding a specific physical store when a customer is nearby. Loyalty programme

FIGURE 13.2 Tiered loyalty programmes: comparison of Ulta Beauty's Ultamate Rewards and Sephora's Beauty Insider

	Ultamate Rewards	Beauty Insider
Year of Launch	The Club at Ulta, the predecessor to Ultamate Rewards, was launched in 1995 and was replaced by the current program in 2014	2007
Number of Members	32 million (as of December 2020)	25 million (as of June 2020)
Membership Tiers	**Basic:** Free	**Insider:** Free
	Platinum: $500 in annual spending	**VIB:** $350 in annual spending
	Diamond: $1,200 in annual spending	**Rouge:** $1,000 in annual spending
Points Earned	**Basic:** one point per $1.00 spent	**Insider:** one point per $1.00 spent
	Platinum: 1.25 points per $1.00 spent	**VIB:** 1.25 points per $1.00 spent
	Diamond: 1.50 points per $1.00 spent	**Rouge:** 1.50 points per $1.00 spent
Points Expiration	For Basic members, points expire at the end of the calendar quarter following the 12-month anniversary of the date when the points were earned by the member; for Platinum and Diamond members, points never expire	All unredeemed points expire if customers do not engage with point activity associated with their purchase for 12 months
Basic Member Benefits	Birthday gift: 2x bonus points in birthday month	Birthday gift, seasonal savings, $15/year for two-day shipping
Higher-Tier Member Benefits	**Platinum:** birthday gift—2x bonus points during birthday month, $10 birthday coupon	**VIB:** birthday gift or points, seasonal savings, $15/year for two-day shipping
	Diamond: birthday gift—2x bonus points during birthday month, $10 birthday coupon; free shipping on orders over $25; annual $25 beauty-services rewards card	**Rouge:** birthday gift or points, seasonal savings, free two-day shipping, early access to products and exclusive events and $100 Rouge reward in exchange for the redemption of 2,500 points

SOURCE Coresight Research, company reports

apps therefore enable users to receive instant updates on purchases, personalized offers and rewards – as well as providing a smoother checkout process, with many retailers offering in-app payment options.

There are a number of retailers that have implemented loyalty programmes through an app. We present a few examples below.

- 7-Eleven launched its 7Rewards points programme on its mobile app in 2015 with a reward of a free drink after a customer purchases six drinks. The retailer subsequently expanded the programme in 2017 to enable customers to earn reward points for hundreds more 7-Eleven product purchases. In December 2020 the retailer launched the 7-Eleven Wallet app through which users can access touchless payment and loyalty offers. As a bonus, the retailer is currently offering 2,000 7Rewards points to first-time users when they load $20 into their 7-Eleven Wallet, for a limited time.

- Casey's General Stores announced the launch of its first loyalty programme, Casey's Rewards, in January 2020. The programme uses the retailer's app, which it updated in July 2019, as a central part of the programme in order to create a seamless experience for its customers.

- Home Depot updated its loyalty programme app for home-improvement professionals in October 2020, adding gamification features. Members of the Pro Xtra programme can earn points when shopping at Home Depot and redeem perks through the app. The app offers members greater transparency into the loyalty programme and enables them to avoid the inconvenience of carrying membership cards and key fobs that could wear out or get damaged easily.

GAMIFICATION IS BECOMING MORE INTEGRAL TO LOYALTY PROGRAMMES

Gamification in loyalty programmes encourages recurring behaviour, incentivizes specific actions, spurs engagement beyond transactions and offers a more fun and memorable customer experience.

Consumers across age groups in the US are showing growing affinity toward gamified programmes. According to Merkle's 2019 Loyalty Barometer Report focused on US consumers, almost one-third of all participants – and 40 per cent of Millennials – said that there should be games within loyalty programmes (HelloWorld, 2019). Additionally, 80 per cent of Millennials and almost two-thirds of baby boomers are interested in gaining rewards not just for purchases but also for engaging with their favourite brands.

- Luxury cosmetics company Lancôme offers reward points to consumers for social sharing and brand advocacy.

- Home Depot introduced gamification features (including bonus rewards) to its loyalty programme app in October 2020 to encourage repeat store visits and drive purchases as members track their advancement to the next reward level.

- Victoria's Secret created an app in September 2018 which the brand integrated with its PINK Nation customer loyalty programme. Users could gain points for signing up to the 'Fashion Show Sweeps' contest, giving them the opportunity to win a trip to the Victoria's Secret Fashion Show. Users could gain additional points by sharing the promotion on Facebook and playing daily trivia games. Apart from gathering a lot of customer data, the promotion led to increased visits and more participation on the website, according to the company.

Other examples of retailers that gamified parts of their loyalty programmes to drive longer-term usage include CVS Pharmacy and Wendy's.

Retailers are increasingly recognizing that including gamification elements in loyalty programmes is an effective way to drive sales and boost consumer engagement. We expect to see more brands and retailers adopting this approach.

PERSONALIZATION WILL HAVE A GREATER ROLE TO PLAY WITHIN LOYALTY PROGRAMMES

Loyalty programmes are becoming more digitally focused and tailored, giving consumers relevant and personalized offers in real time. According to global marketing firm Epsilon (2018), 80 per cent of US consumers are more likely to make a purchase when brands offer personalized experiences.

Introducing new loyalty offers for consumers without appropriate personalization and segmentation of those offers runs the risk of the promotions being irrelevant to the consumer.

One obvious example of implementing personalization through loyalty programmes is in email marketing campaigns. Blender manufacturer and retailer Vitamix sends a monthly email to its loyalty club members with information about the customer's total points earned over time, overall spending over time and total redeemable points, as well as relevant reward offers. According to the company, this strategy attracts more customers to its e-commerce site to redeem their rewards. The retailer launched its loyalty programme in June 2019 and as of August 2020 had almost 120,000 loyalty club members.

Another example is home-furnishings brand Jonathan Adler, which hosted an online event exclusively to its loyalty club members. The brand sent each of its loyalty programme members a private code that could be entered on its website to access the event. Members who made eligible purchases gained 1,000 loyalty points, amounting to $100 off.

USE OF NFTS AS REWARDS

The popularity of NFTs has increased significantly over the past two years. We expect loyalty programmes to take advantage of this avenue to interact and engage with tech-savvy global audiences. We believe that NFTs will become an increasingly common feature in loyalty programmes going forward.

In October 2021 Estée Lauder-owned beauty brand Clinique started offering NFTs to drive loyalty and add marketing weight to its top products. With this new strategy of modernizing loyalty programmes, Clinique is offering reward points in the form of its first NFT, called MetaOptimist, to its Smart Reward members. Along with the NFT, Smart Reward members will also receive an assortment of Clinique products each year for the next decade. Carolyn Dawkins, Senior Vice President of Clinique Global Online, Consumer Engagement and Product Marketing, stated that 'In the world of NFTs, brand authenticity and consumer excitement are critical, and we think our approach really delivers. These NFTs are a uniquely contemporary way to celebrate loyalty and put our consumers in the driver's seat, with storytelling and engagement at its core' (Weinswig, 2021).

Canada-based customer loyalty rewards platform Drop launched Superpower, its first NFT rewards programme, in January 2022. The startup ran a contest through which it gave away $25,000 in Drop and Amazon NFTs to participants. Some members also earned limited-edition NFTs and received a 10 per cent cashback offer on all Amazon purchases.

> Companies can issue their own tokens as part of a crypto-based loyalty programme – a 'perfect flywheel effect' will see a two-sided market of buyers and sellers rewarded.
>
> Sanja Kon, CEO, Utrust (2021)

Loyalty implications for brands/retailers

Customer loyalty programmes are an effective way for brands and retailers to increase customer lifetime value and thus enhance the top line and achieve sustainable growth. Retail organizations are focusing on adopting customer-centric initiatives to drive their top line. Attractive loyalty programmes foster consumer value and improve retention rates, driving incremental business growth. Brands and retailers should keep the following principles in mind as they create their own loyalty programmes:

- Basic/free programmes can fail to provide sufficient benefits that are deemed valuable enough by consumers or drive true engagement among members. Offering a clear path for members to access greater benefits is a way to overcome this challenge – and this can be done through tiered loyalty programmes.

- Retailers should look to introduce or improve the gamification and personalization elements in their loyalty programmes to enhance the overall efficacy of the programmes, both in driving sales and boosting engagement.
- Retailers should invest in improving the mobile app-based loyalty programme experience that they offer to their consumers, ensuring that the benefits, rewards and experience on offer stand out against those offered by competitors.

Using technology to innovate loyalty programmes

New startup technology companies are increasingly focusing on the loyalty space by creating new and innovative ways for retailers to develop engaging loyalty programmes that connect on mobile, create attractive programmes for consumers, gamify the process and tap into leading trends such as the Metaverse.

Below we will profile some of these global startups and explore how they are working with retailers to offer innovative customer loyalty platforms. We have identified 29 startups across five categories:

- blockchain loyalty programmes
- cashback loyalty programmes
- gaming loyalty programmes
- personalized loyalty programmes
- tiered loyalty programmes

Blockchain loyalty programmes

Blockchain loyalty companies are helping retail players to enhance their loyalty offerings using blockchain-enabled technology. Examples of these types of startups include:

- US-based startup Aetsoft is a blockchain automation consulting company. It helps brands to offer blockchain-enabled tokens as rewards.

FIGURE 13.3 Customer loyalty programmes ecosystem

RETAIL-TECH LANDSCAPE: CUSTOMER LOYALTY PROGRAMMES

PERSONALIZED LOYALTY PROGRAMMES

9minds	PErx
App Card	Swiftly
Bonat	wlamoo
Loyalize	zeal

BLOCKCHAIN LOYALTY PROGRAMMES

aetsoft	KomChain
digitalbits	loyyal
fidly	myntcoinz
gft	qiibee

TIERED LOYALTY PROGRAMMES

antavo	novus loyalty
BAYIQ	yotpo
kangaroo	

CASHBACK LOYALTY PROGRAMMES

bitback	bon	Cashback App
gainon	HappyCredit	thank u cash

GAMIFIED LOYALTY PROGRAMMES

PugPharm
Unotag
Untie Nots

SOURCE Coresight Research

- Digitalbits, a US-based startup, focuses on enhancing the loyalty and rewards industry through its flexible blockchain technology. It allows businesses to tokenize its blockchain reward points into secured, transferable and tradable points. Customers can easily trade these digital points on Digitalbits blockchain for hotel points or airline points.

- French startup Fidly offers blockchain technology in the customer loyalty industry. It provides consumers the option to convert loyalty points into crypto assets or fiat currency in a secure digital wallet.

- Gft Exchange is a US-based blockchain optimized marketplace that allows retailers and brands to develop, distribute and settle coupons, rebates and rewards.

- KornChain is a UK-based startup focused on creating a blockchain-based global loyalty points exchange marketplace called LoyalT. The company is currently working to onboard a variety of small and medium-size businesses in more than 20 countries to create new options for loyalty members.

- Loyyal is a US-based blockchain solution provider that helps businesses to set up their own loyalty and rewards programme. The company utilizes blockchain and smart contract technology to reduce costs of setting up and operating a loyalty programme.

- US-based MyntCoinz is a blockchain-as-a-service platform for loyalty and rewards. The startup operates a blockchain ecosystem that helps its clients to trade digital loyalty tokens as a subscription service.

- Qiibee is a Switzerland-based software startup that helps brands to operate their loyalty reward programmes on blockchain. The company focuses on unifying all loyalty programmes under one platform, offering multiple options to customers for redeeming their loyalty points.

Cashback loyalty programmes

Cashback loyalty programme companies are helping retailers to launch instant cashback programmes for customers. These include:

- Canada-based Bitback is a cashback reward platform that connects people across Africa. The company allows users to earn cashback for every purchase from selected retailers on their Bitback app.

- Founded in 2020, Bonaz offers online shopping cashback services to users based in Azerbaijan and Turkey.

- Africa-based startup CashbackApp! allows users to get cash discounts on myriad household products at supermarkets in Kenya, helping fast-moving consumer goods (FMCG) brands to build loyalty. The company secured funding of $475,000 during its pre-seed round in August 2021.

- Gainon is an Indian startup that offers instant loyalty cashback to users on every successful payment transaction. According to the company, it has registered more than 100 leading brands and has more than 10,000 members on its platform.

- HappyCredit is an Indian cashback startup that was founded in October 2020. In 2021, the company launched its cashback reward programme Aishback, wherein users can get instant cashback on their purchases sent directly to their linked bank accounts.

- ThankUCash is a US-based rewards and loyalty programme platform setup for businesses and banks operating in Africa. It enables its customers to earn cash rewards for every offline and online transaction.

Gaming loyalty programmes

Gamified loyalty programmes are helping retailers to introduce gamification into loyalty programmes to boost consumer engagement, including:

- PugPharm is a Canada-based startup that operates as a customer loyalty and engagement technology provider. The company's gamification platform Picnic was launched in 2014. The technology platform delivers engagement, motivation, rewards and item-based gameplay to its users.

- Indian-based startup UnoTag helps companies to build gamified incentive programmes to motivate employees to improve their performance. Launched in 2018, the startup has raised $100,000 over the past four years.

- French startup Untie Nots offers AI-enabled loyalty and promotion solutions to brands and retailers. The startup allows retailers to offer individual, gamified loyalty challenges to their customers with personalized rewards.

Personalized loyalty programmes

Personalized loyalty programme companies are enabling retailers to curate personalized loyalty programmes for customers based on their profiles and habits and offer personalized offers and discounts. Examples of these include:

- 99-minds is a US-based startup that allows businesses to generate customized offers and loyalty programmes for users.

- US-based Appcard helps brick-and-mortar retailers to build customized loyalty programmes for their customers. The company's AppCard reward programme offers retailers useful customer insights along with item-level transaction data.

- Bonat offers retailers and brands a fully automated and customizable loyalty and reward platform. It also provides an advanced system that collects customer feedback and reviews.

- Loyalize is a London-based customer engagement platform that operates in the banking segment. It allows banks and financial institutions to offer customized loyalty programmes to their customers.

- Perx Rewards operates as a loyalty and rewards software-as-a-service (SaaS) platform. The highly customizable platform allows organizations to offer incentive-based programmes for organizations of all sizes.

- US-based technology solution provider Swiftly offers digital solutions to retailers and e-commerce players. The startup's loyalty programme platform allows retailers to build customized offers and reward programmes for customers.

- Walmoo offers a loyalty-as-a-service (LaaS) and interaction-as-a-service (IaaS) platform for organizations. It helps businesses build and implement customizable, simple to use and affordable loyalty programmes.

- Zeal Rewards is a UK-based digital loyalty platform that offers personalized rewards to customers based on customer data insights. The UK-based startup has secured more than $100,000 funding since its inception in February 2019.

Tiered loyalty programmes

Tiered loyalty programme companies are offering tiered loyalty programme platform for retailers wherein customers can unlock new levels by spending, and engaging more with the business. Some of these global companies include:

- Antavo offers customer loyalty technology solutions that allows retailers and brands to set up tiered loyalty programmes for their customers. Consumers can earn loyalty points whenever they engage with a retailer through social media content, referrals, product reviews or by making purchases. Customers can unlock new levels and get additional benefits such as access to special discounts, invitations to events and free shipping with their accumulated loyalty points.

- BayIQ offers a loyalty platform primarily for the tyre and automotive repair industry. The startup provides a tiered loyalty programme wherein customers can collect points whenever they pay for services. Based on the number of points accumulated, customers can unlock new levels. At each level, customers receive higher benefits, including better discounts on services. These points can also be redeemed for further services based on customers' convenience.

- Kangaroo Rewards is a Canadian customer loyalty solution provider. The technology firm helps businesses to improve customer engagement by offering rewards points, dollar discounts and benefits to customers who shop, spend and engage more.

- Novus Loyalty offers end-to-end loyalty solutions to businesses. It helps retailers to develop and manage tier-based loyalty programmes with incremental rewards available to customers when they reach higher levels.

- yotpo. is a US-based e-commerce platform that helps direct-to-consumer brands to expand and improve their businesses. The technology firm offers multiple solutions, including consultative services for deployment and customer analytics.

INTERVIEW
Diane Randolph, Board Member/Retired CIO (2022)

Diane has deep expertise as a retail technology professional. She was previously the CIO of Ulta Beauty, and currently serves on the board of directors/advisers to of several retail and technology companies, including Shoe Carnival, Flexe, MyPlanet and Newmine.

Diane views the near-total adoption of omnichannel retail by consumers as the most significant change to the retail industry in the past few years, which was dramatically accelerated by the pandemic. Covid forced people who had only interacted in the physical channel to utilize the digital channel. Since the pandemic, many people have returned to in-store shopping, but a large majority of consumers have switched to shopping both online and offline. And as a result, consumers' expectations of a seamless shopping experience are now paramount.

Retailers now need to make sure that their e-commerce experience is very efficient for transacting, but it also needs to serve as an information source and as a community. Consumers should be educated about products when they are shopping on the digital channel, just like a salesperson would educate them in store. In fact, brands and retailers are now so good at adding education to their e-commerce experience that retailers are struggling to ensure that the same level of education filters down to every salesperson in every store.

Diane tells us that innovation in retail is much more important now than it was in the past. Every retailer is now looking for speed and agility and how they can differentiate themselves. And as a result, retailers are increasingly becoming involved with technology companies at the forefront of this innovation, with some retailers acquiring or investing in these companies and some simply wanting to partner and learn from them. And, while most retailers had an innovation mindset when it came to product, it now extends through the entire organization, including technology, process and business models. This new focus on speed is partially driven by the rapid changes in consumer demand, and partly by the speed of technological improvements.

One key area that Diane sees changing is the advent of personalization and loyalty. Consumers are becoming more and more sensitive to privacy rights, and it is important for retailers to not violate their consumers' trust. At Ulta Beauty, for example, approximately 95 per cent of its sales were to loyal customers. With high levels of loyal customers, it is even more crucial for brands to make sure they get loyalty and personalization right.

Diane's most important advice to retailers and brands as they consider how to integrate technology and innovation into their business is to *ensure consistency of the customer experience*. In most well-run retail stores with qualified sales associates, you as the consumer feel warm and cared for. The consumer should feel that same level of warmth and care when they shop online – through the entire cycle of their customer journey, down to the product delivery and after-sales service. By being able to interact with consumers throughout this journey, brands and retailers have new opportunities afforded to them to surprise and delight their customers.

But Diane cautions: do not sacrifice brand DNA to speed. Many people equate innovation to speed. But if you innovate without the brand DNA in mind, you can go very wrong. The brand needs to feel consistent to customers across all touchpoints. Innovation must be done in an authentic way that is congruent with brand principles and personality and reaches the customer in the manner and tone that they have come to expect from your brand.

TEN THINGS RETAILERS NEED TO KNOW ABOUT LOYALTY

1   Retailers can choose whether to offer a proprietary loyalty programme or a coalition loyalty programme – each has its own advantages and disadvantages.

2   Some consumers value premium loyalty programmes, allowing retailers to differentiate levels of benefits and service for consumers who are willing to pay for enhanced loyalty rewards.

3   Loyalty gamification is an ideal way to more actively engage consumers.

4   Personalization can be improved with loyalty programmes, elevating the consumer experience.

5   NFTs and the Metaverse are being increasingly woven into loyalty programmes.

6   A wide variety of innovators are emerging in the loyalty space – retailers should look to these startups for new and innovative ways to enhance their loyalty programmes.

7   Loyal customers are a key asset for retailers – companies should be careful to maintain their trust and commitment to the brand.

8   Getting customer loyalty right is more important for retailers than ever before.

9   Retailers should look to blockchain for enhanced loyalty options.

10 The pace of technological change will continue to advance options for loyalty programmes – retailers should ensure they stay up to date on the latest loyalty technology.

KEY TAKEAWAYS: CUSTOMER LOYALTY PROGRAMMES

As the retail and consumer brand industry increasingly shifts to a direct-to-customer model, all brands and retailers should be examining their customer loyalty programme to ensure that they are in line with consumer preferences, data privacy laws and retailer best practices. Key takeaways from this chapter on customer loyalty programmes include:

•   Customer loyalty is more important than ever, with loyal customers tending to spend more and stay with brands longer.

- Retailers can develop their own proprietary loyalty programme, or they can join a coalition loyalty programme to take advantage of existing infrastructure.

- Loyalty programme best practices include: recognition, registration and reward redemption.

- Retailers should ensure that they are addressing key trends in the loyalty market, such as mobile app integration, gamification and NFTs.

- There is a wide array of new startups across the globe helping retailers to enhance their loyalty programmes with the use of new technology.

References

AT Kearney (2018) Realize the full potential of your customer loyalty programme. www.kearney.com/strategy-and-top-line-transformation/article/-/insights/realize-the-full-potential-of-your-customer-loyalty-program (archived at perma.cc/7RUS-E3BZ)

Avionos (2019) *Shoppers Demand Superior Ecommerce Experiences*. www.avionos.com/wp-content/uploads/2019/06/Avionos_B2C_Datareportv3.3.pdf (archived at perma.cc/QZ9K-HYAZ)

Boudet, J, Huang, J and von Difloe, R (2020) Coping with the big switch: How paid loyalty programmes can help bring consumers back to your brand, AT Kearney. www.mckinsey.com/business-functions/growth-marketing-and-sales/our-insights/coping-with-the-big-switch-how-paid-loyalty-programs-can-help-bring-consumers-back-to-your-brand (archived at perma.cc/PY2Y-6ND5)

Brown, P, Burns, T, Harris, T, Lucas, C and Zizaoui, I (2022) The rise of the inclusive consumer, McKinsey & Company. www.mckinsey.com/industries/retail/our-insights/the-rise-of-the-inclusive-consumer (archived at perma.cc/9ETP-2RCY)

Caporaso, T (2018) How the 80/20 rule applies to premium loyalty, Nasdaq. www.nasdaq.com/articles/how-the-80-20-rule-applies-to-premium-loyalty-2018-09-27 (archived at perma.cc/7CGC-NVDX)

Clarus Commerce (2020) *What Do Your Customers Expect in 2020?* Rocky Hill. www.claruscommerce.com/wp-content/uploads/2020/06/clarus-commerce-premium-loyalty-data-study-2020-web.pdf (archived at perma.cc/DS9K-R8TR)

Epsilon (2018) New Epsilon research indicates 80% of consumers are more likely to make a purchase when brands offer personalized experiences. www.epsilon.com/us/about-us/pressroom/new-epsilon-research-indicates-80-of-consumers-are-more-likely-to-make-a-purchase-when-brands-offer-personalized-experiences (archived at perma.cc/M9TE-9JLU)

HelloWorld (2019) 2019 loyalty barometer report: What consumers think of loyalty and reward programmes, Merkle. www.merkle.com/thought-leadership/white-papers/2019-loyalty-barometer-report (archived at perma.cc/QA5V-MF2W)

Randolph, D (2022) Interview with the authors.

Weinswig, D (2021) Loyalty programs: How can US retailers drive growth and engagement? Coresight Research. https://coresight.com/research/loyalty-programs-how-can-us-retailers-drive-growth-and-engagement/ (archived at perma.cc/JG8D-8BE7)

14

Headless commerce

WHAT IS HEADLESS E-COMMERCE?

At the dawn of the e-commerce sector, most e-commerce players built their own platforms (such as Amazon and Pets.com). Then, full-stack/integrated platforms such as Shopify entered the space, offering off-the-shelf solutions to new and smaller entrants, while enterprise players such as Salesforce Commerce Cloud and SAP provided more customized, costly solutions for larger players. Now, a new segment has emerged and is rapidly growing: commerce-as-a-service (CaaS). This segment builds on the increasingly modular nature of the broader online space and is enabled by the decentralized nature of the cloud.

CaaS offers new/smaller retailers and brands the ability to both spin up a new e-commerce site with speed and efficiency as well as quickly customize the back end (data access and processing layer) and front end (presentation layer, containing user interface) of the site, including extending/integrating the site's front end outside of the base website (into social media, blogs, etc.).

E-commerce had been gradually gaining share of the total US retail market prior to Covid-19, but the pandemic-led acceleration saw online sales reach a high of $222 billion in the fourth quarter of 2020 – representing online penetration of 20.1 per cent – according to Coresight Research analysis of US Census Bureau data (Weinswig, 2021). In the third quarter of 2021 e-commerce penetration stood at 17.0 per cent (Weinswig, 2021).

While older and/or larger players already had the infrastructure in place to expand and capitalize on consumer-driven tailwinds, smaller players have been limited in their ability to innovate. We believe that by leveraging CaaS solutions these companies can build the infrastructure needed to effectively and quickly adapt and scale. Such solutions also enable retail teams to remain focused on core strategies, which is critical in the ever-changing environment – macroeconomically, technologically and within retail.

The impact of, and response to, Covid-19

The recent widespread consumer shift to the online channel presented e-commerce sales opportunities. However, retailers had to adapt quickly to the pandemic-led disruption, and many measures they put in place negatively impacted margins – such as increased costs around personal protective equipment and socially distant scheduling reducing relative productivity. In addition, some companies may have seen a shift in sales to low-price/low-margin items, even if sales volumes did not decline. In a Coresight survey of 153 e-commerce leaders (Weinswig, 2021), two-thirds (67 per cent) of respondents reported that Covid-19 caused a moderately or highly negative impact on margin.

Many retailers made changes to their e-commerce operations in response to Covid-19: 56 per cent of respondents to the Coresight survey reported that their organizations found ways to reduce shipping costs – making it the most widespread operational adjustment. This change was likely necessary as retailers rapidly scaled up e-commerce operations and invested in logistics/delivery services to meet stronger consumer demand for shorter fulfilment times, as well as being driven by the need to stand out against other online players offering competitive delivery options.

In addition, with the absence of more traditional offline ways to reach consumers, 52 per cent of survey respondents said that their businesses looked for alternative ways to drive sales, and 44 per cent began moving part of their offline business online.

From offline to omnichannel and beyond: The evolution of commerce

Commerce infrastructure and strategy continue to evolve both online and in the brick-and-mortar channel. We highlight the five key types of commerce in Figure 14.1 and explore the evolution of retail in more detail.

At the dawn of the internet age, over 20 years ago, companies such as Pets.com, eBay and, of course, Amazon, sought to disrupt the traditional retail space by offering a less capital-intensive (no stores) and more accessi-

FIGURE 14.1 The evolution of retail

	Offline Commerce	Bespoke E-Commerce	Platform-Enabled E-Commerce	Omnichannel Commerce	Decentralized Commerce
Core Strategy	By offering an optimal selection for the target segment and a superior in-store experience, these retailers create repeat customers who subsidize the high cost of operations (labour, land, etc.)	By leveraging access to the internet, retailers can access and target a broader base of customers with a more varied set of products, delivered through a self/partner-built infrastructure	While commerce platforms take care of online operations, retailers can focus on effectively delivering the right products to their customers	By consolidating back-end operations and optimizing the offline/online customer experience, retailers can provide a more consistent experience while keeping costs down	By fragmenting the commerce stack, platforms provide retailers (large and small) greater flexibility in how to reach, sell to and deliver to customers, as well as to scale
Key Player	Walmart	Amazon	Shopify	Target	Emerging (newer players include BigCommerce, Nogin)
Key Innovations/ Enablers	• POS • Back-end software	• Internet access • Online payments	• Cloud • Search • Social media	• Smartphones/ apps • Centralized data/systems	• APIs • Decentralized data/systems

ble (online) shopping experience, with a potentially larger selection of items. Building up these websites took significant time and investment, as they were built from scratch (in the absence of the current landscape of tools and cloud infrastructure). Many of these companies, like Pets.com, went bust when the late 1990s internet bubble burst, funding ran out and they could not pay off their debts.

As the e-commerce space evolved, players started to emerge to provide support for various aspects of e-commerce (PayPal and others for the payments side, for example), culminating in the full-stack offering of Shopify and other e-commerce platforms, offering a quick and easy solution for retailers to spin up a website and online sales operations. These platforms, while user-friendly, did limit retailers to a locked-in set of features emulating a 'traditional' e-commerce store (comprising a storefront, catalogue of items, shopping cart and purchase functionality).

Around the same time, offline retailers made investments to move further online; a little later, they made concerted efforts to better merge these operations, particularly in the back end (infrastructure, warehousing, supply chain, data) to achieve the particular synergies that came from operating in an omnichannel manner. The embedded, generally immutable nature of these companies' existing IT systems required them to typically extend these operations online, bringing large enterprise players such as Salesforce and SAP more directly into e-commerce. The fragmented e-commerce landscape therefore became a more centralized, standardized space, which worked to accelerate market growth overall but also reduced the ability for individual players to innovate and break out of the shell.

However, enabled by tools such as the cloud, the commerce stack has recently evolved toward decentralization, as retailers look to better reach and serve their consumers (decentralized here meaning a system built up of and driven by disparate components instead of being dictated to/guided by one central system). With the use of standard application programming interfaces (APIs) and consistent underlying architectures, retailers building their e-commerce operations on decentralized platforms have the ability to further innovate to compete directly and indirectly with larger players, while accelerating their own development with more agile research and development (R&D) and operational tools.

The e-commerce infrastructure market landscape

We see five types of e-commerce platforms in the infrastructure market:

- *Proprietary:* Proprietary solutions are home-grown platforms that are built internally and highly tailored/customized to the core, with original products and strategy – as implemented by Amazon, for example.

- *Simple DIY*: An off-the-shelf offering provides smaller retailers with a full-stack solution that allows for a range of basic to more advanced e-commerce functionality, but generally limits the retailer to the capabilities and foundations of a third-party offering, with less ability to expand outside the core. The largest player in this segment continues to be Shopify, although other players such as Wix and Weebly compete in this space.

- *Enterprise*: Sophisticated, typically costly enterprise solutions are built with a key, larger partner and are typically deployed by large multinational companies. Legacy market leaders include Salesforce, Adobe and SAP.

- *Modular/headless*: This newer model separates the back end from the front end but allows for integration/flexibility through APIs. Headless solutions are built through numerous third-party vendor offerings. Emerging players in the space include ElasticPath, CommerceTool and Skava.

- *CaaS*: This is another new model that offers greater separation between the front and back ends with different capabilities/functions. This provides retailers with the flexibility to innovate and expand but also more standardization/consistency due to greater ownership/integration of the stack through a single CaaS vendor. Emerging players in the space include Nogin, BigCommerce and Cart.

Interestingly, the largest retailers (those with revenues of $150 million or above) are already deploying more decentralized CaaS solutions (75 per cent) or modular/headless technology (25 per cent), according to the Coresight survey (Weinswig, 2021). Unsurprisingly, smaller retailers are still leveraging legacy proprietary, DIY and enterprise solutions, with no companies with under $50 million in revenue deploying modular commerce or CaaS solutions. Meanwhile, mid-size retailers are leveraging and experimenting with a greater variety of solutions.

The adoption of decentralized solutions, CaaS in particular, among larger retailers indicates that e-commerce infrastructure is evolving to prioritize flexibility, scale and innovation.

In Figure 14.2 we summarize how different facets of e-commerce infrastructure, ranging from development, platform/maintenance, marketing/conversion, site/purchasing to delivery/operations work in different e-commerce platform types.

Why should retailers move to headless commerce?

The Coresight survey shows that there is room for improvement in e-commerce infrastructure: at least 3 in 10 respondents reported that they are not satisfied with any outcomes of their existing platforms/solutions (Weinswig, 2021).

FIGURE 14.2 How e-commerce platforms work

	Development		Platform/Maintenance		Marketing/Conversion		Site/Purchasing		Delivery/Operations		
	Research and Development	Back-end platform and systems integration	Platform hardware, software and hosting	Platform annual maintenance	Marketing and analytics	Front-end customer/user experience	Payments and merchant services	Platform per-transaction fees	Fulfilment (pick, pack, storage)	Freight (shipping and returns)	Customer service
Proprietary Solution — Amazon	Architecture and systems potentially leveraging some online tools (cloud, etc.) but generally built internally, with full customization of the back end				Separate marketing operations, with some sync on branding/messaging		Home-built, customized operations and interface, with partner modules for high-risk functionality (payments, sensitive data)		Sellers usually work with third-party logistics partners, typically lowest cost/best fit		
DIY Solution — Shopify	Ongoing R&D produce improvement in platform	Out-of-box developed by solution provider; no customization for a seller; consistent back-end platform operations			Sellers typically work separate agencies/solution providers		Shell interface with front-end customization allowed within platform constraints		Sellers typically work with third-party logistics partners, sometimes referred by solution provider		
Enterprise Solution — Magenta	Most/all R&D conducted internally, with some development outsourced, as needed, to specialists	Architecture developed by solution provider; high level of customization for a seller including back-end platform operations			Sophisticated CRM likely in place; integrated with high-end marketing/analytics		Customized front-end that likely leverages best practices and techniques form top consumer sites		Partner and/or build operations to minimize costs and maximize positive experience		
Modular/Headless — elasticpath		Architecture developed by solution provider incorporating API flexibility to allow for more dynamic systems building			Sellers typically work with separate agencies/solution providers		Flexible front-end with numerous possibilities/configurations to allow for and test different go-to-market models		Sellers typically work with third-party logistics partners, sometimes referred by solution provider		
CaaS Solution — nogin	Ongoing R&D produce improvement in platform	Out-of-the-box offering developed by solution provider; limited customization for a seller; modular back-end platform operations			Individual/integrated solution modules developed; can easily be integrated with existing solutions/partner solutions as needed				Supporting solutions more closely integrated with modules, allowing for easier addition/expansion of operations		

Sourced to platform   Sourced to various third parties   Sourced internally

This indicates a clear opportunity for different point solutions (covering a particular capability/area of the stack) and integrated solutions to offer more value.

Of the outcomes the survey asked about, the ability to diagnose problems had the greatest satisfaction level (69 per cent of retailers rated this outcome 8, 9 or 10 out of 10 on a scale of satisfaction), followed by ensuring quality customer service and the ability to enhance brand strength (cited by 67 per cent of respondents). Increasing conversion and leveraging predictive analytics both fell to the bottom of the pack, with 39 per cent rating these outcomes at 7 or below.

The survey data show that retailers have incurred significant upfront costs when setting up their e-commerce operations, with a greater focus on infrastructure/back-end operations and R&D over front-end features. The front end, however, requires ongoing investment into development, expansion and improvements. Setting up key services such as logistics and payments also requires upfront investment.

Solutions that reduce or eliminate these upfront costs while rolling them into operating expenses could be valuable down the line, to allow for easier scaling and expansion.

Addressing the profitability of mid-size e-commerce players

Mid-size brands or retailers (companies with annual online revenues of between $5 million and $150 million) struggle to compete with e-commerce giants such as Amazon because they do not have a comparable amount of data or the funds to invest as heavily in technology and R&D.

Consumers now have enterprise-level commerce expectations – i.e. a seamless online shopping experience coupled with one-click checkout and fast, cheap/free shipment (associated with giants such as Amazon, Target and Walmart) – when interacting with mid-size brands/retailers, making it even more difficult for these mid-size businesses to maintain superior customer experiences. Many e-commerce companies try to play Amazon's game by offering heavy discounts and free shipping, which negatively impacts both the top and bottom lines – resulting in businesses often losing money in the online channel.

In this chapter we explore the levers of profitability in e-commerce business, how CaaS ensures profitability and growth for mid-size companies, and why mid-size brands and retailers should capitalize on AI, ML and predictive analytics. To set the context for the chapter, we lay out below a few key segments and their respective definitions:

- *Total mid-size*: The overall bracket, comprising companies with annual online revenue of $5 million to <$150 million.
- *Lower mid-size:* Annual online revenue of $5 million to <$50 million.
- *Intermediate mid-size*: Annual online revenue of $50 million to <$100 million.
- *Upper mid-size*: Annual online revenue of $100 million to <$150 million.

Overview of e-commerce costs

The issue of profitability can be analysed through the unit economics of e-commerce – the profit or loss per order (after deducting all variable costs) that contributes to overall business performance. It is therefore of paramount importance to understand the various costs involved in e-commerce, which we outline below.

Direct costs:

- *Platform hardware, software and hosting*: Costs relating to the infrastructure or build of an e-commerce solution.
- *Platform annual maintenance*: Costs around standard upgrades, security updates and tools to boost ongoing traffic growth.
- *Platform per-transaction fees*: The fees businesses pay to process customer payments.
- *Front-end customer experience*: Product, development and maintenance costs to guide and enhance shopper interactions (such as product detail pages and drop-down menus) as well as employee/merchant interactions (such as inventory, shipping and customer service).
- *Back-end platform and systems integration*: Product, development and maintenance costs required to manage the data access layer that holds products, orders and customer information.
- *Marketing and analytics capabilities*: Costs to set up, deploy and manage marketing campaigns (email, SEM, affiliates, paid media, etc.).
- *Customer service*: Costs associated with AI, email and phone support for webstore orders and follow-ups.

- *Payments and merchant services*: Costs associated with facilities handling electronic card transactions.
- *R&D capabilities*: Development costs to build new capabilities, features, optimizations and enhancements.
- *Fulfilment*: Costs associated with pick, pack and storage services.
- *Freight*: Costs associated with shipping and returns.

Hidden costs:

- *Incomplete/disjointed customer data/profiles*: Discounting more than necessary can be due to an incomplete view of a particular customer, caused by a lack of data or siloing of data that limits the ability to properly target and price (can be mitigated/improved with integrated data platforms). More integrated data platforms have led to 20 per cent less discounting with similar conversion rates, according to Nogin (2021).
- *Manual/standard approach to free shipping*: Taking a more manual and/or one-size-fits-all approach to shipping drives up costs and/or discounting without increasing sales. With data and AI, shipping costs can improve considerably, from 9 per cent of sales to 5 per cent, according to Nogin (2021).
- *Inconsistent approach to returns*: A lack of analysis and integrated data leads to 20 per cent greater returns, according to Nogin (2021).
- *'Traditional' merchandising/planning model*: A lack of data-driven planning leads to slow replenishment and excess inventory due to poor technology and fulfilment visibility. Brands and retailers will only make profits if they charge prices higher than the above costs combined and/or develop supplemental revenue sources (such as subscriptions and data monetization). The Coresight survey of e-commerce leaders found that 91 per cent of total mid-size retailers allocate 10 per cent or more of their annual spending on at least one of the above costs – and nearly half of all mid-size companies spend 10 per cent or more on platform hardware, software and hosting alone (Weinswig, 2021).

Brands and retailers will only make profits if they charge prices higher than the above costs combined and/or develop supplemental revenue sources (such as subscriptions and data monetization). The Coresight survey found that 91 per cent of total mid-size retailers allocate 10 per cent or more of their annual spending on at least one of the above costs – and nearly half of all mid-size companies spend 10 per cent or more on platform hardware, software and hosting alone (Weinswig, 2021).

Looking at the initial spend for the three platform-related fees, significant proportions of all mid-size companies will spend $100,000 or more, which is very high. Among all mid-size companies, 11 per cent reported that they initially spend $100,000 or more on platform hardware, software and hosting; 10 per cent initially spend $100,000 or more on platform annual maintenance; and 15 per cent initially spend $100,000 or more on first-year platform per-transaction fees (Weinswig, 2021).

While mid-size respondents indicated that operating the front-end customer experience does not account for a high share of annual total costs, front-end development likely requires upfront and ongoing investment into development, expansion and improvements. For many retailers, it is therefore important to choose build approaches that can bring lower upfront and ongoing platform-related costs, which tend to be higher in enterprise e-commerce platforms.

The costs of fulfilment and freight, which account for 10 per cent or more of total annual costs for low proportions of mid-size companies, can increase per shipment due to efforts to accelerate delivery times and/or offer lower-cost/free shipping. These initiatives can also add to operational expenditure by driving an increase in the number of orders delivered. It is therefore of little surprise that Kroger is fulfilling online grocery orders more efficiently through large, automated hubs operated by Ocado, a UK-based logistics technology company, according to a virtual investor conference in March 2021 (Weinswig, 2022). Fulfilment and shipping are areas in which many mid-size businesses can improve their cost structure. The combined costs for mid-size companies can be overwhelming, especially when competing with the enterprise businesses that have scale, like Kroger.

Last-mile fulfilment

Fulfilment is a longstanding barrier to profitability in online retailing. As a variable cost, fulfilment expenses rise as sales increase – unlike store-based costs, which are largely fixed. Compounding this challenge, shoppers have come to expect ever faster and more convenient, yet inexpensive, shipping, placing the financial burdens of delivery largely on the shoulders of retailers. For retailers without stores to leverage as collection points, home delivery brings higher costs than in-store pickup. For example, Target has claimed that it is about 90 per cent cheaper on average when a customer picks up an online order in one of its stores versus the retailer shipping the item to their home (Weinswig, 2022). It is not surprising that, besides Target, retailers such as Best Buy and Dick's Sporting Goods have also turned stores into mini warehouses and touted curbside pickup in order to save on shipping costs. In fact, the Coresight e-commerce survey found that among currently profitable mid-size retailers, 13 per cent cited last-mile fulfilment costs as a key obstacle to achieving greater profitability through their webstores.

In addition, among mid-size retailers that are not currently profitable, 15 per cent cited the inability to deliver goods at lower operational costs as a key roadblock to their companies being profitable. Mid-size retailers therefore need solutions to reduce per-unit fulfilment costs, especially as they rapidly scale up e-commerce operations, or they may struggle to turn a profit. They need to couple this with investment into logistics/delivery services to meet stronger demand for shorter fulfilment times and to meet industry delivery standards/expectations being set by enterprise retail players. Not surprisingly, more than half of all mid-size companies in the Coresight survey cited improved fulfilment as a current priority, and more than 4 in 10 stated that it will be a priority in the next five years.

Overspending on marketing and promotions

Marketing represents another hurdle to profitability when selling online – especially for those companies that do not have the marketing benefit of physical stores. Ad spending can be high even for large companies with the most sophisticated means of measuring ROI, and the challenges of balancing spending with driving growth can be even greater for mid-size firms. While mid-size retailers must spend on marketing in order to increase brand awareness and so compete with retail giants, they often lack insights into who to target promotions at and what marketing strategies to adopt, leading to overspending on marketing and ultimately impacting profitability.

From the Coresight survey, 21 per cent of total mid-size retailers that were not currently profitable cited overspending in marketing as a key profitability roadblock. That said, the setup of marketing and analytics capabilities does not come cheap: 31 per cent of upper mid-size companies in the survey cited that their initial spend on these capabilities was $100,000 or more, and 8 per cent of intermediate mid-size retailers reported the same.

Among the Coresight survey respondents, 31 per cent of all mid-size retailers – and an even higher 38 per cent of intermediate mid-size retailers – consider overspending avoidance to be a key goal when finding and/or building a platform/solution to facilitate their e-commerce businesses. This poses opportunities for solution providers that have capabilities such as data analytics and ML that can help retailers avoid overspending in marketing.

The importance of AI and technology on revenue

AI can be a powerful tool for mid-size retailers to maximize profitability if they want to compete with retail giants, save fulfilment costs and refrain from overspending on marketing. Since December 2019, Google AI has been helping retailers such as Home Depot and Kohl's in creating better promotions and recommendations, and improving margins through dynamic pricing. Stor.ai, an end-to-end digital commerce platform for grocers, recently launched a grocery picking app that supports retailers in improving efficiency by combining multiple product-picking strategies when managing inventories and fulfilling orders. By using smart tools, retailers can improve pickers' average units picked per hour (UPH), awareness of item availability and real-time decision-making. This means that retailers can maximize the number and range of orders processed without increasing costs.

The Coresight survey found that mid-size retailers leveraged AI and technology to support operations amid the impacts of Covid-19 and to better compete with retail giants. For instance, 51 per cent of intermediate mid-size retailers leveraged AI to further revenue growth due to Covid-19 – the highest proportion among all mid-size revenue segments. Bringing in technical expertise was also a key action taken by mid-size companies – lower-mid size retailers in particular (46 per cent) (Weinswig, 2022).

Among all mid-size retailers, the upper mid-size segment saw the highest proportions report the embedding of AI/ML/predictive analytics across various e-commerce functions – with the top three being customer service (62 per cent), platform hardware, software and hosting (59 per cent) and freight (55 per cent).

How can a CaaS approach help improve profitability?

CaaS is a new model that offers greater separation between the front and back ends of a platform, which have different capabilities/functions. The CaaS model provides retailers with flexibility to innovate and expand but also more standardization/consistency due to greater ownership and integration of the stack through a single CaaS vendor.

CaaS/headless commerce solutions can also bring higher profitability for retailers compared with DIY (off-the-shelf) and enterprise solutions through better internal workflows and processes with a full-managed service model and availability of technical expertise. The Coresight survey found that 39 per cent of all retailers using CaaS/headless commerce solutions are satisfied with how their current e-commerce infrastructure solution increases profitability by optimizing internal workflows and processes (Weinswig, 2022). Only 16 per cent of DIY solution users reported the same.

While just 5 per cent of all retailers using CaaS/headless commerce solutions reported that ROI is too low, 19 per cent of enterprise solution users and 14 per cent of DIY solution users stated the same.

CaaS solutions offer a number of profitability-related advantages to brands and retailers:

- low or no platform development costs through an agile approach
- lower fulfilment costs through order management systems
- lower marketing costs through data-driven intelligent promotions and access to scale
- low or no R&D costs through cloud-based R&D upgrades

Based on these benefits, it is not surprising that 34 per cent of mid-size retailers currently use a CaaS solution for their e-commerce platform, and the remaining retailers are planning to adopt such a solution at some point in the future, according to the Coresight survey. We believe that by leveraging CaaS solutions, mid-size companies can build the infrastructure needed to effectively and quickly adapt and scale. Such solutions also enable retail teams to remain focused on core strategies, which is critical in the ever-changing environment.

The value of external support

Mid-size retailers want technical support to be available when developing and maintaining their e-commerce infrastructure. The need for expert support has been heightened due to the recent pandemic-driven acceleration of e-commerce: 36 per cent of mid-size companies in the Coresight survey reported that the availability of technical support is a current priority, and 32 per cent brought in more technical expertise due to Covid-19 (Weinswig,

2022). Furthermore, more mid-size companies are recognizing the value of technical support in facilitating e-commerce business growth, with 39 per cent of respondents stating that they intend to prioritize technical support in the future. CaaS can potentially mitigate the need for technical support, as it provides the technology and support for mid-size companies needing it, with fast deployment and minimal errors.

Having expert technical support can help mid-size retailers expand operations and realize potential cost savings, but whether this support is provided through in-house resources or external sources is a key consideration.

Internal and external resources: Finding the right combination

There are three ways of providing resources to operate various e-commerce functions:

- *Internal/in-house*: A company licenses a platform or builds its own tech stack to execute its e-commerce strategy and manage retailer platforms in-house, allowing brand manufacturers to internally handle both strategy and execution.
- *External*: A partially managed or fully managed service (CaaS) through a service provider leads to variable instead of fixed personnel and equipment costs. CaaS e-commerce tech platforms, in particular, provide turn-key solutions that allow retailers to better focus in-house on brand building, removing concerns around technology and marketing.
- *Hybrid model*: Some business activities are delegated externally, while some remain in-house. Whether a company utilizes internal or external resources, an e-commerce function will often depend on its strategy, size and operational complexity, as well as the availability of resources on hand.

We present a comparison of the benefits and disadvantages of internal functionality, external resources and CaaS in particular in Figure 14.3.

Interestingly, the degree of internal resources is correlated with a company's annual revenue for platform hardware, software and hosting, the Coresight survey found: the higher the revenue, the more likely a mid-size company is to use internal resources for the e-commerce function. Only 24 per cent of lower mid-size retailers reported that they handle platform

FIGURE 14.3 Advantages and disadvantages of internal functionality, external resources and CaaS

	Internal	External	CaaS
Advantages	• Better handling of sensitive business information • Lower security risks • Better control of spending/budget	• Can focus more on strategic tasks by outsourcing/automating time-intensive, repetitive tasks • Enables access to external technical expertise • Fewer fixed costs	• Security built into the system • Tech expertise/support available • Enables companies to have control over process in parallel • Smoother communications through dashboards
Disadvantages	• Upfront costs of hiring, training • Locked in opex (such as salaries and benefits) on internal staff • Less adaptable/flexible due to more entrenched resources	• Data security risks • Less control over performance of e-commerce functions • Takes time to evaluate vendor performance	• Investment needed to work with a CaaS solution • Entrenched nature, making decoupling (if needed) challenging

hardware, software and hosting internally, while 34 per cent of upper mid-size retailers report the same (Weinswig, 2022). Mid-size retailers that have high annual revenues are more likely to be able to afford the fixed costs of internal technical expertise for platform hardware, software and hosting.

On the other hand, fulfilment is an e-commerce function for which the degree of internal resource deployment decreases with annual revenue: while 46 per cent of lower mid-size companies handle fulfilment and freight internally, only 31 per cent of upper mid-size retailers do the same. Fulfilment is a complex process that involves product storage, picking and packing – and it is often time-intensive. We see companies using external logistics providers for fulfilment services in order to save time and meet high consumer demand quickly. For example, in October 2021 Saks (the e-commerce arm of Saks Fifth Avenue) started using collaborative robots and a shared-space distribution network provided by American logistics company GXO, to meet surging demand for luxury fashion as the holiday season approached.

When using external e-commerce functions, more than one-third of mid-size retailers work with Shopify – and Wix and Adobe are also popular vendors. While these solution providers may be able to integrate with major marketplaces such as Amazon and may have user-friendly interfaces that provide convenience to retailers, they often incur transaction fees; there can be costly monthly subscriptions for premium functionality; and these vendors' solutions can be complex in terms of implementation. CaaS, on the contrary, integrates functionalities such as fulfilment into the platform without incurring extra premium costs.

Implications for mid-size retailers

Mid-size retailers are looking to optimize their operating model by focusing internal resources on their core value proposition, then allocating supporting work to internal teams or external partners. They are typically looking for data analytics and personalization, expert technical support and ease of scaling in order to build their e-commerce infrastructure, many features which can be sourced externally. CaaS in particular is a fully managed e-commerce service that provides expert support on different e-commerce functions, from setup to marketing to fulfilment. Through advanced technologies such as AI, ML and predictive analytics, the data-driven model provides algorithms and insights to support retailers in tailoring their offerings to customers and increasing cost savings. CaaS has a high degree of customization and enables brands and retailers to easily scale up or down depending on their needs.

CASE STUDY
Nogin

Nogin, a CaaS full-stack e-commerce platform, allows for enterprise-level technology with a dynamic mindset and structure. According to Nogin, startups using DIY solutions saw an average of 27 per cent of revenue go to free shipping and 45 per cent to digital marketing (Weinswig, 2021), whereas a CaaS solution could more than halve those cost percentages by better targeting and driving outcomes outside of the standard DIY processes with associated overheads and obsolete systems.

FIGURE 14.4 CaaS case studies: how selected Nogin clients are improving the customer experience

Company	Initiative
Hurley	Hurley surf brands needed to rapidly rebuild its global ecommerce operation after separating from Nike. Hurley replatformed its entire e-commerce operation onto Nogin, converging inventory merchandising, email, paid media and e-commerce under a single, modular platform. Hurley worked with Nogin to build a customer experience that is more integrated and tied with its branded content, better optimizing the conversion funnel and resulting in improved efficiencies, user experience and conversion rates.
Frye	Frye, a footwear company, had suboptimal DTC e-commerce operations due to inconsistent, expensive work being outsourced to multiple agencies and a lack of advanced digital marketing technology tools and associate know-how. Frye employed Nogin to help build and run its online store, including the convergence of multiple teams – including technology, marketing, strategy and planning. Nogin also revamped Frye's shopping funnel, implemented new payment methods and launched new SMS programmes and loyalty programmes to reach and retain customers.
Honeywell	Honeywell, a diversified Fortune 100 company, sought to improve its online DTC operations. The company's back-end and front-end legacy platforms and order fulfilment operating model could not accommodate increased customer demand for select brands. Nogin deployed its CaaS technology platform to implement key drivers for Honeywell's successful multichannel online business and implemented an up-to-date global e-commerce strategy. Nogin also consolidated Honeywell's data under a single architecture, optimized performance through centralized management and fulfilment of all online orders, and enabled Honeywell's online business in real time by syndicating the entire multi-brand catalogue to 10 marketplaces.

Nogin's platform offers mid-size to larger retailers a full-stack solution with the flexibility to let retailers innovate and broaden. The following are some key benefits of Nogin's CaaS platform, according to the company:

- full-stack CaaS platform with R&D investment, sales optimization and machine learning for superior customer knowledge and future predictive commerce
- AI-driven marketing, fulfilment and expert support
- R&D included so clients never have to replatform
- algorithm and advanced promo to increase return on ad spend, lower shipping costs, increase margin and increase sell-through while enhancing conversions
- advanced e-commerce personnel and best practices
- agile development approach to deploy expert enhancements across all clients

Companies deploying CaaS solutions are looking for more flexibility and to decouple from legacy systems. The case studies highlighted in Figure 14.4 (provided by Nogin) are all older companies with an offline and online presence that are looking to break out of the traditional mould toward a more dynamic, innovative, customer-facing experience.

KEY TAKEAWAYS: HEADLESS COMMERCE

- The recent widespread consumer shift to the online channel presented e-commerce sales opportunities. Many retailers made changes to their e-commerce operations in response to Covid-19.
- Commerce has evolved over time from offline to omnichannel and more recently to a decentralized model. Sophisticated e-commerce platforms, including CaaS, are already being used by mid-size and large retailers, signalling the start of a transformation of e-commerce infrastructure into prioritizing flexibility, scale and innovation.
- The Covid-19 pandemic negatively impacted e-commerce margins for mid-size players due to increased fulfilment costs and marketing spending.
- CaaS solution providers can help mid-size e-commerce businesses improve profitability through data-driven intelligence, managed services and ML algorithms.

- Although retailers see obstacles to adopting a CaaS-type solution – most notably a lack of employee support and cost – at least 85 per cent of respondents to a Coresight survey of e-commerce executives indicated that they are 'ready' or 'very ready' for CaaS across the majority of business areas (Weinswig, 2021).

- As retailers look to build on the pandemic accelerated shift to online sales, decentralized CaaS solutions will offer them ways to better innovate and compete.

References

Nogin (2021) Headless commerce: Part 2 – addressing profitability issues for mid-size e-commerce players, Coresight Research. https://coresight.com/research/headless-commerce-part-2-addressing-profitability-issues-for-mid-size-e-commerce-players/ (archived at perma.cc/FKF8-SDRQ)

Weinswig, D (2021) Headless commerce: Part 1 – the evolving state of e-commerce infrastructure, Coresight Research. https://coresight.com/research/headless-commerce-part-1-the-evolving-state-of-e-commerce-infrastructure/ (archived at perma.cc/T2AH-KKYZ)

Weinswig, D (2022) Headless commerce: Part 3 – optimizing e-commerce infrastructure, Coresight Research. https://coresight.com/research/headless-commerce-part-3-optimizing-e-commerce-infrastructure/ (archived at perma.cc/JF8H-TYRY)

15

What's ahead?

The future outlook for retail

In researching and writing this book, we have enjoyed the luxury of interviewing thought leaders, industry experts and digital innovators with the audacious goal of predicting the trajectory of the retail industry through the coming decade.

When we started this scan into the future of retail, looking ahead to an upheaval in consumer mindsets, behaviours and the resulting demands on retailers to adapt, we highlighted emerging consumer demands for: omnichannel retailing, speed and convenience, an inclusive mindset, personalized shopping and a rewarding experience.

We envision a future for retail that meets these disruptive consumer demands and integrates the components of technology innovation we have discussed throughout this book, and even more to come.

The future retail experience

As we look ahead three to five years or even longer into the horizon, what will consumers want, and what will they reward?

Bricks-and-mortar retail will remain

> Retail will still be with us in the future. Consumers will never give up the element of touch, and the social aspects of shopping.
> Terence Ng, Senior Analyst, Coresight Research (2022)

Despite speculation that bricks-and-mortar retail will die with the increase of online shopping and omnichannel retail, we expect that bricks-and-mortar stores will endure in the future. Just as consumers craved personal interaction in the wake of the pandemic, there is still a need for human interaction and face-to-face experiences in the retail world. We believe that the role of physical retail will continue to evolve, but as community-based 'everything' increases in importance, the stores are the future foundation.

The fundamental nature of the in-person retail experience, however, will change and evolve dramatically in the future. We expect that the digital and physical retail experience will merge into a single, blended experience in which the user will seamlessly and simultaneously interact across the digital and real world.

If you or your kids have played *Pokémon GO*, you have seen probably the easiest to understand example to date of a blended offline/online experience. *Pokémon GO* demands that players explore the physical world in real time to find *Pokémon GO* avatars that are digitally augmented upon the real-world landscape, and embark on challenges that can include walking a certain distance, going to a certain place in the real world or interacting with *Pokémon GO* characters that appear digitally in the world around you.

Most kids have been playing *Pokémon GO* for years on mobile phones and have developed a conception of this blending of the real and digital worlds that feels entirely native to them – while their parents have developed a vague sense that something bigger might be happening with this 'game', but can't quite get their heads around what's really happening.

For a simplified application in the typical retail context: imagine walking around a retail store, perhaps with your preferred mobile device – a smartphone or something like smart-glasses – allowing you to interact seamlessly with the products and brands in the physical store.

For example, when you pick up a packaged food item in a grocery store, you could be prompted for recipe suggestions, wine pairing suggestions, nutrition information, matches with pre-set personalized diet criteria scanning for allergies or a Keto diet, similar products – all while in the aisle of the grocery store, delivered seamlessly to you, and filtered algorithmically based on your personalization settings.

And adding the Metaverse layer, even more immersive experiences can enter the grocery aisle scenescape, whether a virtual celebrity hologram, augmented reality environments or interactive product demonstrations allowing the customer to interact virtually within the in-store retail environment.

In-person retail will become more automated

> In the future, retail will be: 1) more automated; 2) more personalized; 3) more experiential.
>
> Ken Fenyo, President, Research and Advisory, Coresight Research (2022)

The retail experience must become faster, more efficient and more streamlined in the future. The customer's indomitable impatience and obsession with 'business' – the expectation of seamless speed and reliability and convenience – will need to be met if in-person retail hopes to stand a chance in a face-off against pure-digital commerce.

The checkout experience is already becoming increasingly automated and efficient, and this will continue to become more and more seamless in the future with the advent of new technologies for fast and seamless checkout, payment and delivery. Retailers will need to continue to adopt the latest new technologies in order to further automate the experience and deliver on customers' high expectations of fast, easy and convenient shopping experiences.

> In the future, we will see more retailers harnessing the power of AI to improve consumer insights and personalized recommendations. We expect to also see retailers using the Internet of Things to improve the store experience and provide a more diverse use of space in the retail environment such as fulfilment centres, DIY corners or experience centres.
>
> Terence Ng, Senior Analyst, Coresight Research (2022)

Retail will be more personalized

> Consumers will grant a premium to brands that create curated products that are tailored to individual needs.
>
> Terence Ng, Senior Analyst, Coresight Research (2022)

Consumers are seeking more personalized experiences that feel customized and tailored to their preferences. In particular, consumers have an expectation that any advertising or recommendations will be relevant and helpful to their shopping experience, and do not want to view retailers as marketing 'at' them.

Retail will offer a sensorial experience

Just as consumers quickly realized that they still wanted in-person experiences after the Covid pandemic subsided, we expect shoppers to continue to come to the retail store for experiences in real life. But they want more than today's retail stores offer – they want to be entertained, to have a sense of discovery and to have meaningful human interaction. Consumers do not want to go shopping just to buy things (they can do that at home) – they want to experience something from the retail environment that they do not have while shopping from home.

> The digital experience tends to lack the emotional connection while shopping, but consumers still want an emotional bond when they shop. The question for the future will be how to inject the emotional experience back into the shopping environment in a new format.
>
> Letitia Webster, SVP E-commerce, Omnichannel and Master Data Management, Tractor Supply (2022)

The 3–3–3 rule

We sum up our view for the future of retail with our 3–3–3 rule. In the future, retailers will have 3 new things to sell, 3 new ways to sell them, to be delivered in 3 new ways.

3 new things to sell

When we think about how retail has changed as a result of the advent of today's technology landscape, three new revenue streams for retailers have emerged.

RETAIL DATA

> The convergence of the increased availability of data, improved human skillsets and enhanced analytical tools has made data a key driver in the decision making process. Whereas hedge funds have been leveraging data to improve their investment and trading decisions for several years, we are now seeing corporations jump head first into leveraging data to improve operational efficiencies, target customers and re-engineer the supply chain.
>
> Daniel Goldberg, Chief Data Strategy Officer, Coresight Research (2022)

With the move to an increasingly digital world, and with the 'cookie apocalypse' (the planned phase-out of third-party cookies) the data landscape will shift dramatically from the big internet companies (Google, Facebook, Instagram) having all of the most valuable consumer data to retailers now having this consumer data.

Retailers will be in a position to sell this data to brands, which can not only provide a new revenue stream for retailers as they sell this data, but will also contribute to a more personalized and rewarding shopping experience for the consumer.

There is a veritable ocean of data that passes retailers' way every day: how many customers enter their stores, their demographics, where they go, what they try on and what they buy and do not buy, in addition to data gleaned online from website visits, dwell times, page views, what items end up in shopping carts and what consumers ultimately buy. This data has historically been trapped in siloes, but there is significant value in retailers sharing it with their supply chain partners. When aggregated and anonymized, this data becomes a hidden treasure to be harvested.

> Retailers are sitting on a goldmine of proprietary data, inside the physical store and online, and they are being propelled into the future to unlock this data to offer more personalized experiences to consumers.
>
> John Harmon, Senior Retail/Technology Analyst, Coresight Research (2022)

RETAIL MEDIA

As brands and retailers are shifting their online advertising budget away from Facebook and Instagram, they are seeking new media that can help them to reach their target audience in today's increasingly fragmented media landscape. Retailers can provide advertising opportunities to brands that they sell that will enable brands to very accurately reach their target customers with personalized offers and messages.

Retailers have begun to understand the value of the time consumers spend on their websites, leading up to the key purchase moment. While Google's business has long been based on selling advertising to consumers on its various platforms, many retailers, including Amazon, Kroger, Walmart and 'instant-needs' player Gopuff, have launched their own retail media networks to monetize consumers' attention during the shopping process. Coresight Research estimates that more than $75 million will be generated in 2022, up more than 80 per cent from last year (Weinswig, 2022).

Retail media is a big opportunity – especially for large multi-brand retailers who can tap into the large number of brands they sell, and tailor these messages via personalized ads or offers that can be delivered seamlessly either in an in-store or digital environment.

Ken Fenyo, President, Research and Advisory, Coresight Research (2022)

VIRTUAL COLLECTIBLES AND NFTs

As the Metaverse continues to develop, we will see more retailers establish new revenue streams from selling virtual items such as clothes or accessories for avatars, tickets to virtual events or NFT launches that can also help to drive interaction, engagement and visits to retails stores – both in the real world and in the Metaverse.

The sale of these virtual items can drive new revenue lines, as well as be additive to existing revenue streams by creating excitement, driving new product development and raising brand engagement with core consumers.

Retailers are unlocking the value of NFTs connected to their brands. For example, Nike and Adidas consistently top sales lists for avatar NFTs, while Macy's dropped its first-ever NFT collection in 2021 in connection with its 95th annual Thanksgiving Parade. In addition to being a revenue opportunity, NFTs are a key building block of the Metaverse.

3 ways to sell them

The changing nature of the retail technology landscape will also bring us three new channels for retailers to sell both virtual and physical goods.

LIVESTREAMING

Livestreaming allows retailers to combine entertainment with direct selling, allowing for sales from an in-person retail store, within the Metaverse or even on a one-to-one basis with a host or salesperson. This new way of selling allows for enhanced engagement with the consumer, increased product education and direct interaction between the consumer and the host.

Livestreaming enables brands and retailers to reach and sell to consumers wherever they are, showcasing products in a live, authentic and engaging format. After becoming a phenomenon in Asia, the adoption of livestreaming is growing in the US, and Coresight estimates that the market will grow from $20 billion in 2022 to $68 billion in 2026 (Weinswig, 2022).

THE METAVERSE

With brands quickly adopting the Metaverse, the future will see more retailers selling both virtual and physical products via the Metaverse. This can encompass a wide variety of formats, including e-commerce in the Metaverse, virtual stores, livestreaming in the Metaverse, integrated offline/online stores, selling of digital assets (NFTs) or transactions made within virtual worlds or games. We expect the number of options to rapidly increase in the next several years as well.

Building upon artificial and virtual reality, blockchain and NFT technology, the Metaverse has sparked a great deal of excitement and investment among retail players looking to stake a claim in this potentially enormous opportunity. The decentralized essence of the Metaverse unlocks the creativity of content creators, who can build virtual worlds that transcend the laws of physics, which will naturally include brands and retailers. Coresight estimates that Metaverse retail sales will hit $2.3 billion by the end of 2022 and double each year for the next five years thereafter (Weinswig, 2022). These new experiences will take brand recognition, engagement and loyalty to a new level.

> The future will be more virtual than it is now, and will include virtual
> e-commerce, virtual stores where avatars can explore and try on clothes, and
> virtual payment – with products shipped directly to the customer's house.
> Scott Eneje, Co-Founder of Yandi Digital Solutions (2022)

QUICK COMMERCE

Consumers are going to continue to want speed and convenience in their shopping environment; and in the future the definition of speed and convenience will accelerate to be even faster and more seamless than it is today.

With the advent of quick commerce, retailers can now sell to their customers via quick commerce channels to enable their consumers to have a shopping experience that meets their needs. Midtown Manhattan is currently replete with storefronts from Getir, Gopuff and other quick commerce (or instant-needs) retailers, whose offers of 15–30 minute grocery delivery have resonated with consumers. These retailers also offer hyper-localized assortments, which can vary significantly by neighbourhood. With quick commerce, consumers are looking at their screens and receptive to advertising as they ready their purchase, driving higher conversion rates, according to Gopuff. We estimate the US quick-commerce market hit $20–25 billion last year, representing 10–13 per cent of 2021 online CPG sales (Weinswig, 2022).

Immediate gratification, just like a short attention span, is today's reality so retailers need to be able to accommodate the demands of today's consumer by either providing same-day delivery or providing convenient curb-side pickup.
Daniela Ciocan, CEO, Access Beauty Insiders and Unfiltered Experience (2022)

3 ways to deliver them

As the future of retail evolves and retailers have new things to sell and new ways to sell them, they need to make sure that they are staying in tune with consumer needs and demands. We see the below as the three most critical ways that retailers need to serve customers in the future of retail.

PERSONALIZED

Consumers will come to expect the level of personalization that they receive when shopping online and to have it brought to them in the retail environment.

The expectations are going to be raised across the retail industry with the convergence of AI in physical retail environments. Personalization can be delivered seamlessly so that consumers can find the best product suited for them and their needs from within the entire store assortment versus the products that the sales associate knows or is affiliated with. AI can now refine merchandising assortments based on a real understanding of data and it allows for customization of inventory at individual store levels taking into account weather patterns and demographics. Rather than a uniform look and same planogram, stores can now reflect unique individuality based on the wants and needs of their neighbourhood and communities.
Daniela Ciocan, CEO, Access Beauty Insiders and Unfiltered Experience (2022)

EXPERIENTIAL

Consumers need more from their shopping trip than just running an errand or accomplishing a task. Retailers have a higher bar to clear to please consumers and entice them to the retail store.

While consumers love to discover products online and read reviews to guide their purchases, we see that the old-fashioned desire to touch, feel and experience products in person is not going away. Gen Zs are a perfect example of using online to discover and offline to experience products.
Daniela Ciocan, CEO, Access Beauty Insiders and Unfiltered Experience (2022)

SUSTAINABLE

Younger consumers are going to force the future of retail to be more sustainable. They will no longer tolerate the same standards of sustainability – they will demand more accountability from retailers, and they will not reward those that do not comply.

> The biggest consumer trend that will have a fundamental impact on retail is undoubtedly sustainability. It will change how much we buy (do we really need another t-shirt or extra pair of jeans?), what we buy (materials, social and environmental impact of the making of the product), who we buy from (which brand has better ESG practice), where to buy (which channel has the lowest carbon footprint).
>
> Janie Yu, Partner, LFX Venture Partners (2022)

Retail responsibility

As we look ahead, we must also keep in mind the responsibility that the retail industry has to the environment. As climate change accelerates rapidly, the reality of the environmental challenges can no longer be ignored. Retailers have the power to not only shape consumer opinion in this area, but to make tangible changes to their entire operations that can have real impacts on the environment for the future.

> In the future, consumers will demand sustainable goods that don't cost more to make. They will want to know the story of the good (which can be trusted via blockchain) and what makes it sustainable. Right now, everyone thinks it has to cost more, which is the antithesis of sustainability. Lots of education needs to happen and companies need near-term measures for investors and consumers and employees. We can't have CEOs saying, 'In 20 years we aim to XYZ.' Because in 20 years they will be G-O-N-E.
>
> Buddy Teaster, CEO, Soles4Souls (2022)

References

Ciocan, D (2022) Interview with the authors, July.
Eneje, S (2022) Interview with the authors, July.
Fenyo, K (2022) Interview with the authors, July.
Goldberg, D (2022) Interview with the authors, July.

Harmon, J (2022) Interview with the authors, July.

Ng, T (2022) Interview with the authors, July.

Teaster, B (2022) Interview with the authors, July.

Webster, L (2022) Interview with the authors, July.

Weinswig, D (2022) Weinswig's weekly: Introducing Coresight Research's 3×3 framework – three new products and three new ways to sell them, Coresight Research. https://coresight.com/research/weinswigs-weekly-introducing-coresight-researchs-3x3-framework/ (archived at perma.cc/KTL5-DYZL)

Yu, J (2022) Interview with the authors, July.

16

Creating your roadmap

My advice to retailers, as they plan for the future: three words – data, technology and mindset. As retail executives think about all the challenges we face as an industry and as a generation – inflation, labour shortage, political instability, supply chain disruption, the only way to drive forward is to leverage data and technologies to improve efficiency in current businesses and design new business models that are relevant in the future (which happens faster than it sounds). More important than data and technology is the mindset of the businesses. To be relevant in the future, retailers must be willing to experiment and change.

Janie Yu, Partner, LFX Venture Partners (2022)

Planning for innovation

As you plan your future roadmap and consider how to change your business practices to account for innovation in retail, we recommend that you start by assessing the areas in this book and evaluate which innovation areas can provide the biggest impact to your business. In addition, a critical aspect is, whom do you have in the seats that would oversee each of these updates/revelations/transformations?

There is no one set answer or playbook to follow to create a strategy to address the rapidly changing nature of the retail industry. Each industry is different. Each brand is different. And, most importantly, any advances in technology and innovation must be closely aligned with your brand DNA and consumer preferences.

The Coresight RESET framework

Coresight Research's RESET framework for change in retail serves is a call to action for retail companies. The framework aggregates the retail trends that Coresight's analysts identify as meaningful for 2022 and beyond, as well as Coresight's recommendations to capitalize on those trends, around five areas of evolution.

To remain relevant and stand equipped for change, we urge retailers to be:

- responsive
- engaging
- socially responsible
- expansive
- tech-enabled

Emphasizing the need for consumer-centricity, the consumer sits at the centre of this framework, with their preferences, behaviours and choices demanding those changes.

RESET was ideated as a means to aggregate more than a dozen of our identified retail trends into a higher-level framework. The framework enhances accessibility, serving as an entry point into the longer list of more specific trends that we think should be front of mind for retail companies as they seek to maintain relevance. Retailers can dive into these trends as they cycle through the RESET framework.

The components of RESET serve as a template for approaching adaptation in retail. Companies can consolidate processes such as the identification of opportunities, internal capability reviews, competitor analysis and implementation of new processes and competencies around these RESET segments. We recommend that you look at your own business through the lens of the RESET framework, allowing you to develop a holistic view of how to adapt your business for the future of retail.

In this chapter we examine each of the components of retail innovation that we covered within this book to provide thought starters and ways to begin to develop your own strategy for that area of retail innovation.

Dip your toes into the Metaverse

Almost every day, we speak to retailers that are creating their Metaverse strategy. As with most strategies, there is no one-size-fits-all approach that

FIGURE 16.1 The RESET framework

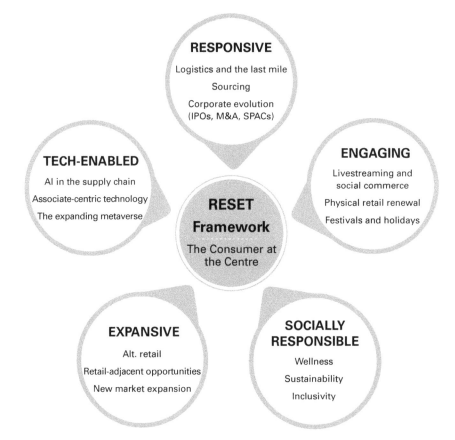

SOURCE Coresight Research

works for every brand or retailer. As you formulate your own Metaverse strategy, a good place to start is to ask yourself a series of questions:

- Who is your consumer community?
- Does your community engage with your brand online? If so, why? If not, why not?
- What does your consumer want from your brand?
- What are examples of other brands' Metaverse strategies that target your consumer community?
- What elements of your brand DNA can you bring to life via your Metaverse strategy?
- Are there brands, artists, influencers, creators who align with your brand that you can partner with for your Metaverse strategy?

As you develop your Metaverse strategy, make sure to align it with your overall marketing plan. Consider adding Metaverse components to your contracts with celebrities. If you are contracting a celebrity for a campaign, consider adding a Metaverse component to the plan, such as creating a digital avatar of the celebrity.

And don't be afraid to experiment with virtual influencers.

As you evaluate your brand's Metaverse strategy we recommend you evaluate how you can take advantage of the Metaverse across the following areas:

- *Create new revenue streams*: This can include creating NFTs, selling digital products or selling in-game or in-virtual world collectibles.
- *Engage consumers in the Metaverse*: Find compelling and interactive ways to engage your customers in the Metaverse, via building virtual stores, celebrity/influencer digital avatars, unique collaborations bringing the brand to life in the Metaverse or relevant virtual advertising.
- *Build digital community*: Utilize the Metaverse to establish deeper level connections with consumers online, incorporate ESG or community giveback and provide brand-linked education.
- *Enhance supply chain capabilities*: Explore opportunities to add efficiencies to your supply chain via NFT barcodes, product authentication or security enhancements.
- *Expand payment options*: Consider accepting crypto payments, enabling cross-border transactions and implementing loyalty tokens or other loyalty rewards.

Test and learn by implementing a livestreaming strategy

We recommend that companies begin experimenting with livestreaming as soon as they can. It does not have high setup costs and your approach can be iterated over time as you experiment with the platform and format.

Start by asking yourselves some questions:

- What are your goals for starting a livestreaming strategy?
- What metrics will you use to judge success besides sales?
- When estimating sales, are you planning for a ramp up?
- How will you engage your consumers?

- What experts, influencers or celebrities know and understand your brand and will connect with your audience?
- Which brand spokespeople would be engaging for a consumer audience online?
- Which locations will be an engaging area for shooting livestreams? Do you have a design room, factory, engaging experience location?

As you build your strategy, start with the following approach.

- *Assess your industry and competitors.* Prior to creating your own livestreaming strategy, make sure you understand what your industry and competitors have been doing in the space. If possible, evaluate who in your space has been successful at livestreaming to date, and why. If there is no one in your space who has been successful to date, look to other comparable industries and seek to understand what has worked and has not worked for them, so that you are incorporate learnings into your own brand plan.
- *Set a plan.* Book a start date and align it with ongoing campaigns for your brand, such as seasonal campaigns like Back to School or new product launches. Make sure that you have planned for a series of livestreams (not just one) and that they happen at a regular cadence. You need to give yourself time to experiment with the channel and adjust – planning only one or two livestreams will set you up for failure.
- *Choose your partners carefully.* Livestreaming will require partners – make you sure do a thorough evaluation and choose carefully. First start with a technology platform partner and ensure that you can easily integrate with your own back-end and e-commerce infrastructure. Also make sure to understand the technology support they provide, as well as data and metrics. Evaluate your consumer base and check that the technology platform will reach *your* consumers on the platform they use in the ways that they like to be engaged.
- *Develop your approach. Start to plan your approach.* What products will you promote? Where will you host your livestream? Who will host your livestream? When will you host it? How often? All of these decisions need to be made with your brand image and assets in mind so that you are presenting the brand in a way that is aligned with your image and is exciting to your customer base.

- *Drive the right traffic to your livestream.* One of the most common problems for livestreams is that there is either not enough people on the livestream or that they are not the right kind of consumers. It is crucial to find ways to drive the right audience for your brand to your livestreams. Experiment with paid social, influencer traffic, customer lists, partners and other ways to drive the right traffic to your livestream. Make sure to provide multiple prompts to ensure engagement at the right time and be sure to promote the recorded sessions after they are done.

- *Assess and iterate.* Once you complete your series of livestreams, make sure to assess against your pre-determined goals and determine your key learnings and opportunities for improvement. Then keep testing and repeat!

Evaluate how quick commerce can impact your business

The rapid adoption of quick commerce as a result of the pandemic has fundamentally altered the food retail sector, specifically the restaurant, grocery and convenience store markets, and is beginning to have a broader impact not only on drug stores and hypermarkets, but also on industries as broad and toys and apparel. Quick commerce will not be relevant to every business and every industry, but even if it is not as relevant to your industry or business, it is a worthwhile exercise to evaluate how it could potentially impact your business positively or negatively.

As you think through this exercise, below are key questions to ask yourself and areas in which you can assess how to build your own quick commerce strategy.

- *Industry*: How has the quick commerce market affected your industry? Have competitors adopted quick commerce as a solution? How has the adoption of quick commerce changed your industry for the positive or negative? How will this change in the future?

- *Consumer experience*: How could quick commerce improve your customer's experience? Could quick commerce enhance convenience, satisfaction or meet unmet consumer needs?

- *Efficiencies*: Could quick commerce enable any efficiencies in your business processes? Could it make your employees' work more satisfying or *efficient*? Could you find efficiencies in supply chain? Could you find ways to enhance your company's sustainability efforts?

- *Ecosystem*: What is the quick commerce ecosystem in the markets where you operate? How can you participate in this ecosystem? If there is not opportunity for participation, how can you partner with those in the ecosystem to find opportunities to reach your end consumers or increase efficiencies?

As you ask yourself these questions, look for ways in which you can incorporate quick commerce into your business to enhance consumer experience, increase efficiencies or find sustainable alternatives to current practices. While the way that companies utilize quick commerce will continue to change, one thing is proven – consumers like it!

Advancing sustainability in your organization

As you assess how to adapt your sustainability strategy for the future of retail, we recommend you utilize Coresight's EnCORE framework to help adapt your business to be more sustainable.

- *Environmental engagement*: First, make sure that you have a thorough understanding of your industry, competitors and company as it relates to sustainability practices. Update your awareness of all current and upcoming regulations across different cities, states and countries. Regulation is shifting quickly and it is not uniform across markets.

- *Circular models*: Start at the end of your supply chain and look for ways to create circular loops in your product lifecycle. Assess whether consumers in your industry and sector are open to second-hand items, and also look for ways to take advantage of previously used products to achieve your sustainability goals. Be ruthless in your quest to get rid of excess waste throughout your products' entire lifecycle.

- *Optimized operations*: Audit your operations to find efficiencies: reduce materials and resource usage, cost and waste. Long-term investments should include renewable energy technology and electric vehicles. Ensure that you have optimized your operations so that you can accomplish two goals: reducing cost and improving sustainability.

- *Responsible supply chains*: Revamp your supply chain to find sustainable inputs, materials and processes. Find industry associations and partners within your sector to join together to achieve overall sustainability goals.

- *Excellence in reporting and communicating*: Be transparent and open about your goals, achievements and setbacks. This level of honesty will resonate with your employees, suppliers and consumers and serves to align the entire organization behind specific goals.

And, most importantly, once you have done the work to develop your sustainability strategy, ensure that it is communicated internally and externally and linked to tangible, measurable goals that can be tracked along the way. Making public and private intentions will align your organization and ensure that these goals are adopted throughout the organization – not just by people with the word sustainability in their title.

Integrating content and commerce with social commerce

Every retail and DTC business should have a social commerce strategy in place and a plan for how to adapt to the fast-moving changes within the industry. As social commerce grows, so too will the links between brands and e-commerce, enabling brands to capture rich data and insights about their customers and deepen the level of engagement with customers.

As businesses seek to build their social commerce strategy, they should consider the following components to craft the strategy that is right for their brand:

- Assess your social engagement with consumers online. Where are you interacting with your customers? What is the quality of that interaction?
- What types of social content does your company produce? Classify the types of social content you create, for example: brand history, promotional, new product, influencer created content, interactive content and others. After you have classified the content, assess how much of each you are posting, and then assess the engagement of each type. See if your goals and plan align with what consumers actually engage with.
- Who is your online community? Why do they follow your brand? What are they seeking?

Once you have assessed your existing community and content, you should create a social commerce strategy that seeks to connect your content with commerce.

As you create your strategy, ensure that you have:

- Met with partners across the emerging social commerce ecosystem. The landscape is changing very quickly, and there are new entrants that are innovating in this space. Make sure your team is up to speed on the new developments and is testing new technologies to create deeper connections with consumers and enable more seamless commerce.

- Created methodologies to track and assess social commerce data. One of the primary advantages of social commerce is that it allows for the linking of content and commerce, so tracking what works and does not work is critical for strategy iteration.

- Make sure you have the right talent asking for the sale. As we discussed in the livestreaming chapter, influencers do not always make the best salespeople due to their need to stay authentic and engaging to their community. Make sure you have someone who is asking for the sale in a credible manner and in the way that your consumer accepts for your brand.

- And, most importantly, as companies look to maximize returns from their social strategies, they must provide authentic content for savvy consumers and inspire more influencers to express enthusiasm for their products

Engage consumers through retail media

We believe that the relevance and popularity of retail media will continue to grow and become a mainstream revenue channel for retailers. We expect to see retailers of all sizes enter into partnerships with technology providers to generate additional revenues from vast amounts of insightful customer data. These technology providers can help retailers to successfully set up, run and manage their retail media networks (RMNs).

To assess whether your brand or retail company can better leverage retail media for its business, start with asking yourself the following questions:

For retailers:

- What customer data do I collect directly?
- Could I launch my own RMN?
- Could I partner with a third-party provider to launch a RMN?
- Can I improve the customer experience with a RMN by making more personalized recommendations or otherwise tailoring the shopping experience to each individual consumer?

- What customer data do I collect that would be valuable to brands we carry?
- How could we launch a RMN without deteriorating our relationship with our consumers?

For brands:

- What are the key consumer data points that would help me sell more or better serve the end consumer?
- Do any retailers we sell through offer RMNs?
- (If you have engaged with RMNs already) What data am I receiving and how is it being used?
- How can I tailor our offering to be more personalized for the consumer?
- What formats are available for retail media networks and how can I stand out?

And if neither of the above applies to your business, the best thing you can do is to start to identify the RMNs in your sector and evaluate how you can partner with them for advertising or other consumer engagement techniques. Make sure to also get to know the ecosystem of technology innovators in this space in order to track their progress and look for newly launched opportunities and capabilities.

And while some retailers may think that they are too small to create their own RMN, they should look to the ecosystem for ways to innovate. For example, regional and smaller grocers who rely solely on delivery-provider marketplaces such as Instacart are automatically excluded from the benefits of advertising. By developing their own e-commerce websites and digital capabilities they could take advantage of the opportunities that exist in retail media and grow new revenue streams. Retailers that adopt solutions that incorporate self-serve platforms to gain insights, activate ads and measure campaigns can enable brands to build and deliver high-quality ads without reliance upon intermediaries – thus cutting costs.

Build an intelligent supply chain

Most retailers and brands have already dealt with a myriad of supply chain issues since the pandemic started. And although many have already made shifts and adjustments, there is always more that can be done to further optimize supply chains.

FIGURE 16.2 Four pillars of a resilient and profitable supply chain

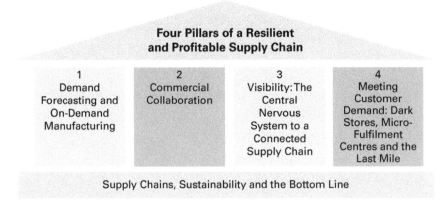

As each retailer faces different challenges with their supply chain, start by asking what your goals are, and then developing strategies to achieve each of these goals.

We identify four pillars of a resilient and profitable supply chain in Figure 16.2 and below. We recommend you approach your supply chain strategic planning by focusing on these four pillars.

- *Demand forecasting and on-demand manufacturing*: How can you partner with external providers to create more sophisticated demand forecasting, down to the local level? Can you benefit from enhanced AI or ML in your supply chain?

- *Commercial collaboration*: Supply chains are no longer unidirectional and need to share data for everyone's mutual benefit. How can you increase your level of collaboration and data sharing across your supply chain to create value for the consumer and efficiencies for your business?

- *Visibility*: Central to supply chain management is visibility, since it is difficult to optimize what one cannot visualize or measure. Assess how you can improve visibility throughout your supply chain, adding supply chain control towers, utilizing AI and identifying ways to find hidden relationships and make predictions.

- *Meeting customer demand*: Can you use creative solutions to increase revenue and enhance customer satisfaction? Consider solutions such as dark stores, micro-fulfilment centres and last-mile efficiencies.

Reward your community with NFTs

The time for retailers and brands to start launching NFTs is now. The market is rewarding early entrants, which allows brands and retailers the opportunity to build community early in the adoption of the Metaverse and create a first-mover advantage within their industry.

Before setting your NFT strategy, make sure you assess your brand against the three Cs: consumers, competitors and content.

- *Consumers*: Define your target consumer. Who are they, and how are they interacting with the Metaverse?
- *Competitors*: Assess competitor activations and initiatives to date, and understand what worked and did not work about each initiative.
- *Content*: Identify the type of content that would be attractive to your consumer base, and then whether you can develop that content in-house or via partners.

Once you have assessed your brand's opportunity within the NFT market, we recommend that retailers and brands ensure that they take into account the following components of their NFT strategy:

- *Revenue*: Develop new revenue streams around your NFTs.
- *Authenticity*: Ensure that you are working with partners who are authentic and understand the needs and priorities of the NFT community.
- *Behaviour*: Influence customer behaviour with your NFTs – whether it be to increase purchase of physical products, drive traffic to your retail stores or enhance loyalty with special rewards.

There is no one-size-fits-all NFT strategy, as each initiative must be extremely targeted to the brand ethos and tailored for the brand's community. Like with many aspects of retail innovation, plan for repeated initiatives to build learnings within the organization and iterate your strategy as you go.

Utilize blockchain to open new opportunities

Blockchain technologies support high-volume digital asset trade, protect ownership and provide authenticity. For retailers and brands, blockchain offers benefits in product quality and supply chain improvement, inventory management, loyalty programmes and payment channels.

Blockchain has a wide array of potential applications for businesses, so creating your blockchain strategy will take time – you and your organization must assess the impact of blockchain on your industry and your brand. We recommend a few ways to start the process below:

- Set up a virtual store or experience on a Metaverse platform.
- Accept cryptocurrency to conduct seamless transactions with customers around the world.
- Look for ways that blockchain could reduce friction in your industry by removing market inefficiencies.
- Find methods to integrate blockchain into your loyalty programmes.
- Get to know the blockchain ecosystem and identify partnerships for your company.

Upgrade in-store and digital payment options

Retailers can benefit from adopting flexible payment methods to appeal to consumers who are increasingly intolerant of friction in the payment process.

- *Contactless payment*: This method became popular during the Covid pandemic, and is one new retail adaptation to Covid that consumers like and want to keep.
- *Acceptance of digital currencies*: There are more than 6 million daily cryptocurrency transactions – and this number will likely increase in the future.
- *Buy now, pay later (BNPL) options*: 20 per cent of US consumers report using BNPL options in the past year, and with increased economic uncertainty we expect this to increase in the future.
- *Smart checkout technologies*: Global smart checkout transactions are estimated to grow by 187 per cent from 2020 to 2025 according to Bankr/CoinMarketCap/Coresight. Make sure not to miss this growth.

Retail data

As you develop your retail data strategy, we recommend you use the Coresight CORE framework as a guide to assess your own business.

- *Communication*: Assess how you can tap into AI's strengths in pattern recognition and finding connections in data to enable new means of communication with computers, leading to the use of virtual assistants, chatbots, voice shopping and visual search functions in retail.
- *Optimize pricing*: Examine how you can improve forecasting, competitive data analysis and dynamic pricing using AI and ML.
- *Rationalize inventory*: How can you use AI to rationalize data forecasting demand, product allocation and for conducting audits?
- *Experiential retail*: Can you utilize data to create a seamless fusion of online shopping, offline shopping and logistics? Retailers can use AI to make the online and offline shopping processes seem unified and seamless. Technologies such as augmented reality, virtual reality and livestreaming can provide a virtual experience of visiting a physical store or mall.

FIGURE 16.3 The CORE framework for AI in retail

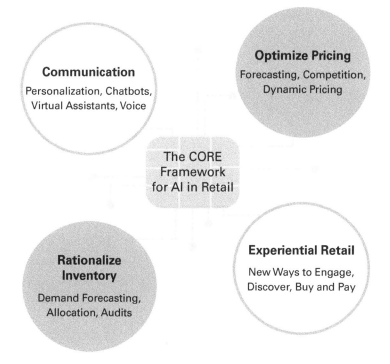

Re-assess your loyalty strategy

During the pandemic, consumers switched brands and retailers at record rates; now, leveraging loyalty programmes to retain these new shoppers is key. And loyalty strategies are becoming more diverse and increasingly vital.

As you re-assess your loyalty strategy, make sure to review each of the following areas:

- *Subscription memberships*: A growing number of retailers are rolling out paid loyalty programmes, following the lead of Amazon Prime. Paid programmes allow retailers to offer valuable benefits that they could not offer for free.

- *Hyper-personalization*: Retailers need to create a 360-degree view of customers, including both offline and online activity, to deliver more personalized experiences. AI and ML are providing retailers with new tools to hyper-personalize their loyalty programmes.

- *Experiential rewards*: Best-in-class loyalty programmes provide benefits beyond earn-and-burn to build loyalty and create a gap between perceived and actual programme costs. These programmes can include benefits such as early access to sale or new products, exclusive products and/or input into new product designs.

- *Loyalty ecosystems*: Retailers are providing more value to customers by integrating a broader range of functionality such as payments, digital offers and online ordering. They are also integrating relevant partnerships to provide more opportunities to earn and redeem awards.

- *Data monetization*: Retailers are monetizing their data assets via retailer media and syndicated data sales. Revenue generated from vendors and other partners can be used to fund omnichannel investments and other initiatives.

Investigate the headless commerce landscape

As new technology enters the market to disrupt the industry as is happening in the headless commerce sector, we recommend you start your assessment by gaining an in-depth understanding of the retail technology landscape. We highlight some of the emerging players in this sector across Europe, North America and Australasia in Figure 16.4. We estimate that even more entrants will be entering this landscape in the future.

FIGURE 16.4 Retail-tech landscape: headless commerce

RETAIL-TECH LANDSCAPE: HEADLESS COMMERCE

NORTH AMERICA

builder	chord
commerce layer	
fabric	Commercejs
Nacelle	nogin
CONTENTSTACK	
SCALEFAST	
shogun	Spryker
swell	uniform

AUSTRALASIA

fluentcommerce   shopistry

EUROPE

AKINON graphcms
ikas   saleor   STYLA
strapi
Vue Storefront

SOURCE Coresight Research

Part of adopting new technologies is meeting the companies leading this change – as with all next technologies, the best way to determine your approach is to meet these innovators!

In summary

Although we often write about the challenges retailers face – supply chains, competition from e-commerce and labour shortages, among others – they also have a new set of products and opportunities to draw on. Retailers are in a unique, exciting position to unlock the value of their data, brands and platforms to generate revenue from these new channels.

Despite the challenges brought on by the pandemic and its aftermath, business and technological innovation have presented retailers with new products and channels, offering new revenue opportunities, many of which monetize the value they have built over the years in collecting data and building their brand identities. As retail is constantly evolving, the definition of a successful retailer could also evolve to mean one that generates a significant portion of revenue from media and selling products via livestreaming and in the Metaverse.

As always, disruptive change will create winners and losers. The challenge is indeed daunting to consider, but for retailers who can be in front of the change in the new retail landscape, they will be the new retailers who will succeed in tomorrow's retail environment. And, we believe that retailers will partner more broadly than ever before – with each other, technology partners and influencers – to evolve to organizations with higher margins, less volatile sales# and a seat at the centre of the data table. This is why we are long retail.

Reference

Yu, J (2022) Interview with the authors, July 2022.

INDEX

CPSIA information can be obtained
at www.ICGtesting.com
Printed in the USA
JSHW071500220223
38092JS00006B/272